Bright Morning Stars Are Rising

50th Anniversary Anthology
Kodály Center at Holy Names University

Anne Laskey and Gail Needleman, editors

Kodály Foundation for Music Education

The Kodály Foundation for Music Education is a non-profit organization. Proceeds from the sale of this anthology will be used to support of the Kodály Center at Holy Names University, Oakland, California.

First Printing: June 2022

Kodály Foundation for Music Education
P.O. Box 318052
San Francisco, CA 94131, USA
www.kodalyfoundation.org

ISBN 979-8-98642-260-2

Printed in the United States of America

Cover design by Robert Lee

This anthology is dedicated to

Gail Needleman

Day is a-breakin' in my soul

TABLE OF CONTENTS

Art Music and Musicianship

Teacher Education and Research

Hungarian Inspiration

Contributors

Preface

The Kodály Center at Holy Names University has played a significant role in implementing Zoltán Kodály's vision for music education in the United States and around the world. In celebration of its 50th anniversary, this anthology presents twenty-six articles by Kodály Center faculty and alumni. The articles reflect on the basic tenets of Kodály's vision: that music is for everybody, that music literacy is a universal right and not a secret language for a select few, that singing is the most human and universal of instruments, and that folk music and art music are the most beautiful and lasting of musical forms. The articles were chosen from the more than 125 articles by Holy Names faculty and alumni which have appeared in the *Bulletin of the International Kodály Society* and the *Kodály Envoy*, the quarterly publication of the Organization of American Kodály Educators.

The Kodály program at Holy Names was founded in 1969 by Sr. Mary Alice Hein, a professor at Holy Names whose encounter with Kodály inspired a lifelong devotion to bringing his vision of education to America. This encounter, at Stanford University in 1966 when Kodály attended a symposium on the Kodály Method, was a turning point; within six years, she had:

- visited Hungary to see first-hand what was happening in the schools (1968),
- organized the first summer course at Holy Names University (1969),
- received an International Research and Exchange grant for herself and six others to spend a year of study in Hungary (in 1971); this led to the establishment of several other courses throughout the United States,
- co-chaired the first International Kodály Symposium at Holy Names, in 1973, with Erzsébet Szőnyi, Head of the Music Education Department at the Liszt Academy, and
- initiated the first advanced degree in music education based on Kodály's philosophy in North America at Holy Names, in 1973.

Sr. Mary Alice (on right)
with Erzsébet Szőnyi

Since its founding, the Kodály Center has become one of the most respected teacher education programs in the country. This is largely due to the close collaboration of American faculty and over twenty Hungarians who have been invited to teach, to conduct, to advise and to establish priorities for the program. This collaboration has included the choice and analysis of American folk songs for teaching, the founding of the Holy Names Children's Choral Festival in 1996, and the translation of Hungarian curricula and textbooks. The Hungarian teachers' incredible musicianship, unfailing musicality, and choice of repertoire have inspired generations of students and faculty at Holy Names. Canadian, Australian and Filipino faculty and students have also been important contributors to the program, and have been leading figures in the spread of Kodály's philosophy in those countries.

One of the distinguishing features of the academic year masters program, from the very beginning, was the student teaching component. Unlike the majority of Kodály teacher education programs in the United States, which take place in three-week summer courses, the academic year program allows students to put theory into practice in neighboring schools immediately while they are learning the methodology. This ability to teach under the guidance of Kodály faculty is cited by graduates as one of the highlights of the program.

Graduates of the Kodály Center now teach throughout the United States and Canada, as well as in Europe, Australia, Japan, Taiwan, the Philippines and South America. Several conduct nationally recognized choirs, while others have assumed leading roles in professional organizations.

This anthology reflects the depth and variety of experience of Kodály Center alumni and faculty in their efforts to realize and implement Kodály's vision. It begins with reflections by Sr. Mary Alice Hein on her work to bring Kodály's ideas to American classrooms, along with articles that investigate Kodály's life and thought, and what these mean for us today. It ends with writings of some of the many Hungarian master teachers who have worked with Holy Names faculty to develop higher levels of musicianship, excellent materials and clear pedagogical goals in music teacher education.

Because folk songs provide the basic material for beginning instruction in Kodály classrooms, several articles are included that deal with specific songs or genres, such as "The Cuckoo in Mythology" and "Sea Shanties: The Hardy Survivors." Others describe folk song research projects and efforts to implement Kodály's ideas in other countries, for example, "Sweet Betsy from Smithfield" and "The Kodály Concept Finds Eager Students in Malawi."

Also included are articles on art music ("Britten's Noye's Fludde") and musicianship ("Good Intonation: Ear or Voice,") and on pedagogical issues ("Teaching Students to Hear, Sing, Play, Identify and Enjoy the Modes").

We hope that readers will find inspiration in these writings for their current and future endeavors.

~ ~ ~ ~ ~

The editors would like to thank members of the 50th anniversary committee who helped with the selection of the twenty-six articles chosen for this anthology: Robert Lee, Miriam Factora and Michele Winter. We are grateful to the International Kodály Society and the Organization of American Educators for permission to reprint these articles.

Special thanks to Michele Winter, who entered almost all of the musical examples in Sibelius for this anthology. Thanks also to Maree Hennessy, current director of the Kodály Center, for continuing the tradition of excellence in music education at Holy Names.

IN RETROSPECT: THE KODÁLY PHENOMENON, 1964–1997

Mary Alice Hein, SNJM

During the thirty years since the death of Zoltán Kodály on March 6, 1967, there has been a phenomenal, worldwide spread of what the International Kodály Society refers to as Kodály-inspired music education. I would like to recount some of the momentous events of those thirty-some years, particularly in relation to the involvement of Holy Names College in this grand enterprise.

Music educators throughout the world first became aware that something extraordinary was happening in Hungary in 1964, when the International Society for Music Education (ISME) Conference was held in Budapest. Because the Eastern European countries had been virtually cut off from the West as a result of events following the Second World War, even the very fact that such an international conference was held in Hungary at that time was extraordinary. It was mainly through the efforts of Erzsébet Szőnyi, then Dean of Music Education at the Liszt Academy of Music and ISME board member, that the conference was held there. Inspired by what they saw and heard during ISME, music educators returned to their respective countries, enthusiastic and determined to introduce some of Kodály's ideas into their own school systems. The well-known quote from the book of Ecclesiastes, "There is a season for everything, a time for every occupation under heaven," seemed to fit the occasion, as the time was indeed ripe for these ideas to filter into our own country.

In 1966, Kodály and Erzsébet Szőnyi traveled to Stanford University at the invitation of Dr. Wolfgang Kuhn to present a workshop. I decided to attend, thinking it would be like others I had attended—where I might be able to pick up a few ideas to use with my students. Little did I realize that those few days would have a profound influence on my life.

During the course of the workshop, participants were given the opportunity to meet in small groups for question-and-answer sessions with Kodály. I was sitting just a few feet from him and was deeply impressed with the utter simplicity and lucidity with which he responded to our questions, pointing out what he considered to be essential aspects of a universal music education.

The experiences of that workshop led me to examine seriously my views about music education and to explore ways in which Kodály music education could be incorporated into our music curriculum at Holy Names College.

Mary Helen Richards and her Portola Valley School students were among the presenters, and shortly after the workshop she called me. Following her visits to the classes of Emma Serényi during a trip to Hungary, she had written *Threshold to Music*, the initial American adaptation of the Kodály approach. We discussed the possibility of her joining our summer faculty to give courses, and planned for the summer of 1969 to incorporate a Kodály master's degree into our existing music master's degree program. Holy Names College thus became the first institution of higher learning in North America to offer a master's degree in Kodály music education.

This was an important decision, and I felt it essential to have a connection with Hungary. Consequently, I wrote a letter to Miss Serényi, assuming that a letter of invitation should go directly to her, as is the usual procedure when inviting someone to give a course. The events that followed reminded me that "Fools rush in where angels fear to tread." Hungary was still very much a closed society; all invitations to travel to the West had to be handled through an official government agency. Not being aware of this policy, I sent Miss Serényi our letter of invitation on our official college stationery. The words "Holy Names College," emblazoned across the top, were a red flag for the communist government. When Miss Serényi took our letter to the official agency, they asked, with disdain, "What kind of a place is this. . . Holy Names College?" She replied, "All the places in California are holy names: San Francisco, Los Angeles, Santa Barbara. . ." After much subsequent negotiating with the official agency, Miss Serényi finally arrived at Holy Names in time for our first Kodály summer program. She returned for the following summers and was a full-time faculty member from 1972 until 1975. It was she who helped establish our Holy Names College Kodály program on a firm foundation.

At the same time that we were having our first summer program on the West Coast, Denise Bacon was starting a Kodály summer program on the East Coast at the Dana School of Music, to which she had invited several Hungarian teachers, among them Erzsébet Szőnyi. I felt it was important to meet with Professor Szőnyi to acquaint her with what we were doing, to show her our curriculum plan for the master's degree and to get her advice. While approving the general outline of the curriculum for the Kodály master's program, she strongly advised me to spend a year in Hungary to ensure that any adaptation would be as authentic as possible.

Fortunately, I found an entry for the International Research and Exchanges Board (IREX) listed in a grant book that our college's director of development had in her office. I saw that IREX, which was funded in part by the Ford Foundation, sponsored exchange programs between our country and Russia as well as other Eastern European countries. Noting that the application deadline for the following year was in two weeks, I applied immediately. In January I received notification that I had been accepted for study in Hungary. IREX had just recently been established and I was the first person to receive a fellowship to study music education in Hungary. Thanks to the foresight of the staff at IREX in anticipating the importance of the Kodály movement in our country, several other music educators also received grants in following years to study in Hungary.

During my year in Hungary, I observed music classes in schools all over Hungary and had the privilege of studying with many Hungarian music educators, too numerous to mention here. I feel a profound sense of gratitude to these excellent teachers, who shared their knowledge and expertise with me. Many of them were later to come to Holy Names College to teach in summers and during the academic year. Also in Hungary that year were Lois Choksy and another valued colleague, Toni Locke. Lois was appointed to our faculty to teach in our full-time academic year program for several years. Toni later came to Holy Names to help set up our Kodály Resource Center, which became an important aspect of our program.

I knew that IREX sponsored what they called Collaborative Project Grants, that is, grants for conferences involving two or possibly three countries. I decided to talk to Erzsébet Szőnyi about the possibility of having a binational symposium between Hungary and the United States. We arranged to meet at her house, but the cleaning lady had come unexpectedly, so we went down the street to a little coffee shop. I explained that I thought perhaps IREX would give a grant for a binational symposium; she replied, "Why not an international symposium?" Why not, indeed? There, in that little coffee house, initial plans were made for the first International Kodály Symposium. History is made with just such small moments.

Again, the time was ripe for such an undertaking. Professor Szőnyi had been in contact with many of the persons working with Kodály adaptations in various countries, so it was decided to invite these persons to present lectures and to give papers. In the end, fifty delegates from seventeen countries came to the symposium. A preliminary plan for the symposium was presented to IREX, and a meeting was arranged for me with Dr. Endre Rosta, then president of the Institute of Cultural Relations, to get his support. (IREX worked through the Institute of Cultural Relations in organizing grants for Hungary.) Dr. Rosta was most gracious and very helpful in arranging for participation of the Hungarian delegates to the symposium. To aid in the planning, a binational committee of American and Hungarian educators met in Hungary during the summer of 1972. The purposes, format and proposed outcomes of the symposium were further clarified, and a two-fold purpose emerged: to offer an opportunity for an international exchange of ideas among Kodály educators from the various countries, and to further stimulate interest in the Kodály concept among American music educators. Erzsébet Szőnyi was appointed general chairperson, Mrs. Sarolta Kodály was the honorary chairperson, and I acted as coordinating chairperson.

The first International Kodály Symposium was set for August 1–15, 1973, at Holy Names College. The invited delegates met during the first few days before the open conference, mainly to get to know each other and to exchange ideas before the more than 350 observers and invited guests arrived for the open conference. In true California tradition, one of the first things we planned for the delegates was a visit to the Christian Brothers winery in Napa and a picnic lunch in their lovely shaded picnic area, where the Brothers, of course, were very generous with the wine. Needless to say, all the delegates were on very good terms after that initial outing.

Among the invited guests were Harold Arburg from the United States Department of Education; John Bice, educational consultant for Boosey and Hawkes; Jack Schaeffer, then president of MENC; John Matthews from IREX; and Richard Kapp from the Ford Foundation, who was to announce their first grant to our Kodály program to establish Kodály fellowships for our full-time academic year program.[1]

After the open conference, the delegates remained for a few more days and met in various national groups. In the United States group, plans were made for the founding of a national Kodály organization. It was also decided that there should be a Kodály publication, and so the

Kodály Envoy came into being at the symposium. The founding conference of the Organization of American Kodály Educators was held in Milwaukee in March of 1975, with Sister Lorna Zemke and Stephen Jay as co-chairs.

The founding of the Kodály Society of Canada was also announced at the 1973 symposium and plans were made for the establishment of an international Kodály organization, which was formalized at the second International Kodály Symposium, held in the summer of 1975 at Kodály's birthplace, Kecskemét, Hungary. During the ensuing eight years, I was privileged to serve on the IKS Board as this newly formed organization developed its policies and programs, including planning for subsequent Kodály symposia.

International Kodály Symposia have been held every two years since 1973 in many countries, including Canada, Australia, Japan, Belgium, England, Greece, and Italy. The meeting in Hartford, Connecticut, in 1993 marked the 20th anniversary of the first symposium, and this year [1997] in Manila one of our Kodály graduates, Miriam Factora, is playing a leading role. There are times when an event acts as a catalyst, providing impetus and direction to an idea or a movement. Such was the impetus of the first International Kodály Symposium.

As mentioned above, the Ford Foundation announced a grant to our Kodály program at the symposium, and later, another grant to establish a Kodály pilot project in the San Jose Unified School District, culminating in a film entitled *Music Lessons*, which featured various Kodály programs in the United States.

When the Ford Foundation grant ended, the Foundation put us in touch with the William and Flora Hewlett Foundation in Palo Alto. This foundation also was convinced of the value of Kodály music education and of the importance of having a strong teacher training program at the graduate level. In 1983, in order to insure the continuance of our Kodály program, the Hewlett Foundation awarded the college an endowment grant to be used for Kodály fellowships.

Seeing the prodigious spread of Kodály-inspired music education around the world, I became more and more attracted to researching the roots of Hungarian music education in Hungary, for I feel that what we are witnessing today is one of the most significant educational phenomena of our 20th century and, I might add, one that will continue into the 21st century. Consequently, through a Fulbright research grant, I was able to go to Hungary during the spring of 1986 to do this research. I felt that the most interesting way to carry out this project would be to collect oral history from Kodály's former students and colleagues. I felt that collectively they could offer, from their direct experiences with him, a living, historical account of the development of Hungarian music education and the actual extent of Kodály's involvement.

In my grant proposal, I stressed the urgency of collecting this oral history before it was too late. A number of Kodály's first students had already died; but fortunately, I was able to interview Lajos Bárdos, György Kerényi, and Benjamin Rajeczky, three men who had studied with Kodály in the 1920s and played leading roles in Hungarian music education. Had I arrived later than the spring of 1986, I would have been too late: by September—the usual Fulbright time frame—Bárdos and Kerényi were too ill for interviews. Both died the following winter.

As I said, using the methodology of collecting oral history was a delightful and most interesting way of doing this research. The following is a little story about my interview with Kerényi, which was conducted in his hospital room. I knew that he had some connection with Fritz Jöde, the great German music educator, and I intended to ask Kerényi to what extent Jöde had influenced Hungarian music education. At the end of the interview, however, before I had a chance to ask him about Jöde, he said, "I am finished—that is all." In my thank-you letter to him I asked if he would write me a few lines about Jöde. He suggested that I should go see a certain lady who would tell me about Jöde. I arranged to see her, but she said she had very little time to spend with me because her dog had new puppies. I must say that I was met with some suspicion—this American woman trying to get some kind of information about Kerényi—and as a consequence, I was getting very little information from her, so I finally said, "Do you think I could see the puppies?" She replied that she would bring the mother out first, and out came a beautiful springer spaniel. She came right up to me, let me pet her, and we had a very nice encounter. The woman kept looking at me and then looking at the dog and finally, she said, "That dog never goes to strangers." We went to see the puppies and then came the coffee and cake and the information I was seeking.

She told me that Kerényi had his unpublished memoirs in the Széchényi National Library. They are entitled *The Disciple, A Life Close to Kodály*. From his memoirs, I learned about his connection with Jöde, which was quite extensive indeed. In fact, Jöde later came to Hungary to give lectures to music educators, and the February 1938 issue of *Énekszó*, the Hungarian music education publication, was devoted entirely to Jöde's visit.[2]

It was Kodály who sent Kerényi to Berlin for a year with the words, "See what they are doing and we will go even further than they." Prophetic words indeed.

My interview with Lajos Bárdos was in his big, sunny apartment. I particularly remember his delightful sense of humor and gentle wisdom, maintained despite the many vicissitudes he suffered when the church music program at the Liszt Academy was dissolved by the government in 1948. Bárdos also established the *Ének Ifjúság* or Singing Youth movement, in which several choirs would gather, first singing as individual choirs, then combining to sing together. That practice is still going on in Hungary. The tradition is being carried at the Holy Names College Children's Choral Festival, begun two years ago by Judit Hartyányi and Anne Laskey, director of the Kodály Program. Vance George, director of the San Francisco Symphony Chorus, was guest conductor at the choral festival last spring.

Another extremely interesting experience for me was the 40th anniversary of the founding of the school in Békés Tarhos, located in the southern part of Hungary. Begun in 1946 by György Gulyás, this was a special music school for children living in the little villages of Hungary who had no opportunity to study music. It was actually a school where the children lived, and the whole school was centered on music. I was able to interview Gulyás and also one of the former students who was there for the anniversary. The Sándor Szokolay interview gives much information about this little-known early implementation of Kodály's ideas. Mr. Szokolay, now a prominent composer, was also a pupil at that school and he speaks of how it was there that he became a composer.

These interviews, I feel, show that Kodály was deeply involved in the lives and activities of his colleagues and that he seemed to be able to recognize and draw out the potential and gifts of each person. That they revered Kodály is very evident. The interviews reveal many lovely, personal details of Kodály's relationship with them, perhaps in a way that would not ordinarily be found in a standard biography. It was a privilege and an inspiration for me to speak with all of these persons who were so beautifully influenced by Kodály and to see a picture of a truly great man emerge from their recollections of him.[3]

Looking back over these almost thirty years of intense involvement in Kodály music education, I can truthfully say that it has been a marvelously absorbing adventure. These past years have seen a continuous development and acceptance of Kodály-inspired music education, not only in the United States but in many other countries as well. Musicians and educators are becoming more aware of the benefits that such a holistic approach to music education can bring to children and adults. What seems to be of most importance, however, is not so much the personal gratification, but the sense of how an all-embracing educational philosophy has the power to change lives. I have seen this happen to so many young teachers who have come to study at Holy Names College. These teachers are enthusiastic about their work and are professionally motivated to assume leadership roles in their professional organizations, in their school districts, and as members of college and university faculties. Such enthusiasm and dedication result from a belief that what they are doing as Kodály educators can make a difference in the lives of the children and adults they can reach by their teaching.

Notes

[1] The complete program of the first International Kodály Symposium can be found in László Vikár, *Reflections on Kodály* (Budapest: International Kodály Society, 1985). For those interested in the history of the international dissemination of Kodály Music Education from the 1960s to the mid-1980s, this book is a valuable resource.

[2] Copies of early issues of *Énekszó* are in the Kodály Resource Center at Holy Names College.

[3] Mary Alice Hein, SNJM, *The Legacy of Zoltán Kodály: An Oral History Perspective* (Budapest: International Kodály Society, 1992).

Originally published in *Kodály Envoy* 23, no. 4 (1997): 10-13. Reprinted by permission.

ZOLTÁN KODÁLY: HIS CONTRIBUTION TO MUSIC EDUCATION

Thomas S. Kite

Zoltán Kodály, the Hungarian musician and composer, was a scholar in the areas of education, linguistics, folk music and ethnomusicology. He was born on December 16, 1882, in Kecskemét, a small town southeast of Budapest. Kodaly's father Frigyes (1853–1926) married Paulina Jalovecsky (1857–1935) in 1879. Frigyes Kodály's position as a railway official required the family to move frequently; hence, there was variety in his children's birthplaces: Emilia (1880–1919) was born in Budapest, Zoltán (1882–1967) in Kecskemét, and Pál (1886–1948) in Galánta. It was at Galánta and nearby Nagyszombat, villages in western Hungary (both now in Czechoslovakia [now Slovakia]), that Zoltán spent his formative years. During his grammar school education, he developed his love for knowledge, displaying a particular proficiency for language.[1]

Kodály received his earliest musical training from his parents, who themselves were accomplished amateur musicians. He displayed his talents by singing in the choir and playing the cello in the orchestra of Nagyszombat Cathedral. Kodály also took part in family chamber music concerts. At the turn of the century, Kodály faced the problem of choosing a career, and, following the advice of his school teachers, chose to pursue that of scholar and musician. (Kodály's parents had wanted him to better himself by studying to be a lawyer.)[2] From 1900-1904 he studied simultaneously at Eőtvos College, a training college for gifted teachers, and the Liszt Academy of Music, where he became a pupil of János Koessler, whom he eventually succeeded as professor of composition. Kodály received a teacher's diploma in 1905.

His early scholastic efforts were directed toward composing and conducting. In 1905, he began collecting Hungarian folk songs as a means of preserving his cultural heritage. Folk songs were to be an important part of his life, since they were to provide the basic material for the system of music education that has come to be called the "Kodály method."

In order to better understand Kodály's contributions to music education, however, it is necessary to understand the political and social climate of Hungary. In 1867, prior to Kodály's birth, the dual monarchy of the Austro-Hungarian Empire was established by Ferenc Deák.[3] By the end of October 1918 it was evident that the Austro-Hungarian monarchy would collapse.[4] During the subsequent revolution in Hungary, the King at that time, Charles, was deposed.[5] Soon after that, the working class established the Hungarian Republic of Councils. Within one year, in August 1919, the dictatorship of the proletariat was overthrown by the communists.[6] This brief communist dictatorship was followed by a twenty-five year regency under Admiral Miklós Horthy. Later, during World War II, the Germans occupied Hungary, but were soon driven out by the Soviets. The communists intensified preparations for the establishment of a Soviet Republic with the assistance of Mátyás Rákosi, the leading Hungarian Stalinist from 1945 to 1956.[7] Eventually, the Hungarian people revolted against Rákosi's repressive regime. Moderate Imre Nagy replaced Rákosi, but was executed soon afterward. In 1956, the Russians suppressed another national uprising, and János Kádár became the First Secretary of the Hungarian National Council, the communist party which ruled over Hungary until 1989.

Because a majority of Hungarians were employed in farming, and because the industrialization of Budapest in the late nineteenth-century attracted foreign skilled labor, especially from Germany, Germans not surprisingly exerted great control over artistic, economic and social mores in the capital. In an effort to break away from the strong influence of the Germanic tradition and the musical language of Wagner and Brahms and to replace it with a new national musical tradition and language, Kodály toured Galánta and its vicinity, collecting over 150 Hungarian folk songs. He then wrote his dissertation, *A magyar népdal strófaszerkezete* (The Strophic Structure of the Hungarian Folk Song), based on his analysis of these folk songs. The dissertation partially fulfilled the requirements for the degree of doctor of philosophy, completed in 1906 at the University of Budapest.

In 1907 Kodály began teaching music theory at the Liszt Academy. When not teaching, he devoted himself to composing chamber music.[8] One of his main teaching goals at the Academy was to implement a systemized approach to ear training using tonic sol-fa.[9] According to Kodály's biographer, László Eősze, Hungary (like Germany) used a fixed-do system at that time, and Kodály was the first to suggest the adoption of two names—absolute (fixed) and relative (movable)—for each note.[10] Referring to its importance, Kodály suggested that the "movable sol-fa system is more definite and lasting than the use of purely staff notation letter names, as it indicates not only the relative pitch, but also the tonal function of each note, along with the feeling for intervals."[11]

In 1919 Béla Reinitz, the administrator of music for the Hungarian Republic of Councils, appointed Kodály to the newly created post of deputy director. According to Eősze, Kodály accepted this position in order to implement a system of movable-do solmization as the fundamental approach to musicianship training in the Academy. Eősze states that Kodály's efforts were opposed by conservatives resisting new ideas.[12] Furthermore, some of Kodály's colleagues, especially Reső Kemény and Béla Szabados, resented his appointment to such an influential post, and caused him much tribulation.[13] Kodály was eventually discharged from his official duties at the Academy of Music for these reasons:

1. He had participated in a strike action by teachers at the Academy.
2. He irregularly issued permits for the qualifying examinations of singing teachers.
3. Instead of signing in his own hand, he used a rubber stamp on official Academy documents.
4. He was accused of being a disorganized administrator.[14]

During the six-month period following his dismissal, Kodály underwent twelve separate hearings in defense of his position as deputy director at the Academy. On one occasion, Jenő Hubay, who had unsuccessfully sought the position of deputy director, attempted to influence public opinion and discredit Kodály. Hubay requested that Izor Beldi, a journalist for the daily paper *Pesti Hirlap*, write an editorial, which was published on January 7, 1920:

The staff of the Academy of Music. . . must be purged of those who, by their conduct under the dictatorship of the proletariat, have proved themselves to be unreliable. The adjustment of salary scales, still bearing strong traces of Reinitz's dictatorship, must be drastically revised. . . Every care should be taken to preserve the younger generation of musicians from the contamination of such 'ultra-modernist' movements as Symbolism and Cubism. Indeed what these people chose to regard as the present, history has already relegated to the past. What we want is an Academy that will train *musicians*, not foster *young Kodálys*. . .[15]

Two men who supported Kodály's leadership at the Academy protested to the chairman of the Committee of Inquiry. Ernő Dohnányi, director of the Academy, wrote a letter, dated January 28, 1920, which stated,

Responsibility for all measures taken during the specified period, apart from those of a purely administrative character. . . rests with the Director of the Academy. I must protest against the procedure which calls Kodály to account for actions, the responsibility for which rests, not upon him, but solely upon myself, as Director of the Academy. I wish to put it upon record that I fully identify myself with Kodály, and assume full responsibility for all measures taken under my Directorship.[16]

This letter was followed by one from Béla Bartók, dated February 3, 1920, which said, "Having myself participated in the executive functions of that body in precisely the same way as Kodály, I feel I must protest against the procedure that calls him alone to account, either for the mere fact of former membership, or for any action to which exception is now taken."[17]

The inquiry to discredit Kodály's work was completed on June 25, 1920, when István Haller, the Minister of Education, ruled that Kodály would be placed on a leave of absence for the first term of the 1920–21 academic year. In Haller's words, Kodály's professional reputation was preserved: "It has been established that neither your conduct under the Communist Government, nor your behaviour as a Professor, was in contravention of the rules governing your terms of professional service."[18]

While irrefutable proof of Kodály's unprofessional behavior seems to be lacking, one may conjecture that the entire ordeal was simply an imposition of a political nature aimed at ruining his academic career. The Ministry of Education suggested that Kodály accept a six-month leave of absence, an idea which originated with Jenő Hubay and his supporters. Eősze suggested that this outcome was, in essence, an effort to extend the time Hubay sought to secure Kodály's dismissal.[19] Hubay again spoke to the Committee of Inquiry: "I see no possibility of harmonious and friendly collaboration with Kodály within (the Academy). . . and therefore consider his return to his Chair both undesirable and inadvisable."[20] Hubay further suggested that since Kodály was a qualified secondary school teacher, the Ministry should arrange for him to be removed from the Academy to some humbler post; or, if that should not prove feasible, to retire him on pension.[21] At this point Kodály was thirty-eight years old.

During his leave, Kodály continued to direct his effort to the education of Academy students; he recognized their lack of ability to appreciate music in a comprehensive manner. In his search to rectify the problem, Kodály found himself drawn toward younger people, eventually arriving at the primary school level. Reflecting his awareness of poor music education, Kodály said,

> Until 1925, I had lived the ordinary life of a professional musician. I was not concerned, that is to say, with our educational system because I assumed that it was satisfactory and that everything possible was being done; and that, as far as music was concerned, those who had no ear for it might just as well be written off. Then an incident occurred that destroyed this illusion. One fine spring day, I happened to come across an outing of young girls in the hills of Buda. They were singing, and for half an hour I sat behind some bushes listening to them. And the longer I listened, the more appalled I was by the kind of songs they were singing.[22]

Kodály was displeased with the quality of song literature sung by these girls, and further displeased to learn that they were students at the teachers' training college. Based on these concerns, Kodály composed "See the Gypsy Munching Cheese," the first of many choral compositions for children's chorus.[23] Eősze, however, suggested another reason why Kodály wrote his first children's composition. Earlier, Kodály had approached Endre Borus, the music teacher at a boys' school in Budapest, requesting the students to learn the "ad libitum" children's chorus part of his *Psalmus Hungaricus*. After attending a rehearsal, Kodály told Borus, "I'm going to write something for your choir. Meanwhile, in my opinion, these boys are really worth taking trouble with."[24] Lois Choksy said that Kodály composed works for children's choirs in an attempt to lead Hungarian children to the appreciation of art music.[25] Regardless of which account is more correct, Kodály, at forty-three years of age, began to direct his attention to young people.

In the years leading to his retirement, from 1925 to 1942, Kodály continued his assiduous work to improve music education in Hungary. In an essay entitled "Music in the Kindergarten," written in 1941, Kodály said,

> The greatest deficiency in our culture is that it is built from above. When, after centuries of constraint in national life, freedom was achieved in this respect as well, we wanted to make up too hastily for what we had lost. There are no leaps in nature. Culture is the result of slow growth. To accelerate it, to change the order of evolution, is impossible.
>
> We put up the fancy spires first. When we saw that the whole edifice was shaky, we set to building the walls. We still have to make a cellar.[26]

Ilona Bartalus, professor of music at the Franz Liszt Academy of Music, Budapest, noted that Kodály was influenced by many pedagogues.[27] One such teacher responsible for the Kodály-inspired approach to music education was Jenő Ádám (b. 1896), a pupil of Kodály, and professor emeritus at the Academy of Music in Budapest. Kodály's *School Song Collection*, coupled with Ádám's *Manual of Singing*, both written in 1943, were compulsory texts in Hungarian schools until 1948. Eősze stated that textbooks adopted since then have been strongly influenced by the Kodály and Ádám publications.[28]

Margaret Stone, former editor of the *Kodály Envoy*, OAKE's quarterly journal, suggested that, circa 1927, Kodály was influenced by the ideas of Englishman John Curwen (1816-1880).[29] According to Erzsébet Szőnyi, a student of Kodály and his successor as professor at the Liszt Academy in Budapest, Curwen's use of tonic sol-fa and the development of a system of hand signs contributed greatly to the improvement of English choral singing.[30] Kodály's interest in this system stemmed from his observation of the results of English choir training, and he incorporated Curwen's ideas in his attempt to improve Hungarian music education.[31] Connie More, a Kodály pedagogue from Victoria, British Columbia, reported that Kodály was also influenced by a number of outstanding musicians and educators such as Guido d'Arezzo, Chevé, Dalcroze, Bertalotti, Weber, Hundoegger, Pestalozzi, Kestenberg, Toscanini, Schumann, Hindemith, Rousseau, Jöde, as well as a host of Hungarian pedagogues.[32]

In addition to compiling ideas from other prominent individuals, Kodály realized that a reform of music education in Hungary would require more than simply composing works for children's choirs. He also wrote a series of articles and essays which were intended to educate both choir directors and singing teachers.[33] In selected articles, he intimated that the songs which children learned in school were of poor quality. He believed that children brought up on substandard music would never associate art with music. In the first essay, entitled "Children's Choirs" (1929), Kodály made suggestions which paved the way for the restructuring of music education in Hungary when he stated,

> If the child is not filled at least once by the life-giving stream of music during the most susceptible period—between his sixth and sixteenth years—it will hardly be of any use to him later on. Often a single experience will open the young soul to music for a whole lifetime. This experience cannot be left to chance, it is the duty of the school to provide it.[34]

In a further development of this idea, he continued,

> Teach music and singing at school in such a way that it is not a torture, but a joy for the pupil; instill a thirst for finer music in him, a thirst which will last for a lifetime. Music must not be approached from its intellectual, rational side, nor should it be conveyed to the child as a system of algebraic symbols, or as the secret writing of a language with which he has no connection. The way should be paved for direct intuition.[35]

To provide a means to this end, Kodály wrote *Énekes játékok* (Singing Games) in 1937, and stated in the preface, as cited by Helga Szabó: "Singing is the instinctive language of the child, and the younger he is, the more he requires movement to go with it. The organic connection between music and physical movement is expressed in singing games. These, particularly in the open air, have been one of the principal joys of childhood from time immemorial."[36]

In his belief that music belongs to everyone, Kodály wanted every individual to have an opportunity to achieve a higher level of musical understanding.[37] In his essay "Musical Life in a Provincial Town," Kodály said, "Education of an elite and education of the masses must go hand in hand: only if we maintain equilibrium between the two shall we obtain results of permanent value. The most urgent step towards restoring such equilibrium is the development—or, more accurately, the creation—of musical training in the schools."[38]

In that same year (1937), Kodály began work on the first of four volumes of progressive two-part songs, entitled *Bicinia Hungarica*. According to János Mátyás,

> Kodály wrote his Biciniums [sic]—like Lassus his two-part cantos—for pedagogical purposes, but they also serve as examples of a great composer's pure lyricism and brilliant humor. They are characteristically individual little masterpieces written in a marvelously condensed manner and with absolute surety. . . . Their style is that of the mature Kodály, based on the pentatony and the modal scales of our folk music, using diatonic melody and harmony with sharp rhythm and clearly defined forms. Their material is particularly characterized by an equal balance between music and text, and spiritual relationship with the vocal polyphony of the sixteenth century, perhaps most of all the diatonic and harmonic polyphony of Palestrina.[39]

Geoffry Russell-Smith, editor of the revised English edition, wrote that most of the songs are based on the music of the Hungarian peasant community.[40] Kodály himself, in his preface to the Hungarian edition, wrote about his songs,

> If in those far-off days we had been taught what I try to teach in this book . . . life would have been very different in our little country. It is left with you who use this book to show that, while singing in itself is good, the real reward comes to those who sing, and feel, and think with others. This is what harmony means. We must look forward to the time when all people in the lands are brought together through singing, and when there is a universal harmony.[41]

This decade (the 1930s) was not exclusively devoted to music education, for Kodály also wrote several works for orchestra. The *Peacock Variations* (1939) is a set of orchestral variations based on an ancient Hungarian folk song. Because these variations use the ancient "Peacock" folksong and because the peacock represents freedom, it reminds the hearers of the period of medieval

Hungarian feudalism. Other orchestral works include *Dances of Marosszek* (1930), *Dances of Galánta* (1933), and the *Concerto for Orchestra*, written in 1939, commissioned by the Chicago Symphony Orchestra.

During the next two decades, especially between 1941 and 1958, Kodály's contributions to music education were prolific. He spent much of his time composing songs for chorus and writing essays in support of music education in the schools. "Music in Kindergarten" (1941) spared neither official feelings nor individual interests and led to a considerable controversy when it was first published. In that article, Kodály made the following observations:

> Some strange professional haughtiness is not rare among musicians. The fewer people who are proficient in the craft, the more valuable they feel. They despise those who do not understand it, but are unwilling to do anything to increase the number of those who do understand it. They consider it particularly beneath their dignity to be interested in schools. This is the heritage of Romanticism: the artist defends himself with haughtiness against a society of Philistines even today. Why, we rear them ourselves. Nothing but Philistines can come from the musical education provided by our schools. For what is a Philistine if not an unfeeling dolt, failing to look for the value of life in the very place where it begins for the man of spirit.[42]

Music education in the kindergarten was not Kodály's sole interest, however, as he devoted increasing attention to a new periodical, *Éneklő Ifjúság* (Singing Youth), founded by his former students who were working to improve the music education skills of their own secondary school pupils. Describing this movement, Kodály said,

> The foundations of a genuinely national musical consciousness have to be unearthed from beneath the accumulated rubble of Hungarian indifference and a misconceived and outmoded method of training. This is the spirit in which *Singing Youth* has been launched. Our movement rejects all distinctions based on class or social status. Music belongs to all.[43]

Many of Kodály's choral compositions during this period were written to provide materials for secondary school choirs. Vocal studies included *Fifteen Two-Part Exercises* and *Let Us Sing Correctly*, both of which were published in 1952. Of the former, Kodály said in his preface, "These fifteen exercises constitute a progressive course in two-part singing. . . . Moreover, they will serve as an introduction to the style of the greatest epoch of choral singing."[44] One example (#12) which typifies these pieces is written on a theme of Antonio Vivaldi—the opening movement (Allegro) of his *Concerto in D minor, Op. 3, No. 11.*

Kodály strongly advocated singing without the aid of a piano because its use is a deterrent to the correct intonation required for vocal excellence. He said,

Most singing teachers and chorus masters believe in controlling the pitch of the voices by the piano. . . . Singing depends on the acoustically correct 'natural' intervals—not on the tempered system. Even a perfectly tuned piano can never be a criterion of singing, not to speak of the ever "out-of-tune" pianos available at schools and rehearsal rooms. . . . The beginners' first steps in the endless realm of notes should be supported not by any instrument of tempered tuning and dissimilar tone-color, but by another voice.[45]

To this end, he wrote *Let Us Sing Correctly*, a collection of 107 exercises for two voices. In the preface, he stated that correct intonation is the main purpose of these exercises, and rhythmic difficulties are therefore avoided. With the exception of the last two, these exercises lack semitones because "correct intonation can better be achieved if semitones are postponed until whole tones are sung with sufficient assurance."[46]

In August, 1942, Kodály, then sixty years old, officially retired from the Academy after thirty-five years of service. As a tribute to his efforts to improve music education, the National Federation of Choral Societies proclaimed 1942 a "Kodály Year."[47] He was further honored by the General Assembly of the Academy of Sciences, which elected him first as a corresponding member and later to the Philological Committee, on which he actively participated.[48]

Many students of Kodály have reflected on his position as a music educator. Among them, Mátyás Seiber (1905–1960) said,

With Kodály, instruction ceased to be merely instruction but became something quite different. He has that curiously compulsive and suggestive power of drawing out from his pupils their latent ability. . . . He makes no attempt to interfere in their development, but allows their personality to unfold in accordance with their individual bent. . . . It would be a complete mistake, however, to suppose that Kodály therefore just leaves his pupils to shift for themselves. . . . On the contrary, he has a clear plan of what he is doing and, without their suspecting it, he firmly leads them towards its fulfillment.[49]

Another student, Pál Járdányi (1920–1966), himself a composer and member of the Folk Music Research Group at the Academy of Sciences, studied composition with Kodály. Reflecting upon Kodály as a teacher, Járdányi said,

He never talked about his own work, and indeed did not like us to refer to it. If he wanted to illustrate a point he would take an example from one of the masters, usually one of the greatest; and his extraordinary capacity for quoting music at will brought home to us the value of erudition. This, and his austerity—his well-known "ruthlessness"—were continual incentives to serious study. . . . It was the combination of his fascinating power as an artist with his sober objectivity as a scholar that made his teaching quite unique.[50]

After his retirement from the Academy in 1942, Kodály devoted his attention chiefly to the primary schools, "which he considered to be the main front in the struggle for a national musical culture."[51] His first post-retirement contribution to music education was the *333 Reading Exercises*, completed in 1943. In the preface, he stated, "Our growing pedagogical literature has up to now (1943) not included sight-reading exercises. . . . The small number of sight-reading exercises found in textbooks are not sufficient. It is necessary always to have plenty of new material in order to present fresh and unfamiliar music."[52]

Kodály's reason for composing these reading tunes was to provide melodies that were well within the capabilities of the student. In further support of these compositions, Kodály said, "If we want our heritage of folksong to regain its old attraction, shining out over the whole nation, we have to prepare our children for it with tunes of limited compass and easy rhythm, but ones with the spirit and structure of the old folksongs."[53] In the 1961 revision to the *333 Reading Exercises*, Kodály addressed the usefulness of this new volume: "Only lively musical activity can produce a musical expert. Listening to music is by itself insufficient."[54]

While Kodály's main efforts were directed to music education through singing, he also recognized the value of using instruments to accompany singing. In the preface to Erzsébet Szőnyi's *Musical Reading and Writing*, published in 1954, Kodály declared, "The teaching of music is best begun with singing, that is, through singing, and before ever touching an instrument, the child should learn to read music."[55] Three years later (1957), however, in his postscript to "Music in Kindergarten," Kodály advocated the use of instruments in the classroom. According to Eősze, Kodály suggested the use of a blockflöte (recorder) or a cimbalom (Hungarian dulcimer) because they were accessible, small enough for children, and inexpensive.[56] Kodály also supported the use of a piano accompaniment—by a good composer, and only after the song was well known.[57] He discouraged the continual use of piano accompaniment because it deprived the child of the pleasure and profit gained through independent singing. He said, "Anyone who always walks with crutches will never be able to walk without them."[58] Further reinforcing his belief that the overuse of a piano cannot lead to correct singing, Kodály said, "If we incessantly accompany singing, the sense of the beauty of pure, unison melodies, which ought to be developed above all, will not develop.[59]

Kodály wrote *24 Little Canons on the Black Keys* in June 1945 to show one possible approach to the use of a piano with singing. This book is his only contribution to what is considered a beginning piano method. It is divided into two sections. The first sixteen canons use tonic sol-fa notation, and the remaining eight use conventional staff notation.[60] Kodály stated his reason for such a division in the preface:

> The musical imagination is more stimulated if two-part canons are played from one stave. . . . It is of great value if one melody is sung and the other played. Although the canons using sol-fa notation can be played in any key, it is nevertheless advisable to remain on the black keys. Introduced later, it can only appear as a defective and incomplete formula.[61]

Since Kodály had spent many years collecting and compiling Hungarian folk songs, he was well acquainted with those materials which were useful for teaching. In order to bridge the gap between his critical writings and the available teaching materials, Kodály composed four volumes of pentatonic music between 1945 and 1947. In the second volume, *100 Little Marches*, Kodály reviewed his position regarding early music education:

> While pondering on the music of the Kindergarten, I decided that more criticism would not bring about any real improvement. It was thus that these little pieces were written in order to make some small contribution to replacing the awful marching and walking songs then customary in such classes. "What is the need for them? Why, there are already folksongs available," somebody might say. Indeed there are, but, as I have declared many times, we have very few pentatonic folksongs of sufficiently limited compass and rhythm. For this reason, smaller children need tunes written in the spirit of folksongs but without their difficulties. In such pieces, by making them into games, we can prepare the ground for genuine folksongs.[62]

The period immediately following Kodály's retirement from the Liszt Academy in 1942 was a relatively inactive one for him. Then, in 1946, he was elected president of the Academy of Sciences. In that same year, Kodály, along with his first wife, Emma, toured Britain and the United States. This tour was followed by a second tour to the Soviet Union in 1947, where he conducted concerts of his own works in Moscow and Leningrad.[63]

On his sixty-fifth birthday (1947), Kodály received the "freedom of his native town," Kecskemét, and was invested with the Grand Cross of the Order of the Republic by the minister of education.[64] Within three months, on March 15, 1948, he was further honored by being one of the first of his countrymen to receive the newly instituted Kossuth Prize "for signal services in the fields of science and the arts."[65]

During the 1950s, Kodály resumed his work to improve Hungarian music education. This decade served as the apex of his career by the fact that he persuaded the Ministry of Education to allow an experiment in music education to be conducted in Kecskemét, the town of his birth. Kodály established a Singing Primary School, in which music was taught daily via his principles and philosophy. Under his personal guidance, Márta Nemesszeghy, who later became one of the master teachers of the Kodály method, taught daily music lessons as a part of the regular curriculum. Lois Choksy, professor of music at the University of Calgary, suggests that because students exposed to the Kodály method began to show improvement in other academic areas, Kodály and Nemesszeghy were able to convince the Ministry not only to continue support of the first Singing Primary School, but also to approve the establishment of additional schools.[66] Where there was only one such school in 1950, there were in 1983 more than 140.[67] This increase in the number of Singing Schools kept Kodály's schedule full because he visited each one for the purpose of advising the teachers and listening to the children's choirs.

In the meantime, Kodály was honored several times. In 1952, he was presented a second Kossuth Prize and awarded the First Division of the Order of the Hungarian People's Republic with the title of "Eminent Artist," as a tribute not only to his accomplishments in music education but in honor of his seventieth birthday.[68] A third Kossuth Prize was bestowed upon him in 1957, the same year in which he was elected president of the Music Council, a newly established post set up by the Ministry of Education. After the death of Emma Sándor, Kodály's first wife of forty-eight years, he married Sarolta Péczely, a conducting student at the Academy, in 1959.

Also during this time, Kodály prepared the accumulated mass of folk materials, some of which he and Béla Bartók had collected during their folk song tour in 1910, for publication by the Academy of Sciences. In 1951, the first volume of the *Corpus Musicae Popularis Hungaricae* (Thesaurus of Hungarian Folk Music), *Gyermekjátékok* (Children's Games), was published. Referring to this effort, Kodály said, "This collection will have a lasting practical influence, and not only on our national life." He continued, "Folk song is one of the mighty cornerstones on which our nation can be rebuilt. The songs of the people are the heralds of life—of life that goes on forever."[69]

Kodály devoted his professional lifetime to establishing his position regarding music education and his retirement years to clarifying these beliefs. According to Eősze, Kodály was provoked into controversy by a widely expressed opinion that music education needed to progress beyond the folk song. To this Kodály replied, "This is quite true. We must, indeed. But before we can begin to do so, we must first get as far as folk song."[70] Music educators who had been observing Kodály's principles being taught in the Singing Schools were sometimes disturbed to see folk songs as the main source of teaching materials. What these observers misunderstood, perhaps, was that through singing folk songs, the student was acquiring good music reading skills, and through these skills, he was gaining a deep and lasting appreciation of art music. In essence, Kodály advocated teaching a love for music supported by a knowledge about music. Because folk song is an accessible product of its people, especially in children's singing games, Kodály supported its use as the point at which one's music education should begin. Subsequent volumes of the *Corpus Musicae Popularis Hungaricae* were published in 1953, 1955/1956, 1959, 1966 and 1973.

In 1954, Kodály's prolific output included five volumes of exercises, all of which were written to improve sight-singing and ear training. These volumes included *Tricinia*, a collection of 28 three-part singing exercises; *Epigrams*, a collection of nine songs for voice and piano accompaniment; and three volumes of two-part singing exercises of graded difficulty. The *55 Two-Part Exercises* require less demanding reading skills, while the *44 Two-Part* and *33 Two-Part Exercises* are more challenging. Of these five volumes, only one (*Tricinia*) included a dedication by the composer, in which he wrote: "To the better musicians of a better future."[71] In the preface to the same work, Kodály wrote that "no one can consider himself as a properly educated musician who cannot sing at sight, easily, confidently, and artistically."[72] In his preface to the *55 Two-Part Exercises* he says,

Every intelligent musician is beginning to realize that if a higher level is to be attained we must change our working methods. We can produce better musicians only if we can bring about a thorough reorganization in our methods of teaching music. . . . There is a need for better musicians, and only those will become good musicians who work at it every day. The better a musician is, the easier it is for him to draw others into the happy, magic circle of music. Thus he will serve the great cause of helping music to belong to everyone.[73]

The singing exercises which Kodály composed in 1954 provided the basic material for the sight-reading program. Three additional volumes of this graded series of two-part exercises are the *66 Two-Part Exercises*, *22 Two-Part Exercises*, and *77 Two-Part Exercises*, published respectively in 1962, 1964, and 1966. These three volumes completed the six-volume sequence of reading exercises. The larger numbered volumes contain sight-singing exercises that are less technically demanding, both rhythmically and melodically.

The *77 Two-Part Exercises*, written in 1966, addressed the need for shorter and easier exercises than those which followed in the *66 Two-Part Exercises*. In the preface, Kodály wrote, "Besides archaic Hungarian songs I have tried to use and adapt into two-part settings some very interesting Ainu[74] motives. . . . Sight-reading must at all times offer fresh material, including some unusual turns of melody and rhythm, but remaining always sound and attractive music, never degenerating into mere mechanical exercises."[75]

According to Percy M. Young, editor of the Zoltán Kodály Choral Method Series, the *77 Two-Part Exercises* was the last work that Kodály prepared for publication before his death. Young stated that this volume was printed in the form in which Kodály wished it to go to press. In a letter to the publishers, dated January 21, 1967, Kodály wrote of his desire to omit annotations, dynamic markings, or indications of a changed tonic center in order to challenge the pupil into "active thinking."[76]

The *66 Two-Part Exercises*, written in 1962, contained no preface by the composer. It did include, however, some observations by Geoffry Russell-Smith, revision editor of the Kodály Choral Method, who wrote, "[T]his book introduces a wider freedom of key through comparatively frequent modulation, and at the same time explores polyphonic devices and styles. The standard of difficulty involved places it after the *15 Two-part Exercises*, along with *Bicinia Hungarica IV* and the easier items from *Tricinia*."[77]

The most demanding sight-reading of this Choral Method is the *22 Two-Part Exercises*, written in 1964.[78] While Kodály did not write a preface, Young declared this series of pieces "a masterly exposition of the art of writing two-part counterpoint which should be gratefully accepted by all students who are either required or wish to gain fluency in this fundamental technique of composition."[79]

During the 1960s, Kodály continued his visits to schools, composing, and writing articles about music education. He was invited to serve as guest conductor of his own compositions and also made recordings of his works. In 1960, Kodály was invited to Great Britain. Here he directed performances of his own works and lectured at Oxford University, where an honorary doctorate was conferred on him.[80]

In 1961, at the age of 79, Kodály was elected president of the International Folk Music Council. In that same year, he completed his *Symphony in C Major*. He was further honored in 1964 by his appointment as a lifelong honorary president of the International Society for Music Education (ISME).

Kodály remained active in many areas, not just music education. In 1966 the American Guild of Organists (AGO), Atlanta chapter, commissioned him to write a piece for mixed chorus and organ to be premiered at the 1966 national AGO Convention in Atlanta. This composition, *Laudes Organi*, is a fantasia on a sequence from the twelfth century.[81] In the same year, he toured Toronto, attended the ISME Conference at Interlochen, Michigan, and visited Stanford University.[82] In addition to his extensive travel schedule, Kodály prepared the fifth volume of *Corpus Musicae Popularis Hungaricae* for publication. He also composed and arranged the *77 Two-Part Exercises*, making his final years comparably productive to those of his youth.[83] He died on March 6, 1967.

Sarolta Kodály, Zoltán's second wife, reflected on her husband's work: "It was essentially the personal relationship between Zoltán Kodály and the teachers who understood his ideas, that created and developed Hungarian music teaching. This personal interest—his advice and encouragement—spurred on teacher and pupil alike to achieve increasingly better results." She continued,

> He would accept the invitation of the smallest village school, if the work in progress there was worthy of encouragement. He gave his last address on the sixth of November, 1966, at Dunapataj, a village of six thousand inhabitants. It may not be superfluous to quote a few sentences from his speech in order to signify how, out of all the activities of his life, music education was indeed so dear to his heart.[84]

Former OAKE board member Betsy Moll explains one possible reason for Kodály's broad spectrum of accomplishments:

> I think that one of the reasons [for his influence] is the fact that Kodály had such a long life—nearly eighty-five years. . . . He worked alertly and actively up to his death. . . . He was considered a great man among his intellectual peers at home and abroad. He was known and respected among scientists, poets, linguists, artists, and he was undoubtedly a scholar of the highest honor. The fact that such a man among men was so vitally interested in education and children gave an uplift to the whole teaching profession.[85]

Helga Szabó cited Kodály, whose work illuminated the importance of music as a compulsory, daily subject: "Music is an indispensable part of human culture. Imperfect is the culture of him who lacks it. There is no complete man without music. . . . Dealing with music every day stimulates the mind so that it grows more receptive to everything else."[86]

Kodály was a voluminous composer and writer of essays on a variety of subjects. In addition to his prolific contribution of choral compositions for children's and adult choruses,[87] he wrote instrumental solos, transcriptions of selected pieces of J. S. Bach, chamber music, and orchestral works. He wrote many essays on folk music, and he frequently paid tribute to his predecessors and contemporaries by writing and delivering lectures in their honor. Some of Kodály's writings are focused on his own compositions. He presented and published sixty-three essays in an effort to raise the caliber of music education. It is improbable that Kodály ever thought of this means of teaching music as his own method. Instead he realized it was the common effort of many: musicians, teachers, psychologists, ethnomusicologists and students.

Lois Choksy has suggested that *Énekes ABC*, a songbook compiled by György Kerényi and Benjámin Rajecsky (published in Budapest in 1938 by Magyar Kórus), should be considered the precursor of the Kodály method.[88] It was five years later that Kodály, in cooperation with Kerényi, wrote *Iskolai Enekegyüjtemény* (School Song Collection). Published in Budapest, this text contains two volumes, one for ages six to ten and another for ages eleven to fourteen. Kodály composed his *333 Reading Exercises* to accompany this singing book.[89]

Erzsébet Szőnyi, a composition student of Kodály and a professor of music at the Liszt Academy, was the first to outline a complete teaching sequence and incorporated many of the techniques of Kodály pedagogy into books for the use of students enrolled in the Zeneiskola, a Hungarian school whose curriculum was specifically designed for the training of young musicians.[90] Szőnyi's three volumes, entitled *A Zenei Irás-Olvasás Módzsertana* (Musical Reading and Writing), combine all the elements of what has come to be known as the Kodály method.[91]

The Kodály method has received considerable attention in the United States through summer courses, workshops, seminars, and publications. Lois Choksy suggests that it was Kodály's vision that gave breath to this method of education: "Books alone do not make a system of education. It was in the schools and in the hands of the teachers that the Method truly evolved and is still evolving, for the Kodály Method is a living method, not a static one. As better ways are found, they are incorporated."[92]

Choksy cites other educators who expressed their interest in the Hungarian music education system by visiting Hungary and studying the method firsthand.[93] During the 1960s, Estonian educator Heino Kaljuste introduced the Hungarian singing school textbooks to the U.S.S.R., and Jacquotte Ribière-Raverlat, after a year of study in Hungary, wrote the first French language exposition of the method, titled *L'Education musicale dans Hongrie*. In the United States, Mary Helen Richards published *Threshold to Music* after her brief visit to Hungary. Denise Bacon, founder of the Kodály Musical Training Institute (1969) and the Kodály Center of America (1977), became the first American to spend an academic year in Hungary studying the method in 1968–1969. In Tokyo, Hani Kyoto founded the Japanese Kodály Institute after spending an academic year of study in Hungary. According to Choksy, it was the quality of music education itself that attracted musicians and educators to Hungary after 1964. She adds, however, that foreign interest in Hungarian music education actually began in 1958:

> International awareness of the Hungarian music education system perhaps began with the International Society for Music Education (ISME) Conferences in Vienna in 1958 and in Tokyo in 1963, where reports of the method were presented, and the 1964 Conference in Budapest, where Kodály gave an address and was elected Honorary President. It was the latter conference that seemed to cause the beginnings of widespread international interest, since those attending it could see the results of the system firsthand.[94]

In the years following his death in 1967, Kodály's ideals are becoming more universally accepted among music educators. By 1964 musicians in the United States were introduced to his principles via workshops. Five years later, colleges and universities were offering programs leading to certification in Kodály methodology.[95] Resulting, in part, from these programs, the Organization of American Kodály Educators (OAKE) was established in 1974 in Anaheim, California to disseminate knowledge and support activities beneficial to both the music educator and the profession at large. Contemporary society, by its highly complex nature, requires the support of professional organizations to represent the interests of a specific area. OAKE exists to assist its members in continued development of Kodály's philosophy, both in tribute to the man who inspired so many people, and as an informational resource for music educators who wish to communicate accurate knowledge about Kodály to others in the music education profession. It is the hope of this author that Kodály's message of humanism continues to influence all of humankind.

THE MUSIC OF ZOLTÁN KODÁLY

CHAMBER MUSIC

Trio for two violins and viola (previous to 1900)
Intermezzo for string trio (1905)
String Quartet No. 1 (1908-09)
Sonata for violoncello and piano (1914)
Duet for violin and violoncello (1914)
String Quartet No. 2 (1916-18)
Serenade for two violins and viola (1919-20)

CHILDREN'S CHORUSES AND CHOIRS FOR EQUAL VOICES

The Straw Guy (1925)
See the Gypsy Munching Cheese (1925)
St. Gregory's Day (1925)

Children's Song (1927)

Jesus Appears (1927)

Shepherd's Song (1928)

The Deaf Boatman/Gypsy Lament/God's Blacksmith (1928)

Children's Song/Whitsuntide/Dancing Song/New Year's Greeting (1931)

A Birthday Greeting (1931)

Epiphany (1933)

Bunnykin (1934)

Rorate (1935)

The Angels and the Shepherds (1935)

Seven Easy Children's Choirs and Six Canons (1936)

Huszt (1936)

To the Magyars, canon (1936)

The Geneva Psalm No. 150 (1936)

Bells (1937)

Angel's Garden (1937)

The Peacock (1937)

Children's Song/Three Folk Songs from Gömör (1937)

The Filly (1937)

Gee-Up, My Horse (1938)

Treacherous Gleam (1938)

Evening Song (1938)

Hymn to King Stephen (1938)

Don't Despair (1939)

Solmization Canon (1942)

Hungarian against Hungarian (1944)

The Son of an Enslaved Country/Still, by a Miracle, Our Country Stands (1944)

St. Agnes' Day (1945)

To Live or Die/Hey, Bandi Bungozsdi (1947)

Hymn of Liberty (1948)

Motto (1948)

Peace Song (1952)

Children's Song (1954)

National Ode (1955)

Dedication to András Fáy/The Guard at the Tower of Nándor (1956)

Wonderful Liberty, canon (1957)

Children's Song (1958)

Honey, Honey, Honey (1958)

Tell Me, Where is Fancy Bred (1959)

Lads of Harasztos (1961)

To the Singing Youth (1962)

FEMALE VOICES

Two songs from Zobor (1908)
Mountain Nights (1923)
Mountain Nights II-IV (1955-56)
Mountain Nights V (1962)
Four Italian Madrigals (1932)
Ave Maria (1935)
Rorate (1935)
Hymn to King Stephen (1938)
Don't Despair (1939)
I am Lonely (1953)
Children's Song (1954)
Woe is Me (1957)

A CAPPELLA CHORAL WORKS

Mixed Voices:

Evening (1904)
A Birthday Greeting (1931)
Matra Pictures (1931)
The Aged (1933)
Székély Lament/Jesus and the Traders (1934)
Too Late (1934)
Horatii Carmen II (1934)
To Ferenc Liszt/Molnar Anna (1936)
To the Magyars, canon (1936)
The Peacock (1937)
Hymn to St. Stephen (1938)
Evening Song (1938)
Greeting to St. John, boys' mixed choir (1939)
Norwegian Girls (1940)
The Forgotten Song of Bálint Ballassi (1942)
First Communion (1942)
Invocation of Peace/To the Székélys/Cohors generosa/Song from Gömör (1943)
Advent Song (1943)
Battle Song (1943)
Lament (1947)

The Hungarian Nation (1947)
The Hymn of Liberty "La Marseillaise" (1948)
Adoration (1948)
Motto (1948)
The Geneva Psalm No. 50 (1948)
Wish for Peace (1953)
Zrinyi's Appeal (1954)
The Arms of Hungary (1956)
I Will Go Look for Death (1959)
Sík Sándor's Te Deum (1961)
Media vita in morte sumus (1961)
Mohács (1965)

Male Voices:

Stabat Mater (ca. 1900)
Two Choruses (1913-17)
Jesus Appears (1927)
Canticum nuptial (1928)
Songs of Karád (1934)
Whom to Marry (1934)
Horatius: Justum et tenacem (1935)

EDUCATIONAL MUSIC AND SINGING EXERCISES

Fifteen Two-Part Exercises (1941)
Bicinia Hungarica (1937-42)
Let Us Sing Correctly (1941)
333 Reading Exercises (1943)
Pentatonic Music I-IV (1945-48)
33 Two-Part Exercises (1954)
44 Two-Part Exercises (1954)
55 Two-Part Exercises (1954)
Tricinia (1954)
Epigrams (1954)
Fifty Nursery Songs (1961)
66 Two-Part Exercises (1962)
22 Two-Part Exercises (1964)
77 Two-Part Exercises (1966)

Editor's note: For a more complete listing of compositions, see https://www.iks.hu/zoltan-kodalys-life-and-work/compositions.html

WRITINGS OF ZOLTÁN KODÁLY

The Hungarians of Transylvania, Folk Songs (1921)
Hungarian Folk Music (1937, 1943, 1951, 1960, and 1966)
School Song Collection I-II (1943)
Sol-Fa I-VIII, in collaboration with Jenő Adám (1944-45)
Song Books for Forms I-VIII, with Jenő Adám (1948)
The Folk Song Collection of János Arany, with Agost Gyulai (1953)
Retrospection I-II, a collection of Kodály's Essays and Writings (1964)

Notes

[1] László Eősze, *Zoltán Kodály: His Life and Work*, trans. István Farkas and Gyula Gulyás (Budapest: Corvina Press, 1962), 13.

[2] Eősze, *Zoltán Kodály*, 14.

[3] Ferenc Deák (1803-1876) was a political leader who became ruler over the Hungarian nationalists in 1849. By 1867, he was instrumental in drawing up the Ausgleich (compromise) that established the Dual Monarchy. This government provided each country its individual freedom in domestic concerns, although the areas of economy and defense were the concern of a central administration.

[4] Rudolf L. Tőkes, *Béla Kun and the Hungarian Soviet Republic* (New York: Frederick A. Praeger, 1967), 79.

[5] Charles I (1887-1922), the last Hapsburg ruler, was, from 1916-1918, concurrently Emperor of Austria and King (Charles IV) of Hungary. In 1918, Hungary declared her independence, after which Charles abdicated and went into exile in Madeira.

[6] Eősze, *Zoltán Kodály*, 23.

[7] Tőkes, *Béla Kun*, 257.

[8] See "The Music of Zoltán Kodály" (listing at end of article).

[9] Tonic sol-fa is a system of movable do solmization designed to facilitate sight-singing.

[10] Personal letter from László Eősze, November 14, 1984.

[11] Helga Szabó, *The Kodály Concept of Music Education*, trans. Geoffry Russell-Smith (London: Boosey and Hawkes, 1969), 10.

[12] Personal letter from László Eősze, November 14, 1984.

[13] Eősze, *Zoltán Kodály*, 23.

[14] Eősze, *Zoltán Kodály*, 23.

[15] Eősze, *Zoltán Kodály*, 23-24.

[16] Eősze, *Zoltán Kodály*, 24.

[17] Eősze, *Zoltán Kodály*, 24.

[18] Eősze, *Zoltán Kodály*, 25.

[19] Eősze, *Zoltán Kodály*, 25.

[20] Eősze, *Zoltán Kodály*, 26.

[21] Eősze, *Zoltán Kodály*, 26.

[22] Eősze, *Zoltán Kodály*, 69.

[23] See Listing "The Music of Zoltán Kodály."

[24] Eősze, *Zoltán Kodály*, 29.

[25] Lois Choksy, *The Kodály Method* (New Jersey: Prentice-Hall, 1974), 9.

[26] Zoltán Kodály, *The Selected Writings of Zoltán Kodály* (London: Boosey and Hawkes, 1974), 127.

[27] Interview with Ilona Bartalus, July 14, 1982, at the University of Calgary, where she was a visiting professor.

[28] Eősze, *Zoltán Kodály*, 79.

[29] Margaret Stone, "Zoltán Kodály 1882-1967," *Kodály Envoy* 9, no. 2 (Fall 1982): 2.

[30] Erzsébet Szőnyi, *Kodály's Principles in Practice*, trans. John Weissman (London: Boosey and Hawkes, 1973), 20.

[31] According to Peggy D. Bennett, assistant professor of music education at the University of Texas at Arlington, the English tonic sol-fa system was authored by Sarah Glover circa 1830. John Curwen subsequently adapted and popularized Glover's work after 1841. See "Sarah Glover: A Forgotten Pioneer in Music Education," *Journal of Research in Music Education* 32, no. 1 (1984): 49-65.

[32] Connie Foss More, "Kodály: The Eclectic Approach," *Kodály Envoy* 4, no. 2 (Nov. 1977): 2.

[33] The complete writings and speeches of Zoltán Kodály, *Visszateintés kintes I-II*, published by Zenemükiado Vallalat in 1964. Some of these essays are available in an English translation entitled *The Selected Writings of Zoltán Kodály* (London: Boosey and Hawkes, 1974).

[34] Kodály, *Selected Writings*, 120.

[35] Kodály, *Selected Writings*, 120.

[36] Szabó, *Kodály Concept*, 6.

[37] Kodály, *Selected Writings*, 37.

[38] Eősze, *Zoltán Kodály*, 71.

[39] János Mátyás, notes on record jacket, *Kodály Choral Works 5: Two-Part Singing Exercises*, Budapest "Zoltán Kodály" Girls Chorus, Ilona Andor, conductor, Hungaroton LPX 11469.

[40] Zoltán Kodály, *Bicinia Hungarica*, vol. 1, ed. Geoffry Russell-Smith (London: Boosey and Hawkes, 1968), 4.

[41] Kodály, *Bicinia Hungarica*, 3.

[42] Kodály, *Selected Writings*, 128.

[43] Eősze, *Zoltán Kodály*, 40.

[44] Zoltán Kodály, *Fifteen Two-Part Exercises* (New York: Boosey and Hawkes, 1952), 3.

[45] Zoltán Kodály, *Let Us Sing Correctly* (New York: Boosey and Hawkes, 1952), 3.

[46] Kodály, *Let Us Sing*, 3.

[47] Eősze, *Zoltán Kodály*, 40.

[48] According to Eősze, the Academy of Sciences is an institute of scholars in various faculties and fields. Personal letter from László Eősze to author, November 14, 1984.

[49] Eősze, *Zoltán Kodály*, 68.

[50] Eősze, *Zoltán Kodály*, 69.

[51] Eősze, *Zoltán Kodály*, 78.

[52] Zoltán Kodály, *333 Reading Exercises* (New York: Boosey and Hawkes, 1954), iii.

[53] Kodály, *333 Reading Exercises*, ii.

[54] Kodály, *333 Reading Exercises*, iii.

[55] Erzsébet Szőnyi, *Musical Reading and Writing*, trans. Lili Halápy (Budapest: Corvina Press, 1978), i.

[56] Personal letter from László Eősze, November 14, 1984.

[57] Kodály, *Selected Writings*, 151.

[58] Kodály, *Selected Writings*, 150.

[59] Kodály, *Selected Writings*, 151.

[60] In Kodály's *24 Little Canons on the Black Keys*, the tonic sol-fa consonants (*d, r, m*) are attached to a corresponding conventional rhythmic notation.

[61] Zoltán Kodály, *24 Little Canons on the Black Keys* (New York: Boosey and Hawkes, 1957), 2.

[62] Zoltán Kodály, *Pentatonic Music, Volume II* (New York: Boosey and Hawkes, 1970), 3.

[63] Eősze, *Zoltán Kodály*, 42-43.

[64] Personal letter from László Eősze, November 14, 1984. He stated that "freedom of a native town" is comparable to an honorary degree, and also known as "honorary freeman" throughout the world. Also consult Eősze, *Zoltán Kodály*, 51.

[65] Eősze, *Zoltán Kodály*, 43.

[66] Choksy, *Kodály Method*, 10.

[67] Lois Choksy, interview at University of Texas Kodály Summer Course, Dallas, TX, June 15, 1983.

[68] Eősze, *Zoltán Kodály*, 45.

[69] Eősze, *Zoltán Kodály*, 84.

[70] Eősze, *Zoltán Kodály*, 84.

[71] Zoltán Kodály, *Tricinia* (New York: Boosey and Hawkes, 1964), 3.

[72] Kodály, *Tricinia*, 2.

[73] Zoltán Kodály, *55 Two-Part Exercises* (New York: Boosey and Hawkes, 1965), 3.

[74] Aboriginal Caucasian people inhabiting the northernmost islands of Japan.

[75] Zoltán Kodály, *77 Two-Part Exercises* (New York: Boosey and Hawkes, 1967), 2.

[76] Kodály, *77 Two-Part Exercises*, 2.

[77] Zoltán Kodály, *66 Two-Part Exercises* (New York: Boosey and Hawkes, 1969), 2.

[78] Zoltán Kodály, *22 Two-Part Exercises* (New York: Boosey and Hawkes, 1964).

[79] Kodály, *22 Two-Part Exercises*, 4.

[80] Personal letter from László Eősze, November 14, 1984. Eősze stated that the University of Toronto also bestowed Kodály with a second honorary Ph.D. in 1966.

[81] Thomas S. Kite, "Kodály and the Organ," *The American Organist* 16, no. 10 (October 1982): 62.

[82] Stone, "Zoltán Kodály," 2.

[83] Kodály, *77 Two-Part Exercises*.

[84] Szabó, *The Kodály Concept*, 3.

[85] Betsy McLaughlin Moll, "The Significance of the Kodály Conception in America," *Musart* 23, no. 3 (1971): 5-6.

[86] Szabó, *Kodály Concept*, 3.

[87] See Listing, "The Music of Zoltán Kodály."

[88] Choksy, *Kodály Method*, 9.

[89] Kodály, *333 Reading Exercises*.

[90] Lois Choksy, interview, University of Texas Kodály Summer Course, Dallas, TX, June 15, 1983.

[91] Erzsébet Szőnyi, *Musical Reading and Writing*, Volumes I, II, III, trans. by Lili Halápy, rev. Geoffry Russell-Smith (Budapest: Editio Musica Budapest, 1978).

[92] Choksy, *Kodály Method*, 10.

[93] Choksy, *Kodály Method*, 12.

[94] Choksy, *Kodály Method*, 11.

[95] Sr. Mary Alice Hein, "Kodály at the College Level: Undergraduate and Graduate," in *Kodály Envoy* 2, no. 1 (June 1975): 3.

Originally published in *Kodály Envoy* 16, no. 3 (Winter 1990): 5-30. Reprinted by permission.

MAKING (WHICH?) MUSIC TOGETHER

Lois Choksy

When I think of my childhood, certain things come back to me with crystal clarity. I remember my grandmother's huge black iron stove with its warming shelf that always held left-over bacon and cornmeal pancakes for me, mid-morning. Nothing before or since ever tasted so good. I remember summer days, walking barefoot on hot sand, jumping from one shady spot to another.

I remember hating school. Being tall for my age, I was always seated at the back of the classroom. Being very nearsighted, I couldn't see anything written on the blackboard. The teachers simply assumed that I was slow. And the one thing I really wanted to do—sing in the choir—I was never allowed.

Recalling those days and those teachers, I am put in mind of a cartoon I once saw:
A teacher is sitting behind her desk talking to a parent, saying "I'm afraid your son can never have a career in music. He doesn't seem to hear very well, Mrs. Beethoven!"

I do not mean to equate myself and my meager talents with those of Beethoven; however, I think there is a lesson for all of us in this. It is our job as teachers not to prejudge our students, but rather to open the world of music to them all, whatever we may think of their talents. We could be wrong, you know.

Kodály's principal dictum was "Music for all." This should be for us and for the children we teach our overriding goal.

The happiest days of my childhood were Saturdays. From the time I was twelve years old I spent all day Saturday at the Peabody Conservatory in Baltimore, Maryland. I took voice and piano lessons, I sang in a choir, I learned to sing in sol-fa, took musical dictation, studied harmony and music literature. And made friends. For the first time I realized that I wasn't really weird—or that if I was, I had a lot of company. I lived for Saturdays.

Somehow I grew up, and somehow I managed, in spite of teachers, to acquire an education of sorts.

And then, fifty-five years ago, I walked into my first classroom as a teacher. It was shortly after World War II, and I, as someone with only three years of university and no teaching experience, was given something called a "War Emergency Teaching Certificate" and turned loose to teach all subjects to a class of forty-seven third and fourth grade children. I had only the fuzziest idea of how to teach reading, and my own math and science skills were limited, to say the least. But I had studied music for fourteen years, and whenever I wasn't sure what to do next, I taught the children a song or told them about one or another of my favorite pieces of music and played it for them on the school's one and only, rather dilapidated, portable record player.

The school principal was so impressed that I managed to keep forty-seven children more or less occupied and quiet that he came to the (mistaken) conclusion that I was a "good" teacher.

Other teachers in the school were not so easily fooled. But they did see and hear that my children sang every day and that they sang well. I began to get invitations:

"I'll teach your math (spelling, science, geography) on Tuesday and Thursday if you'll teach my music." Before I knew what was happening, about 50% of my teaching time was spent in music. I was a much happier teacher and I dare say my children learned a great deal more math, science and geography than they would have with me.

This went on for five years, with me gradually assuming responsibility for all the music in the school, including a choir and Christmas and spring programs. At this point the district decided to institute school music programs in all of its thirty-three elementary schools, and I was the first "music teacher" hired.

After that I happily taught music to my 500 children on a twice-weekly schedule.
I used movable-do sol-fa in my teaching because it was how I had learned music (Peabody Conservatory being one of the few music schools in the U.S. progressive enough to use movable rather than fixed do).

Still, I had an uncomfortable feeling that I wasn't doing justice to my charges. My "curriculum," if such it could be called, was a hodge-podge of singing and listening in no particular order. I was considered to be a "good" teacher (whatever that is) and other teachers were brought to observe my classes—but, in truth, I had no idea where I was going with my teaching or why I was doing the things I did. I was simply teaching as I had been taught, and I really hadn't been taught very well.

It was an enlightened supervisor who pointed me in the direction of Kodály, and a three-week summer course at Esztergom in Hungary in 1968 changed my life. There, I met Erzsébet Szönyi—the Liszt Academy professor and composer of whom musicologist Alexander Ringer said, "she wears the mantle of Kodály"—and she invited me to return to Hungary for a year to study with her and to observe in the schools. I think it was already in her mind at that time that I should write a book in English about teaching the Kodály way, but I'm not sure—she is ever the master of gentle persuasion.

I spent the academic year of 1970-71 in Hungary, at the Franz Liszt Academy of Music, and in the schools of Budapest, Kecskemét, Székesfehérvár, Miskolc, Pécs, and outlying villages. At first exposure to the Hungarian schools, one is bowled over by the apparent ease with which children sing, read, write, improvise and analyze music. It simply does not seem within the realm of possibility.

That initial glimpse of extraordinary technical facility is both impressive and misleading. One does not necessarily see the carefully constructed foundation underlying all that flash and dash. Indeed, while I was there, there were a number of what I still think of as "one week wonders"—people who came to Hungary from far and wide to observe in the schools, spent one or two weeks and went home to write music books based on what they saw—books usually full of Hungarian songs and cute pictures. They observed sequence without perceiving its philosophic and pedagogic basis; they saw the technical facility without understanding its roots in musical understanding. They mistook the vehicle for the destination.

"Why is it always the incompetent people that force their way to the scene of action, spoiling things to such an extent that twice as much work is needed to put things right again. . . ."[1]

While that remark of Kodály's may seem harsh, it is one with which I am in complete accord. I think we have all seen materials presented under the banner of Kodály that were quick and slick—highly commercial, but with little educational or musical value—what I think of as the Mickey Mouse or McDonald's approach to music education. There is no quick fix for what we as dedicated music educators must do. It's hard work all the way.

I think that good teaching is probably 49% science, 49% art, and 2% black magic. We can plan carefully, fully aware of child development, fully cognizant of correct sequencing for learning, knowledgeable in music, and still have no idea what people, either children or adults, are taking away from our teaching. When we are young we assume that once we have said something to a class, once we have imparted some bit of knowledge, naturally, those upon whom we bestowed it then "know" it. As we acquire age and experience we learn that, sadly, this is by no means the case. Nothing could be further from the truth. It is a simple fact that what the learner brings to the learning is at least as important as what the teacher brings. And there is no test or evaluation device on earth that can give us an accurate picture of what children bring to or carry away from a music lesson. I am appalled at the so-called "tests of musical aptitude" that seem to flourish, particularly in the United States. I'm not sure what they test (other than an ability to take tests), but it isn't musical aptitude.

I have a home on a small island in the Caribbean. For many years, whenever I was there, I volunteer-taught music to the children in the school. In a first grade class, there was a child, Raymond, who never sang. I used to sit with the children clustered around me for their singing lessons. Raymond always placed himself close beside me, one thumb firmly in his mouth and the other hand clutching my skirt. He never uttered a sound. If I directly addressed him he looked at the floor and squirmed. Then one Saturday I was in the car outside a village shop, waiting for my husband, when Raymond approached, leaned in the car window, smiled, and started singing in a clear, accurate voice. In a period of 30 minutes, he sang every song I had taught the class in the preceding three months. You can well imagine my astonishment!

The following Tuesday he was back in my class, clutching my skirt, thumb firmly ensconced in mouth once more. But I no longer worried that he wasn't learning anything.

The mind is a wonderful thing. We should never underestimate the capabilities of those we teach.

I have taught long enough now to have known the children, even the grandchildren, of children I taught. Many times former students have approached me to recount some moment they particularly recalled. And do you know what? Not one of them has ever said "That was a wonderful lesson on fa that day in 4th grade" or "I've never forgotten ta-ta-ti-ti-ta!" They have, variously, recalled specific songs we sang, pieces of music we listened to, concerts we gave, concerts we attended.

I'm not suggesting that fa and ti-ti-ta are not important, but rather that they are only the vehicle. Music, real music, must be the destination.

If I seem to be downplaying the importance of musical literacy or of carefully sequencing material for instruction, such is not my intention. Indeed, my Australian colleague and good friend Frank York once referred to me as the "queen of sequence" (if I'm given a grocery list, I tend to sequence it).

Yes. Sequencing learning so that it proceeds seamlessly from simple to complex within each musical element is important. We cannot possibly teach effectively unless we first organize learning in this way.

Yes. Musical literacy is a worthy goal, and sol-fa and rhythm syllables are useful in achieving that goal. We would be foolish not to use such efficient tools.

But they are means, not ends. They are vehicle, not destination.

Of what use is it to teach linguistic literacy if our students aspire to nothing better than comic books or computer games?

Of what use is it to teach musical literacy if our students aspire to nothing better than the latest pop music? Music Kodály referred to as "the refuse of street music."[2]

There is a world of great literature to be lost if our children are not made hungry for it.

There is a world of great music to be lost if we do not bring it to our children and our children to it!

Kodály stated the principal goal of music education as:

"To make the masterpieces of world [music] literature public property, to convey them to people of every kind and rank."[3]

And later, in a lecture presented at the University of Toronto on the occasion of his being granted an honorary doctorate, he said:

"The final purpose of all this must be to introduce the students to an understanding and love of great classical music—of the past, present and future."[4]

This then must be our promise and our commitment: to bring the best music to our children—to create in them a hunger that can be satisfied only with music of unquestionable quality.

How can we do this?

We must make up our minds first never to use the cheap and tawdry, never to use edutainment music, never to use the expedient, commercially contrived and marketed slosh that permeates our society. Perhaps the only time and place in which our young charges will encounter good music is when they are with us for one or two hours a week. We cannot afford to waste a moment of that precious time on transitory music.

"Whatever 'lessons' are contained in music that is worthless from an artistic point of view, these works are harmful from the pedagogical aspect, too."[5]

"Let us stop the teachers' superstition that only some diluted art-substitute is suitable for teaching purposes. A child is the most susceptible and the most enthusiastic audience for pure art. . . . Only art of intrinsic value is suitable for children. Everything else is harmful."[6]

Judit Hartyányi, in her keynote address to us last Monday morning, said,

"Our task as music teachers is to bring people closer to one another with the help of music, to turn the face of the individual towards his fellows again: to make music together. Let us teach and learn good quality music!"[7]

Once we have made the commitment to good music, the rest is easy.

What are the enduring songs of early childhood? Each culture has its own, passed from generation to generation of children, often without the intervention or even knowledge of adults: the nursery songs and acting-out games, the chase games, games of mock courtship and even songs and games depicting death, through which children attempt to decipher the incomprehensible world of the adults around them. These are a microcosm of life. They have survived in some cases for hundreds of years, and they exist in every culture. They have intrinsic value.

And after the nursery songs and games, what? The world of each people's own folk music heritage, of course. How better to understand oneself than through the music of one's own culture, country and peoples. How better to understand other people than through their music. Speech is mirrored in music; the stress patterns, the natural flow and rise and fall of a language is reflected in the folk music and composed music of each language. It is right for people in Hungary to use Hungarian children's songs and folk songs in teaching their young. Those same songs translated into English or Greek or Chinese are not only inappropriate, they are unmusical.

But folk music is not the destination. Our goal is "to make the masterpieces (of music) public property." And to do this we must spend significant time finding and organizing masterworks into age-appropriate sequences for children. This is the step I see missing most often in Kodály programs. It's as if teachers take the long journey with their children, reach their destination, and then don't bother to open the door and go in. Of what use is it to teach children to sing, read, and write if we are not at the same time teaching them to value their heritage of music—and by this I mean far more than folk music. I've taught children in a conservatory setting, advanced performers on their instruments, who when they came to me could not name a single important composer, let alone sing a fragment by memory of any important composition. I am not the first to observe this strange phenomenon of the gifted performer who is culturally illiterate. Kodály, in 1946, wrote:

"Are there also illiterates in the Music Academy? They are not only in it—they have been receiving diplomas from it for decades."[8]

I believe that everything one needs to know about music may be found in music—real music. That "exercises" not directly drawn from the music being studied and performed are both pointless and counterproductive. Worse, they tend to be deadening. Ten minutes of a lesson, two minutes of a lesson, are too much time to spend on exercises not drawn from worthy music. If children experience difficulty with a particular melodic turn or rhythmic figure, we should take it out of the musical context long enough to practice and perfect it—then return it to the original context. We should always begin and end with students performing the music. It is all there, everything we want to teach—all we have to do is follow the music!

The two most important aspects of our teaching are, first, the value we convey when we use only the highest quality music in our teaching at every level, whether that music is folk or composed, whether it is pentatonic, diatonic, tonal or atonal; and, second, the musicality with which we present that music—the modeling we do in the process of teaching. Every time we sing a new song to a class, we should think of it as a musical performance. That is, we should sing expressively, with attention to dynamics and phrasing, breathing correctly, making the text clear and understandable. And when we present masterworks to children, we should choose compositions we love, for our feelings about that music are communicated as well. Children learn by what they see and hear us do to a much greater extent than they learn by what they hear us say.

I am a music teacher. I am a music teacher who deeply believes in the Kodály philosophy and carefully observes Kodály's teaching principles. I practice what is commonly called "the Kodály method." But what is the Kodály method? It is certainly more than a set of pedagogical tricks.

László Dobszay, in an early lecture at the Kodály Institute in Wellesley, Massachusetts, stated:

> He who hopes that Kodály has worked out a system of education, a manufacturing process, which causes ideal musical education to be brought about infallibly, does not understand Kodály's world of thought and will be greatly disappointed. What is called the Kodály Method does have some elements which can, with more or less certainty, make the child learn—but learn what? . . . Means without purpose. . . . Behind the so-called Kodály Method there is a basic educational thought, an educational idea. If we fail to grasp it we proceed on a paved way—in the wrong direction![9]

So, what is the Kodály method?

It is a philosophy, a body of beliefs, a set of values, supported by (but not consisting of) a collection of pedagogical practices. These practices have existed in many places and for many years, and although it was the early followers of Kodály who put them all together with such great effect, there was nothing new or revolutionary in them. It was the purpose of these practices that was and is different. That pedagogy was only the vehicle.

The destination was music.

To cite Dobszay again: "To be able to achieve a purpose, we must be in constant contact with the purpose, we must understand it well, we must own it. We must have the necessary insight, intuition, to enable us to use the means correctly."[10]

What are the purposes, the beliefs, the foundations of the Kodály method? They are really very simple and straightforward. Yet if we subscribe to them they have the capacity to change our teaching practices (and our lives) forever. They certainly did mine. For me, they became the credo of my professional life.

I believe that music education begins (for better or worse) at birth—with the music children hear in their homes.

I believe that the nursery songs and games of the child's language should be his or her earliest singing experiences and that folk music should be the next. And that the best of the world's art music should be core teaching material for older students. That it is our responsibility to "instill a thirst for finer music in [children], a thirst which will last for a lifetime."[11]

I believe that the human voice—the instrument everyone is born with—is the best instrument through which to teach music. Kodály emphasized this again and again:

"You have an instrument in your throat, with a more beautiful tone than any violin in the world. . . . With this instrument you will come invigoratingly near to the great geniuses of music—if there is only somebody to lead you on!"[12]

"A deeper culture of music always developed only where it was based on singing."[13]

"The root of music is singing."[14]

And I believe that music should occupy a central place in school curriculum—that music should be taught daily—that it should be the obligation of the schools to musically educate all children—and that education should include musical reading and writing. Not with the idea of producing professional musicians, but as Kodály said: just to complete them as people.

This is the "Kodály method." It is not composed of specific Hungarian teaching materials. Each country, indeed each teacher, must choose musical materials and a sequence for teaching, based on his or her own music and children. Kodály reiterated this many times in many places, as, for example, in an interview conducted by Ernő Daniel in Santa Barbara, California in 1966: "If the system is to be adopted in foreign countries, each country must use its own motivic and musical material."

Of course, I've written a number of books (which some of you may know) telling teachers of English speaking children what to teach, when and how to teach it and even what music to use. I only hope that teachers using these books bring understanding, intelligence and musicality to the task. And I hope they realize that there is no one "right" order or process. And that only they can know what is "right" for their children.

Finally, there is no substitute for the well-trained musician-teacher. It is not possible for anyone less to teach music effectively. In my country, it is still thought in some places that any classroom teacher of five- or six-year-olds is competent to teach music, even if he or she is not a musician—or even musically literate. It is thought that band programs begun in the secondary schools are enough music for the schools to offer. Would these same schools think it rational to wait until eighth grade to begin teaching math or reading?

Would they consider someone who couldn't count capable of teaching math or who couldn't read or write capable of teaching language? I think not.

We should have the best musicians teaching the youngest children. Only they can lay the foundation for lifelong musical learning.

Where did the idea that anyone can teach music spring from? I'm afraid only the minds of culturally deprived individuals who control budgets and who, having been given no musical values in the course of their own education, see no need for them in the education of others. It is a notion we must militantly reject.

We are told that it is a matter of not enough money. At the height of the Depression, in the 1920s, Kodály wrote:

"That the economic crisis is the cause of everything? Everything will be set right as soon as the economy is in order? I do not think so. Penury may hamper development but wealth does not always promote it either. . . . The greatest trouble is not the emptiness of the purse, but the emptiness of the soul."[15]

I have fought all my life against the idea that music is some kind of frill—that it is peripheral to education. I will continue to fight this notion verbally and in print with every opportunity afforded me as long as I have breath.

When I retired from university teaching five years ago at the age of 70, a number of my former students chose to speak at the ceremony. One not-so-young man said that my teaching was like a pebble dropped into a pond. The initial splash is small, but the rings from it spread out and out until they reach the far shores. I hope that this is so. If it is, then it means that I in Canada, Wojciech in Poland, Michalis in Greece, Takao in Japan, Jerry in the U.S., Judy in Australia, Mihály in Hungary, and all the others who really care can make a difference.

Once when I was particularly discouraged, my Hungarian mentor and friend Erzsébet Szõnyi told me that I had to think not in days or months or even years, but in generations.

I believe that we have made a difference. I believe that our students, if we have taught them well, can make more of a difference, and that someday there will be a musically educated public—a public that values music as we do. And that their children will not have to fight to be musically educated.

Notes

[1] Zoltán Kodály, "A Hundred Year Plan," in *The Selected Writings of Zoltán Kodály*, ed. Ferenc Bónis (London: Boosey & Hawkes, 1974), 160.

[2] Zoltán Kodály, "Children's Choirs," in *Selected Writings*, 119.

[3] Kodály, "A Hundred Year Plan," 160.

[4] Zoltán Kodály, MacMillan Lecture #3 (Royal Conservatory of Music, University of Toronto, July 14, 1966).

[5] Zoltán Kodály, "Music in the Kindergarten," in *Selected Writings*, 142.

[6] Kodály, "Children's Choirs," 122.

[7] Judit Hartyányi, "Making Music Together," *Bulletin of the International Kodály Society* 28, no. 2, (2003): 22.

[8] Zoltán Kodály, "After the First Solfège Competition," in *Selected Writings*, 163.

[9] László Dobszay, "The Kodály Method and Its Musical Foundations" (paper presented at the Kodály Institute, Wellesley, MA, ca. 1970). A later version of this paper was published as "The Kodály Method and Its Musical Basis," *Studia Musicologica Academiae Scientiarum Hungaricae* 14, no. 1 (1972): 15-33.

[10] Dobszay, "Kodály Method."

[11] Kodály, "Children's Choirs," 120.

[12] Kodály, "Children's Choirs," 123.

[13] Zoltán Kodály, "Éneklő ifjúság" (Singing Youth), in *Visszetekintés,* ed. Ferenc Bónis (Budapest: Zeneműkiadó, 1964) 1: 117, quoted in Dobszay, "The Kodály Method," 25.

[14] Zoltán Kodály, "Zenei nevelésünk reformjáról" (On the reform of our music education), in *Visszetekintés,* 1: 287, quoted in Dobszay, "The Kodály Method," 25.

[15] Kodály, "Children's Choirs," 126.

Keynote address presented at the 16th International Kodály Symposium in July 2003, Ourimbah, New South Wales, Australia. Originally published in *Bulletin of the International Kodály Society* 28, no. 2 (2003): 3–9. Reprinted by permission.

THE CIRCLE OF LIFE: MUSIC, NATURE AND HUMAN POSSIBILITY

Gail Needleman

I am deeply honored to be here today and to have been given the opportunity to think with you about Zoltán Kodály's vision and our shared task in the world: a task that puts us in relationship to a great symbol, the circle, the fundamental symbol of the oneness of reality. And I would like to begin with one of the images evoked by the theme of this symposium, of the medicine wheel, including the mysterious stone circles of the Alberta plains; because the true medicine wheel, as I have been told, is the circle of the horizon: a powerful symbol of the relationship between the self and the world.

What is this symbol telling us? I am here, at the center. The circumference of the circle, the horizon, is created by the center. I stand between Heaven and Earth, at the center of the four directions, at the center of myself. That is the place of the human being, the place of my essential nature, through which I am connected with all beings. And my relation to the horizon is most vivid, it seems to me, at sunrise and sunset, when the sun touches the horizon, calling me to a sense of the greater world.

And the horizon also includes the vertical dimension, in the great dome of the sky. Here, in the open prairies, we are always under that sky. But no matter where we are, surely it is the night sky that calls us to this vertical dimension, revealing the vastness of Creation and my place in it as a human being.

All the peoples of the earth have known in their bones what it is that we are called to be: they have sung it in their songs, told it in their stories, taught it to their children. We are a part of Creation, no less than sun and sky, and we are called to play our part. We who have been given the power to see the order of the universe are obliged to attune ourselves to it, to transmit the order of the heavens to the Earth; or, as the Buddhists say, to work for the salvation of all beings.

The ancient Chinese sages called this the Mandate of Heaven. Among the first peoples of the Earth, it has been called the Original Instructions; and every nation has its own tale of humanity receiving that holy obligation, to express the greatness of this mandate from above.

And across the globe, across the centuries, in culture after culture, this gift, and our response to it, have been expressed in the form of music. The people of the nation of Georgia say: In the beginning was the Song. In India, it is the Bhagavad Gita, the Song of God. It is the sound of Orpheus' lyre, says the ancient Greek myth, which actually made us human. Across the globe, across the millennia, music is said to have come from a level higher than ordinary life: from the gods, from the cosmos, from universal law. And surely the forces of universal order and goodness do not waste their powers on what is not needed. What *are* the gifts of the gods? Fire. Bread. The breath of life. The soul. The gods give what is needed for human life. What is the gift of music? Why do we need music? Why is so much of our brain devoted to it? What is it for?

And why, especially, do we need to bring music—and why is it so crucial that it be given in the right way—to our children, who are the future of humanity?

From the traditional teachings of the world a vision emerges, and its outlines are something like this: To be a real human being, a certain development of the power of feeling is essential—as essential as language is for the development of the mind. It is through this quality of feeling that we perceive, directly, the unity of all things. This capacity to perceive the whole is what enables human beings to be in relationship—with each other, and with all the beings of the universe—with trees and stones, rivers and mountains, deer and eagle, sun and moon and stars. This quality of feeling is the source of compassion, of hope, of love, of a finer sensitivity and intelligence. *And this power of feeling is developed through music*, which alone has the capacity to break down the barriers that separate us and enable us to feel, with our whole being, the wholeness of the world.

Without music, we cannot be human, truly human, because music is how we learn to listen—to ourselves, to each other, to all the beings of the living Earth.

In our present world of increasing fragmentation and loneliness, we need, more than ever, to receive the ancient and universal vision that the essence of life is relationship. But from where will this vision come? Because if we are sincere we see that ideas alone are too weak; they cannot stand against all the forces of division in ourselves and in the world.
What is missing?

This is what we, here, now, need to say to the world—the world we live in, the world beyond the gates. We need to say this: Something absolutely essential is going out of our lives, something that has been part of human life for as long as humanity has existed. Something that connects us to each other and to the greater world, something necessary both for our inmost development as individuals, and for our participation in and responsibility to our common life.

This is what we need to say to the world. We need to say: Something that has sustained us for a million years is beginning to disappear.

We are no longer singing together.

In a world of wars and violence, of the rampant despoiling of nature—a world of so much suffering, so much despair—this loss may seem a very small thing, so marginal, even trivial, as to hardly deserve our notice.

But it is not a small thing! It is an immense thing! As people all over the world have known since the most ancient times, it is an indispensable part of what makes us human.

What we call the crisis of the environment, the crisis of the task of human beings on the Earth, is not primarily a crisis of "policy," of economics or even of ethics. *It is at its root a crisis of feeling*, which means a crisis of our inner development, our very existence as human beings. The real crisis is our *inability to feel*, to truly feel the truth of our interrelated existence. This is what lies, hidden from us, behind the manifestations of greed, egoism and lack of empathy that increasingly threaten our very world.

Yes, we are beginning to feel this lack in our lives. Yes, people are beginning to talk about listening. Can I listen to others with whom I disagree? This is absolutely necessary for our life together. But this is a very advanced form of listening! To try to begin there, without having listened to a mother's voice singing a lullaby, without having participated in the call and response of children's games, without having experienced the community and the freedom from fear that can come from making music together, is a handicap too great for our fragmented culture to bear.

From where will our help come?

And just here, in this fragmented culture itself, hidden in plain view, in the roots of our own cultures, just here is the knowledge we seek, the nourishment we need. In North America it is embedded in the music of the Native American, African-American, and Anglo-American cultures, and the many other cultures that contribute to our common life. The traditional music of these cultures carries a vision of human nature and human community that is exactly what we need.

This vision connects us to all the peoples of the world, both past and present, because it is a vision of the human being *in relationship*—to family, community, nature and the universe. It is a vision of the possibility of music not only sustaining but actually *creating* community, even in the most difficult of conditions. And it is a vision of the spiritual dimension of music, not only transmitting the depths of human experience but opening us to the possibilities of what human beings are meant to be.

There is great wisdom about music, and its role in the life of our planet, in the traditional cultures of the world. But we do not have much time left.

And yes, we can begin to recognize the outlines of this vision by listening, by studying; but the truth of it, the reality, the transforming power, will only enter us through singing.

This is what we need to say to the world. And we can say it, because we know it is true.

Our culture has placed a great emphasis on the development of the mind. Our resources and our intelligence are devoted to it, our values have formed around it. But we have neglected the development of real feeling, and we are seeing the results in our current cultural crisis. And the descent of our culture is happening very quickly, as Kodály foresaw when he prophesied: "Our age of mechanization leads along a road ending with man himself as a machine; only the spirit of singing can save us from this fate."[1]

Think of it! Kodály lived through conditions far worse than anything most of us have experienced. He saw very clearly the forces of disintegration operating in the world. *And he did not lose faith in the power of music.* "Only the spirit of singing can save us." Singing: a power and a practice, absolutely essential for the full development of the human being, that calls us into relationship with the harmony of the universe, that calls us to discover what Kodály said was the true end of education: to find genuine values in the depths of one's heart.

Does this vision actually reach us? Do we follow in his footsteps? Can we bring it into our lives?

Kodály drew great strength from the natural world. He encouraged students to carry their music books out of doors, to sing in the forests and by the streams. He modeled for us another way, a way of long walks in the mountains, listening, listening, until, like the singers of old, he

40

began to hear their voices. He brought to us the timeless truth that music has the power to draw all of nature, all of *our* nature, to listen.

Because nature is not just "out there." This is about us, our inner nature, our essential being.

There is a movement in the world called *rewilding*, which seeks to restore the balance of nature in lands despoiled by civilization. Our inner world, too, is despoiled, assaulted by the excesses of modern life, by its constant stimulation, by the noise pollution which, one Tibetan lama has told us, is far more dangerous than the pollution of the air we breathe.[2]

Can traditional songs, which carry the vision and the values of a life immersed in Great Nature, serve to begin the rewilding, the healing of our inner lives? Can these songs be like a keystone species, enabling the whole inner ecosystem to begin to restore itself? With their help, can we learn again how to listen—to our inmost hearts, to our brothers and sisters, to the Earth and all its beings—and by listening, begin to feel?

These songs carry what human beings have learned over the centuries, from all the beings of Heaven and Earth. We are obliged to listen to them, and to carry forward their wisdom into the future. In Kodály's words, "Of the old treasures [the village] has preserved that which is most precious—the ancient furniture of the soul... It is our job to take over from it and to cultivate them further. *The fire must not die out.*"[3]

The Tao Te Ching says: Human beings follow the Earth, the Earth follows the Heavens, the Heavens follow the Way, the Way follows Nature. Think how different the world would be if it were inhabited by people who had been raised with a sense of kinship to all of Nature. Think how deeply folk and traditional songs are connected to our relationships to the natural world, and to the feelings that allow these connections. Think of what we owe to the profound knowledge of human nature that these songs carry. Think how through them we may discover in ourselves a new voice.

From myself to the horizon, and back, the circle is completed.

The Cree traditional singer Pat Kennedy received from his elders, and transmitted to others, the traditional songs of his people—and then began to hear the songs of the other beings of the world. He said: "The Creator made our voices to sing together." The other beings of the earth, he said, needed us to sing.[4]

What are the gifts of the gods? The greatest gift is the holy obligation to pass on what we have received. Something is up to us.

Notes

[1] Zoltán Kodály, *The Selected Writings of Zoltán Kodály, ed.* Ferenc Bónis (London: Boosey & Hawkes, 1974), 206.

[2] Kalu Rinpoche (1905–1989), on his first visit to Europe in 1975, was heard to say: "People here are very worried about air pollution, but you can deal with that. What is much more dangerous is noise pollution, because it disconnects the inner world from the outer world, and then you cannot

practice." Personal conversation with Andrea Andriotto, Swiss religious scholar and filmmaker, in 1995.

[3] Kodály, *Selected Writings*, 31.
[4] Personal conversation in 2016 with Lorna McMurray, Second Singer of Pat Kennedy's Starr School Drum (1996–2004).

Keynote address presented at the 23rd International Kodály Symposium in August 2017, Camrose, Alberta, Canada. Originally published in *Bulletin of the International Kodály Society* 42, no. 2 (Autumn 2017): 11–14. Reprinted by permission.

THE IMPORTANCE OF FOLK MATERIALS: THE "LITTLE STORY" AND THE "BIG STORY"

James Cuskelly

Kodály believed that folk songs were of the greatest importance, and his manifesto for music education places singular emphasis on the inclusion of folk materials within the pedagogical framework. While Kodály believed that the folk song was "the mirror of the spirit of the entire Hungarian people,"[1] he spoke more broadly of the value of folk song in terms of the embodiment of cultural identity, societal values and personal meaning. In this paper, I suggest that the use of such materials as the building blocks of teaching and learning not only elegantly and comprehensively achieves desirable educational outcomes, but also provides all those involved—students, teachers, parents and the wider society—with a deep sense of meaning, in both intrinsic and extrinsic senses of that concept. For the purposes of this paper, I intend to reflect upon the ways in which that sense of personal and shared meaning is engendered by the inclusion of folk materials within the overall context of teaching and learning.

The most obvious benefit of working with folk materials in music education is the way in which such materials are used to promote true musicality in children, even at the very earliest levels. László Dobszay explains that the "most essential material for music education lies in monophonic *folk-songs*."[2] There is a vast amount of folk material suitable for teaching and learning within the classroom context. Further, this repertory exhibits key musical characteristics in simple, explicit or miniaturized form, thereby presenting students with unparalleled opportunities for learning. The simple and appealing nature of these materials encourages active engagement and fosters learning through the development of discipline-specific skills and knowledge. A great deal of energy and expertise has already been dedicated to the collection, analysis and sequencing folk songs and games drawn from, and employed across, a range of linguistic and cultural contexts, thus giving further proof of the efficacy of such repertoire choices for teaching and learning. Kodály's emphasis on folk materials, alongside his understanding of the benefits of sequential learning—appropriate to the maturity, development and context of the learner—provided the basis for the evolution of an educational philosophy and practice that is breathtaking in its simplicity and effectiveness.

However, if it were simply a matter of finding materials and carefully sequencing them to maximize learning, then surely other materials would serve just as well? Could we not use pop music or jazz? Why not just write some music which would start with the simplest elements and then progress steadily on to the more complex elements? Indeed, such thinking is often seen in a myriad of publications; but few of these sorts of materials persist, and it is clear that a staged progression in learning is but part of the solution.

I suggest that the inclusion of the folk materials does much more than just provide access and a logical progression in learning. First of all, the basic musical activity within the Kodály approach is singing, and Kodály himself considered singing as the "essence" of his ideas on music education. From a broader educational perspective, it is important to note that singing requires the active involvement of learners. Dobszay states that:

> Music education must firstly aim at the active participation of the pupils and not at passive listening to music and voice is the only instrument accessible for all. Besides, singing evokes the fundamental experience of music since music originates, according to Kodály, in singing . . .[3]

Singing as a fundamental stimulus for active engagement

The idea that learners need to be actively engaged is one that is universally endorsed by many researchers,[4] and indeed active engagement in the processes of education is fundamental to the idea of the construction of knowledge. Constructivism is predicated upon the fact that students learn more by doing and experiencing than by observing.[5] At its core, constructivism holds that humans are not mere empty vessels waiting to be filled with knowledge, but rather that they are motivated by the search for meaning. In this vein, Brown contends that learning is most meaningful when the students are "actively connected to the creation and comprehension of knowledge."[6] In a Kodály-based classroom, children sing and chant, dance and play music games; they are involved in a range of literacy tasks, such as notating or sight-reading; and they apply their knowledge through combining rhythms and improvising melodies—in short, a Kodály-based classroom is fundamentally characterized by active, minds-on learning.

Given this scenario, it is important to emphasize that students are not only experiencing the music and constructing knowledge. The music itself is a product of the students, and the quality of that product is a reflection not only of the careful guidance of a teacher, but also of the actualization of the latent musical abilities within the children themselves. The essential point to be made here is that music education in this sense is not condescending, a watering down of music so that the children are able to do it, but rather the elevation of the children into authentic musical activity. There is an increasing trend to patronize children and to diminish their potential for learning and intelligent engagement, but it seems clear, to me at least, that children are perfectly capable of precise and excellent musical performance. Even very young children may be performing as musicians in the earliest classes; the students are evidencing the behaviors and attitudes of performing musicians, and this experience of music-making forms the basis for a personalized understanding of music more broadly. The point here is not that the children lack ability, but rather that our education systems fail to provide suitable opportunities for the students to achieve their potential.

This induction into the world of music and music-making has profound import in terms of the long-term development of a sense of meaning. A key component of this framework is the process of experience before intellectualization; for me, this is fundamental to the development of a sense of meaning. Laurens van der Post explains:

It is one of the laws of life that the new meaning must be lived before it can be known, and in some mysterious way modern man knows so much that he is the prisoner of his knowledge. The old dynamic conception of the human spirit as something living always on the frontiers of human knowledge has gone. We hide behind what we know. And there is an extraordinarily angry and aggressive quality in the knowledge of modern man; he is angry with what he does not know; he hates and rejects it. He has lost the sense of wonder about the unknown and he treats it as an enemy. The experience which is before knowing, which would enflame his life with new meaning, is cut off from him. Curiously enough, it has never been studied more closely. People have measured the mechanics of it, and the rhythm, but somehow they do not experience it.[7]

I believe that we could insert the word "music" here and the significance would be all the more apparent:

The experience of music comes before knowing, this experience of music which would enflame life with new meaning. Curiously enough, the experience of music has never been studied more closely. People have measured the mechanics of it, and the rhythm, but somehow they do not experience it.

Long before van der Post wrote this, Kodály understood that it is only through the experience of music that a person could be awakened to the potential of music in the human spirit: that it is the experience, not the knowledge, of music that must come first, and that it is the experience of music which forms the basis of all the meaning. I believe that this also explains in part why Kodály had such admiration, almost a reverence, for folk music and the people who sang it.

The importance of text

Singing is important for another very significant reason. Singing is based upon text, and the texts themselves inevitably engage the imagination, portray the natural world and the creatures in it, or describe an event which involves characters in some way; in short, the text tells a story. Storytelling is fundamental to our very humanity, and people everywhere and of all ages respond on the deepest level to storytelling. The great mythologist Joseph Campbell reminds us that story and symbol are universals, stretching across cultures. According to Bill Moyers, stories and myth are full of the essential components of meaning which are most directly relevant to the human condition, and he explains that the remnants of the "stuff" of mythology "line the walls of our interior system of beliefs."[8] He goes on to explain that myths and stories provide an interior road map of experience, drawn by people who have travelled it.[9] The presence of such fundamental attributes in all human endeavors highlights a "constant requirement in the human psyche for a centering in terms of deep principles."[10]

From the work of Campbell and others, we have come to understand the significance not only of folk song and story, but of all cultural artifacts, in that these artistic endeavors serve to remind us of who we are and where we have come from. However, in thinking about folk songs, there is another aspect which I would like to consider here. We have already discussed the idea that folk songs tell stories, and the ballad in particular has served as a particularly notable way of transmitting the story.

It worth investigating an example to illustrate the point, and to do that I would like to use the well-known English ballad, Barbara Allen.

Barbara Allen

In Scarlet Town where I was born there was a fair maid dwellin',
Made every youth cry "Welladay"; her name was Barbara Allen.

All in the merry month of May, when green buds they were swellin',
Young Jemmy Grove on his death bed lay for love of Barbara Allen.

Then slowly, slowly she came up and slowly she came nigh him;
And all she said when there she came, "Young man I think you're dyin'."

As she was walking o'er the fields, she heard the dead bell knellin',
And every stroke the dead bell gave cried "Woe" to Barbara Allen.

When he was dead and laid in grave, her heart was struck with sorrow;
"Oh, mother, mother make my bed, for I shall die tomorrow."

"Farewell" she said, "ye virgins all, and shun the fault I fell in;
Henceforth take warning by the fall of cruel Barbara Allen."

I would like to reflect upon the text and to summarize the story from two perspectives, that of the "Little Story" and of the "Big Story." From the point of view of the little story, this is a tragic tale of ill-fated love, of the vagaries of beauty and attraction, and of the sad loss of two beautiful young people. Do we hear of similar instances of doomed love in the modern world? And do we also all too frequently hear of the tragic consequences of such unrequited love in contemporary times? Such stories feed the sensationalism that is the modern-day press, but I am always deeply saddened to hear of such events.

However, from the perspective of the "Big Story," this song recounts a sadly recognizable tale which may have happened anywhere, to any group of people, at any time. This is not an experience unique to a particular group of people or relevant only to a specific point in history. The commonality of human experience is embedded in the tale, and in the telling of it through singing we are reminded of such events within our own worlds. While the recounting of such a story serves to directly tell the "Little Story," it also transmits a deeper message. Thus the song represents a certain wisdom, distilled from a myriad of human responses, and it is in this way that the folk song serves the purposes of the "Big Story." I am not suggesting that these songs overtly serve as morality tales, but rather that such materials serve to artistically capture and recount this essence of human experience that is both particular and universal.

The significance of the "Big Story"

One final point to briefly consider here is the connection which Kodály always made between folk song and the best of art music. For me at least, it is clear that this dual purpose of recounting the "Little Story" and the "Big Story" is evident in the finest folk materials, and that this same process is in play in the masterworks of the great composers. Thus Moyers' "stuff" of mythology apparent in folklore, which "lines the walls of our interior system of beliefs," is both the foundation of and the basis for great works of art.

Kodály stated that Hungarian folk music was important because "there is not a single experience of a single segment of the Hungarian people which has not left its mark on it."[11] Such thinking is echoed by Dobszay, who asserts that that there are "profound relations between music and other manifestations of folk life," and that folk cultures give "elaborated forms to the great events of life by means of folk customs."[12] Equally, the great works of music literature—the lieder and songs, the oratorios and masses, the symphonies and operas, the chamber music and solo works—are laden with the archetypes, stories and symbols of our deepest, but often tacitly held, beliefs and values.

These defining aspects of our culture and community are captured in the folk materials and laid down in us all. Standing on the shoulders of those who have gone before, gifted composers are able to draw upon this interior world and engage us directly in the story—both the "Little" and the "Big" stories. The search for meaning is a basic human instinct, evident in all peoples irrespective of culture or history. Indeed, van der Post would posit that it is meaning, not happiness, that has the most profound impact and long-term influence upon the human condition. He says:

> There's nothing wrong in searching for happiness. But we're using the term happiness as if it were the ultimate of human striving. And actually what we found in prison, and I find in life, which gives far more comfort to the soul, is something which is greater than happiness or unhappiness and that is meaning. Because meaning transfigures all. And once what you are living and you are doing has for you meaning, it is irrelevant whether you are happy or unhappy. You're content. You're not alone in your spirit. You belong. [13]

For me, Kodály had a deep understanding of the potential of music to engage us, to give us meaning, to connect with ourselves and others and place, and to give us a sense of belonging. His philosophy for education provides a framework in which we can eloquently speak the music of the spheres with our children, and in so doing share the wisdom of the ages. He said, "Folk songs are . . . the ancient furniture of the soul," and he admonished us to "cultivate them further."[14] I encourage you to cultivate your own awareness of the importance of folk songs. I urge you to sit on the "ancient furniture of the soul" and to feel its comfort and support. And I exhort you to share the beauty and depth of folk songs with the children, so that they too may know that sense of belonging that comes with being connected.

Notes

[1] Zoltán Kodály, *The Selected Writings of Zoltán Kodály*, ed. Ferenc Bónis (London: Boosey & Hawkes, 1974), 24.

[2] László Dobszay, *After Kodály* (Kecskemét, Hungary: Zoltán Kodály Pedagogical Institute of Music, 1992), 52.

[3] Dobszay, 52.

[4] Julie K. Brown, "Student-Centered Instruction: Involving Students in Their Own Education," *Music Educators Journal* 94, no. 5 (May 2008): 30-35; Dobszay, *After Kodály*; David J. Elliott, *Music Matters: A New Philosophy of Music Education* (Oxford: Oxford University Press, 1995); Howard Gardner, *Frames of Mind: The Theory of Multiple Intelligence* (New York: Basic Books, 1993); Mel Silberman, *Active Learning: 101 Strategies to Teach Any Subject* (Boston, MA: Allyn and Bacon, 1996).

[5] John Dewey, *Democracy and Education* (New York: Macmillan, 1963).

[6] Brown, "Student-Centered Instruction," 31.

[7] Laurens van der Post, *Patterns of Renewal* (Lebanon, PA: Pendle Hill Publications, 1962), 3.

[8] Joseph Campbell and Bill D. Moyers, *The Power of Myth* (New York: Doubleday, 1988), xiv.

[9] Campbell and Moyers, xvi.

[10] Campbell and Moyers, xvi.

[11] Kodály, *Selected Writings*, 24.

[12] Dobszay, *After Kodály*, 80.

[13] Laurens van der Post, *Hasten Slowly: The Journey of Sir Laurens van der Post*, directed by Mickey Lemle (New York: Lemle Pictures, 1996), VHS.

[14] Kodály, *Selected Writings*, 31.

Keynote address presented at the 20th International Kodály Symposium in July 2011, Brisbane, Australia. Originally published in *Bulletin of the International Kodály Society* 36, no. 2 (2011): 3–7. Reprinted by permission.

THE CUCKOO IN THE MYTHOLOGY AND FOLKLORE OF EUROPE

Lily Storm

Traditional cultures have often noted and delighted in bird-song, drawing connections both to the spirit world and to human music. In Europe, many birds have taken up particular places in folklore, and symbolize different aspects of existence: the nightingale symbolizes romantic love, the swallow symbolizes freedom, the dove, domestic bliss, and the lark, joy.[1] But of all the birds in European mythology, the one with the most complicated and ambiguous set of meanings was probably the cuckoo. Throughout Europe, the cuckoo was simultaneously associated with verdant spring and summer, fertility, abundance, sexual energy, and also with sadness and separation, madness, infidelity, treachery, death, prophecy, and the spirit world.[2] All of these were folk interpretations of various aspects of the European cuckoo's behavior: its song, its migration patterns, and its breeding habits.

The cuckoo as harbinger of spring

A widespread English rhyme, with many regional variations, has the following form:

> Cuckoo, cuckoo!
> What do you do?
> In Aperill, come I will,
> In flowery May, I sing all day,
> In leafy June, I change my tune,
> In bright July, away I fly.[3]

The common cuckoo (*cuculus canorus*) migrates twice yearly, from its fall/winter grounds in eastern central Africa to its spring/summer breeding grounds throughout Europe and western Asia. In Europe, therefore, spring was synonymous with "cuckoo-time." According to Grimm, old German law specifies the beginning of spring by the formula "wan der gauch gucket," or "when the cuckoo sings."[4]

The oldest recorded English song (written down around 1250) features the cuckoo:

> Sumer is icumen in,
> Lhude sing cuccu;
> Groweth sed, and bloweth med,
> And springth the wde nu,
> Sing, cuccu!
> Awe bleteth after lomb,
> Lhouth after calve cu,
>
> Bulluc sterteth, Bucke verteth,
> Murie, sing cuccu!
> Cuccu, cuccu,
> well sings thu, cuccu,
> Ne swike thu naver nu,
>
> Sing, cuccu, nu, sing, cuccu,
> Sing, cuccu, sing, cuccu, nu.[5]

It was sung as a round and imitated the cuckoo bird's distinctive call, and in these respects closely resembles many continental rounds. It would have been sung on "Cuckoo Day," which was set in each region on the day the cuckoo could be expected to call for the first time, a day of silliness, frivolity, singing, and playing pranks, identical to the tradition of April Fool's Day, previously "feul-gowk day" (literally, "fool-cuckoo day").[6] In addition to the planned celebration, there would be an impromptu one: "As soon as the first cuckoo has been heard all the laboring classes leave work, if in the middle of the day, and time is devoted to mirth and jollity over what is called Cuckoo Ale."[7] Possibly from such frivolity and mischief, the word "cuckoo" came to signify the adjective "silly," or "crazy."

These celebratory cuckoo songs have been preserved in many of the Western European languages, often in the form of rounds. The following French children's round (and its Spanish twin) is probably descended from just such a spring ritual:

Dans la forêt lointaine[8]

French	English	Spanish
Dans la forêt lointaine,	In the faraway forest,	En la selva lejana
On entend le coucou.	You can hear the cuckoo.	Se oye el cuco
Du haut de son grand chêne,	From the top of the big oak,	Desde el alto de su encina
Il répond au hibou :	It answers the owl:	Contesta al buho:
"Coucou, coucou,"	"Cuckoo, cuckoo,"	"Cucú, cucú"
On entend le coucou.	You can hear the cuckoo.	Se oye el cuco.

These springtime associations of the cuckoo provide a deeper explanation for its appearance in the old Irish song which traditionally celebrated the first day of summer (called Bealtaine in the Gaelic):

Thugamar féin an Samhradh linn[9]

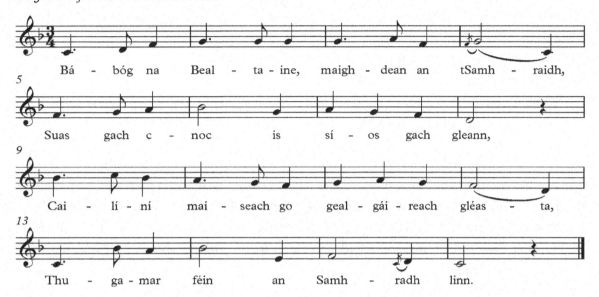

Bábóg na Bealtaine, maighdean an tSamhraidh,
Suas gach cnoc is síos gach gleann,
Cailíní maiseach go gealgáireach gléasta
Thugamar féin an Samhradh linn.

Tá an fhuiseog ag seinm 'sag luascadh sna spéartha,
Thugamar féin an Samhradh linn.
Tá an chuachis an fhuiseog ag seinm le pléisiúr,
Thugamar féin an Samhradh linn.

Flowering branch of May, Summer's maiden,
Up the hill and down the valley,
Graceful girls dressed in shimmering white,
We brought the summer with us.

The lark is playing and swinging the skies,
We brought the Summer with us.
The cuckoo and lark are singing with delight,
We brought the Summer with us.

In addition to its role in merrymaking, the cuckoo had important information to impart. The arrival of the cuckoo was a signal to farmers, not only when to plant, but, by observing its timing, what to plant, or indeed whether to plant at all:

> When the cuckoo comes to the bare thorn,
> Sell your cow and buy you corn.
> But when she comes to the full bit,
> Sell your corn and buy you sheep.[10]

Hesiod, seven centuries before Christ, was already giving advice based on the first notes of the cuckoo: "When the cuckoo sings in the oak trees, it is time to plow."[11] And "according to Aristophanes, the cuckoo formerly governed all Egypt and Phoenicia, because when [the cuckoo] appeared it was time for wheat and barley harvest."[12] This, however, was in the fall, on the other end of the cuckoos' migration, after they had returned to Africa.

51

Where did they go?

> Seven sleepers there be—
> The bat, the bee, the butterflee,
> The cuckoo and the swallow,
> The kittiwake and the corn-craik,
> Sleep all in a little hollie.[13]
>
>   --English nursery chant

Because of a limited understanding of natural history and geography, the ancient Europeans had no idea what happened to the cuckoos when they disappeared. Pliny the Elder believed hawks and cuckoos were the same, transforming themselves into each other. (When he saw a hawk capture and eat a cuckoo, he condemned the bird as cannibalistic.)[14] A common belief was that they hid themselves inside trees, as in the rhyme above, and implied in the following Czech children's song:

Kukulienka, kde si bola[15]

Kukulienka, kde si bola,	Cuckoo, where have you been,
Keď tá tuhá zima bola?	When the severe winter was?
Hajajaj, kukuku,	Hajajaj, kukuku,
Sedela som na buku.	I was sitting on a beech.
Keď som včera prala šaty,	When I was washing clothes yesterday,
Stratila som prsteň zlatý.	I lost my gold ring.
Hajajaj, kukuku,	Hajajaj, kukuku,
Hľadajme ho tu i tu.	Find it here and here!

The cuckoo as a sacred bird of prophecy

Another explanation for the mysterious nature of the cuckoo's disappearance was that it travelled to the spirit world, with the cuckoo becoming either a messenger of the gods or a powerful god in its own right. This, combined with the subtle and portentous shifts in the exact timing of the cuckoos' arrival, caused the cuckoo to become associated with augury. A widespread custom throughout Europe was to ask the cuckoo when one would die (the number of calls equaling the number of years), or the fate of a loved one, and for girls to ask the cuckoo when they would be married.[16] But, Grimm tells us, "if the bird cries oftener than ten times, they say it sits upon a silly bough, and they pay no heed to its augury."[17] Another widespread tradition with many variations was to turn the money over in one's pocket upon hearing the cuckoo's first cry of spring, in order to ensure plenitude in the coming year.[18]

The cuckoo as a messenger of fate can be seen in the following Ukrainian lament, in which a young woman is told of her mother's death:

Letila zozulja[19]

Letila zozulja z gory ta v dolynu,
ta i sila kuvaty kolo mo tynu.

Zozule zozule des' ty ghore chujesh,
kolo mojej khaty na kalyni kujesh.

Zozulja kuvala, pravdon'ku kazala,
shcho mojeji nen'ky na sviti ne stala.

Pobighla do khati stala na porozi,
zabilos' serden'ko pokotylys' sljozy.

Oj matinko-maty de zh tebe uzjaty,
chy pity kupyty chy namaljuvaty.

Najikhaly maljary z dalekoy storony,
zmaljuvaly nen'ku na bilij oseli.

Zmaljuvaly ochi zmaljuvaly brovy,
ta ne smaljuvaly shchyroji rozmovy.

The cuckoo flew from the mountain to the valley,
She perched on my fence.

Cuckoo, what is the news from the mountain,
From the house where I grew up?

The cuckoo sang, and spoke truthfully
That my mother was no longer in this world.

I ran to the house, stood on the threshold,
With pounding heart, tears flowing.

Oh Mama, Mama, who will I turn to?
Who will paint your portrait lovingly?

Artists came from distant lands,
They painted her on a white canvas.

They painted her eyes, and her eyebrows,
But they could not paint our conversation of the heart.

Because of its association with spring and with the spirit world, especially in cold northern latitudes, the cuckoo was considered a sacred bird. In Finland, "the cuckoo . . . is sacred, and is believed to have fertilized the earth with his songs."[20] To Nordic peoples, the cuckoo was a messenger of Thor, telling people how long they had to live, and when they would be married.[21] And,

> In Poland long ago it was a capital crime to kill a cuckoo. The apparent reason was that Zywiec, who in old Slavonic mythology was the ruler of the universe, used to change himself (as Zeus once did and Indra too) into a cuckoo, in order to announce to mortals the number of years they had to live; a belief so real that multitudes used to flock every May to Zywiec's temple on the mountain that was called after his name, to pray for long life and prosperous health.[22]

Negative images of the cuckoo

In addition to being revered, however, the cuckoo was also despised. Although some people hear only sweetness in its call, others heard it as dull and monotonous and contrasted it unfavorably to other songbirds, the nightingale especially. This is implied in the proverb, "Nightingales and cuckoos sing in the same month."[23] Whereas the nightingale was considered the perfect singer, the cuckoo could do nothing but echo a single, simple call (perhaps driving people "cuckoo"; yet another possible explanation for its meaning "crazy"?).

Many folktales relate or compare the nightingale and the cuckoo. A European folktale tells of a singing contest between the cuckoo and the nightingale, with the donkey as the judge (as, by his long ears, he was clearly the best judge of music.)[24] When the donkey ruled in favor of the cuckoo, because he could "understand what it said," the nightingale appealed to the judgment of mankind, "who alone could properly appreciate it, and the judgment was reversed."[25] In a Romanian myth, Sava, the cuckoo's wife, falls in love with the nightingale. When the cuckoo leaves her in anger, she repents, and for a whole month calls after him.[26]

The following old round, *Well fare the nightingale,*[27] illustrates the unfavorable comparison of the cuckoo to the nightingale:

Well fare the nigh - tin - gale,

Fair fall the thrush cock too, But foul

fare the fil - thy bird that sing - eth "cuck - oo."

54

The cuckoo as a symbol of infidelity and treachery

The negative images of the cuckoo were not just a result of its simple and monotonous call, however. The bird had a far more sinister side, ultimately related to the biological fact of its breeding habits. Besides being migratory, the European cuckoo is a brood parasite. In other words, it does not make nests or raise its own young, but instead removes an egg from the nest of a "host bird" and deposits one of its own. The chick, when it hatches (earlier than other birds), rolls the other eggs out of the nest and becomes the lone inheritor of the adoptive parent's attentions.[28] This gave the bird a reputation for treachery and deceit, from which we get the word "cuckold" (probably borrowed from Old French sometime before 1250.)[29] The apparent lack of normal maternal/parental instincts was interpreted as both treacherous and insane (perhaps a third interpretation of the word "cuckoo" as "crazy"). The destruction of another bird's nest and eggs explains the reference found in many folksongs to the cuckoo sucking "little bird's eggs to make his voice clear."

The treachery of the cuckoo, as well as its role as messenger of death, explains its hateful presence in the following old French song:

Quand je menai mes chevaux boire[30]

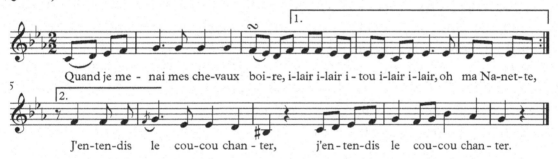

Quand je me - nai mes che-vaux boi-re, i-lair i-lair i - tou i-lair i-lair, oh ma Na-net-te,

J'en-ten-dis le cou-cou chan - ter, j'en-ten-dis le cou-cou chan - ter.

Quand je menai mes chevaux boire,	When I led my horses to drink,
ilair ilair itou ilair	la la la la la
ilair oh ma Nanette	la la oh my Nanette
Quand je menai mes chevaux boire,	When I led my horses to drink,
J'entendis le coucou chanter.	I heard the cuckoo sing.
Il me disait dans son langage,	He told me in his language,
Ta bien aimée vont l'enterrer.	Your beloved will be buried.
Ah que dis-tu méchante bête ?	Ah what do you say, you nasty beast?
J'étais près d'elle hier au soir.	I was with her yesterday evening.
Mais quand je fus dedans la lande,	But when I was on the moor,
J'entendis les cloches sonner.	I heard the bells ringing.

Mais quand je fus dedans l'église,	But when I was in the church,
J'entendis les prêtres chanter.	I heard the priests chanting.
Donnai du pied dedans la chasse,	I gave a kick to the reliquary,
Réveillez-vous si vous dormez.	Wake up if you sleep.
Non je ne dors ni ne sommeille,	I do not sleep nor slumber,
Je vous attends dedans l'enfer.	I await you in hell.
Vois ma bouche est pleine de terre,	See my mouth is full of earth,
Et la tienne est pleine d'amour.	And yours is full of love.
Auprès de moi reste une place,	Near me is a place,
Et c'est pour toi qu'on l'a gardée.	For your sake it has been kept.

An ancient Greek myth perfectly captures the twin aspects of the cuckoo (as both joyful harbinger of spring and agent of treachery): Hera, the queen of the pantheon and the goddess of fertility, has a pomegranate in one hand and in the other a scepter with a cuckoo at the end. When Zeus was first attempting to win her affections (and perhaps knowing her special affinity for this bird), he transformed himself into a wet, storm-bedraggled cuckoo and appeared at Hera's window. She took pity on it and brought it into her room, whereupon Zeus returned to his usual self and raped her, convincing her to marry him to cover her shame.[31] This seems to be an ancient Indo-European myth, as the Indian god Indra also transforms himself into a cuckoo in order to increase the attractiveness of the nymph Rambha in her attempts to seduce the sage Vicvamitras.[32] Furthermore, in the Rigveda (a collection of sacred hymns from India composed around 1700-1100 BCE) we already encounter in the cuckoo a bird of augury: it "proclaims the future, predicts, launches its voice as the boatman his boat."[33]

The cuckoo as mourner

Sometimes, and particularly in Eastern Europe, the sound of the cuckoo is interpreted as mournful and melancholy, rather than glad. Many Eastern European songs containing cuckoo imagery are sad laments, personifying the cuckoo as a tragic female, mourning her lost lover, brother, or son. "The Slavonians always represent the bird as a female—Zezhulice, who sits on an oak and bewails the transitoriness of spring. . . . So also in Russian songs it is a bird of mourning and melancholy, and Russian traditions speak of her as a young maiden changed by an enchantress."[34]

For the Southern Slavs, the cuckoo, or "kukavitsa," is a girl who lamented her brother's death so long that she was turned into a cuckoo. But the Albanians (originally a Northern European people) give a more complete explanation: A sister accidentally kills her brother with a knife or pair of scissors and then is fated to search for him eternally, crying out, "Ku, ku?" which in Albanian literally means, "Where, where?"[35]

The following Albanian song uses the image of a cuckoo/turtle-dove to convey loss and nostalgia, although juxtaposed with the cheerfulness of spring:

K'no moj qyqe[36]

Sing, cuckoo, because spring is coming,
Because the maiden has grown up.

I'm weeping, my dark eyes,
the maiden has left me,
I'm weeping night and day.

Oh the turtle-dove is singing every morning,
Oh the time has come, my soul, to part,
Jarnana, oh, crying, lale.

It is not only in Eastern Europe, however, that we find the cuckoo associated with a mourning maiden, and many English folk-songs also pair the cuckoo with various "floating verses" of lost love. For instance, Cecil Sharp and Charles Marson collected a variant of the following song in Somerset, England, in 1906:

The Cuckoo[37]

As I was a-walking and talking one day,
I met my own true love, as he came that way;
O, the meeting was a pleasure, though the courting was a woe,
For I found him false hearted, he'd kiss me then he'd go.

I wish I were a scholar and could handle the pen,
I'd write to my lover and to all roving men;
I would tell them of the grief and woe that attend on their lies,
I would wish them have pity on the flower when it dies.

The cuckoo as a homeless orphan

In Czech mythology, the cuckoo's brood parasitism is interpreted, ironically, as punishment for over-industriousness. The festival of the Virgin Mary (akin to the Cuckoo's Day of England perhaps?) was a day of enforced leisure and "held sacred, even by animals; the birds, for instance, took particular care not to work at their nests on those days. The cuckoo, having infringed that custom, was cursed, and obliged to wander perpetually, without ever a nest of its own."[38]

In Slavic cultures, even until very recently, girls became something like orphans on their wedding day, as they left their parents and joined their husbands' families, often far away. This was often interpreted as a kind of death, as they passed to another state of existence, and wedding customs often borrowed from funeral rites. These marriages would take place in spring, at the time of the cuckoo's call, and perhaps that is why the Slavic bride felt a mournful kinship with the lonely cuckoo, abandoned by its parents and reared by strangers. One researcher suggests an even more grim association, namely that cuckoos may be linked to the souls of dead children who have died in the winter, but who still "fly wailing through the air," and who must be baptized before they depart to the spirit world in the summer; therefore Russian women sing songs to "christen" the cuckoos in the spring.[39]

The cuckoo in the New World

When Europeans first came to the New World, they brought their cuckoo songs with them, but gradually adapted them to the new continent and the different species of cuckoos there. In general, the New World species are not brood parasites, but rather build flimsy nests of twigs, and their cry is also quite different: a low chuckling sound. They are valued for eating tent caterpillar larvae, which most birds will not touch.[40] The transplanted folksongs reflect some of these changes, and preserve faithfully other references which must have become obscure.

One of the most popular transplants, at least lyrically speaking, is "the popular Scotch song," although the song is more usually expressed in the feminine:

> The cuckoo's a fine bird, he sings as he flies;
> He brings us good tidings, he tells us no lies.
> He sucks little bird's eggs to make his voice clear,
> And when he sings "cuckoo" the summer is near.[41]

The cuckoo's eating habits in American folk songs favor the more refined reliance on nectar. The cuckoo is still a symbol of spring, as indeed are most songbirds in cold climates. He (or she) still "tells us no lies," although the connection to augury seems to have transformed into a more general association with gambling, as we find in the American version by Clarence Ashley, first recorded in 1929:

The Coo Coo Bird[42]

59

Jack of Diamonds, Jack of Diamonds,
I know you of old,
You done robbed my poor pockets,
Of my silver and gold.

I've played cards in England,
I've played cards in Spain,
I bet you ten dollars,
I'll beat you again.

American folk variants often retain the imagery of the mourning maiden, although it is sometimes playfully altered, as in this version sung by Jean Ritchie from her own family's store of songs:

Come all you young women, take warning by me,
Never place your affection on the love of a man.
For the roots they will wither, the branches decay,
He'll turn his back on you and he'll walk square away.

If you do forsake me, I'll not be forsworn,
And they'll all be mistaken if they think that I'll mourn;
For I'll get myself up in some higher degree,
And I'll walk as light by him as he does by me.[43]

As for the melody, most versions in the New World retain the minor character of their English or Scottish progenitors, often la- or re-pentatonic rather than full Aeolian or Dorian (although the complete modes are still found as well, as in the Dorian example collected by Sharp and Karpeles in the Southern Appalachians.[44]

In the version recorded by Clarence Ashley in 1929, and taken up by innumerable performers since, the original melody of the English/Scottish song has been thoroughly altered, and a blues influence is strongly apparent, not inconsistent with the banjo accompaniment. The text, however, is in places remarkably conservative.

Pedagogical uses

Because of their very ancient calendrical, agricultural, and mythological significance, cuckoos are found in the oldest layer of ritual songs throughout Europe, often preserved in children's game songs. Pedagogically, this could make an intriguing introduction to rounds and medieval music, or to cross-cultural studies, and even could furnish a link to nature and ecological studies (sadly, as with all migratory animals, human settlement and climate change are severely impacting the cuckoo population). The repertoire offers appropriate challenges for any level of student, and is a window into many facets of traditional song. For example, this particular collection could be an introduction to the use of modes in the folksongs of Europe, as it includes all the most common folk modes, and even offers interesting examples of modulation within the Dorian and Mixolydian modes (see song analyses at end of article).

In this context, we include one last song, a modern Romanian folk song in the Phrygian mode, in which the image of the cuckoo as the bird of spring and renewal, and also as a hapless orphan, has been used as a symbol of the rebirth of a nation recovering from bitter decades of totalitarianism:

Cântă puiul cucului[45]

Co-lon frunza codrului,
Cântă puiul cucului,
Tot cu dor şi de noroc,
Cântă când are-un foc,
Şi pe crengi se tot înalţă,
Cântă să-l audă fraţii.

Câte-o fost, câte-o trecut,
Pe noi toate ne-o durut,
Dară nu ne-o înstrăinat,
Că Dumnezău o lăsat
Apa apă, vinul vin,
Şi de sânge nu-i străin.

Doamne Sfinte, să nu leşi
Ca din fraţi să fim răzăşi,
Că Prutu-i punte cu flori,
Pentru fraţi, pentru surori,
Făcută ca să unească,
Mândră ţară strămoşească.

There in the leaves of the wood,
Sings the little cuckoo,
From his longing and misfortune,
He sings when he has an inner fire,
And from his branches high,
Sings to call his brothers.

What was was, and what has passed,
On all of us, brought hurt,
But it did not estrange us from one another,
Because God grants that
Water is water, and wine is wine
And blood is not foreign.

Holy Mother, do not allow
That from our brothers we become estranged,
The river Prutul, adorned with flowers,
For our brothers, for our sisters,
Let us unite,
Our dearest country so ancient.

Song Analyses

Dans la forêt lointaine (French)
scale: major
tone set: s, t,drmfs
meter: 2/4
rhythm set: ta, ti-ti, anacrusis, 8th rest, tim-ri

Thugamar fein an Samhradh linn (Irish)
scale: Mixolydian
tone set: s,l,tdrmfs
meter: 3/4
rhythm set: ta, rest, ta-a, tam-ti

Kukulienka kde si bola (Slovak)
scale: major
tone set: t,drmfsl
meter: 2/4
rhythm set: ta, ti-ti, rest

Letila zozulja (Ukrainian)
scale: Aeolian/harmonic minor
tone set: l,t,drmfs(si)lt
meter: 6/8 + 9/8
rhythm set: tam, ta-ti, duple, tie

The Coo Coo Bird (Appalachian)
scale: la-pentatonic
tone set: s,l, drm
meter: 2/4
rhythm set: ti-ti, rest, taa, anacrusis, ti-tam, tiri-tam, tim-ri

Well fare the nightingale (English)
scale: major, modulation to 4th scale degree (ta=fa)
tone set: d   sl(ta)td'r'm' s'
meter: 4/4
rhythm set: ta, ta-a, 1/2 rest, tam-ti

Quand je menai mes chevaux boire (French)
scale: Aeolian/harmonic minor
tone set: (si,)l,t,drmfs
meter: 2/2 (or 2/4)
rhythm set: ta, ti-ti, rest, anacrusis, tam-ti, 8th rest

K'no moj qyqe (Albanian)
scale: Mixolydian
tone set: drmfsl(ta) or s,t,l,drmfs
meter: free + 7/4
rhythm set: ta, ti-ti, rest, taa, 1/2 rest, tam-ti + ornamentation

The Cuckoo (English)
scale: Dorian, modulating to 5th scale degree (fi=ti)
tone set: drmf(fi)sltd'r'm'
meter: 3/4
rhythm set: ta, ti-ti, rest, ta-a, anacrusis, tam-ti

Cântă puiul cucului (Romanian)
scale: Phrygian
tone set: mfsltd'r'm' + ornamentation
meter: cut time
rhythm set: whole note, ti-ti, tam-ti, ti-tam +

62

Bibliography

Chevalier, Jean, and Alain Gheerbrant. *Dictionnaire des Symboles*. Paris: Robert Laffont/Jupiter, 1969.

Choksy, Lois. *Kodály Method I: Comprehensive Music Education*. Upper Saddle River, NJ: Prentice-Hall, 1998.

Lönnrot, Elias, complier. *Kalevala, the Epic Poem of Finland*, vol. 1. Translated by John M. Crawford. New York: John B. Alden, 1888.

De Gubernatis, Angelo. *Zoological Mythology*, vol. 2. Edinburgh and London: Ballantvne, 1872.

Farrer, J.A. "Animal Mythology; Or, Stories of Birds and Beasts." *Cornhill Magazine* 47 (1883): 463–480.

Gaster, Moses. *Rumanian Birds and Beast Stories*. London: Sidgwick & Jackson, 1915.

Hardy, James. "Popular History of the Cuckoo." *The Folk-Lore Record* 2 (1879): 47-91.

Kammen, Shira. *Music in A Circle: Medieval, Renaissance & Early Baroque Rounds, Canons, Catches & Other Forms of Musical Imitation*. Richmond, CA: Average Press, 2006.

Locke, Eleanor. *Sail Away*. London: Boosey & Hawkes, 1981.

Negrotti, Rosanna. *William Wordsworth: A Biography of Selected Poems*. London: Brockhampton Press, 2001.

Ralston, W. R. S. *The Songs of the Russian People: As Illustrative of Slavonic Mythology and Russian Social Life*. London: Gilbert and Rivington, 1872.

Ronnberg, Ami, editor-in-chief, and Kathleen Martin, ed. *The Book of Symbols: Reflections on Archetypal Images*. Cologne: Taschen, 2010.

Sharp, Cecil J., and Maud Karpeles. *Eighty English Folk Songs from the Southern Appalachians*. London: Faber and Faber, 1968.

Sharp, Cecil J., and Charles L. Marson. *Folk Songs of Somerset*, vol. 3. London: Athenaeum Press, 1906.

Svensson, Lars, and Peter James Grant. *Birds of Europe*. Princeton, NJ: Princeton University Press, 2009.

Discography

Ashley, Clarence. *American Roots Collection*. Smithsonian Folkways, 1996.

Matvienko, Nina. *Ukrainski Narodni Pisni*. Folklore Ukrainien, 2006.

Malicorne. *Almanach*. Griffin, 1976.

McLaughlin, Mary. *Sacred Days, Mythic Way*. Rowan Records, 2012.

Pentangle. *Basket of Light*. Sanctuary, 1969.

Ritchie, Jean. *Mountain Hearth and Home*. Rhino/Elektra, 2004.

Notes

[1] Jean Chevalier and Alain Gheerbrant, *Dictionnaire des Symboles* (Paris: Robert Laffont/Jupiter, 1969).

[2] Chevalier, *Dictionnaire*, 292.

[3] James Hardy, "Popular History of the Cuckoo," *The Folk-Lore Record* 2 (1879), 3.

[4] Hardy, "Popular History," 8.

[5] Hardy, "Popular History," 1. A translation runs: Sumer is coming in, loudly sing cuckoo! Grows the seed, and blooms the mead(ow), and springs forth the wood anew. Sing cuckoo! Ewe bleats after lamb, lows after calves the cow, the bullock jumps, the stag leaps. Merrily, sing cuckoo! Cuckoo, cuckoo, well you sing cuckoo, don't ever you stop now. Sing, cuckoo, sing cuckoo!

[6] Hardy, "Popular History," 39.

[7] Hardy, "Popular History," 38.

[8] Mama Lisa's World, a website dedicated to collecting international children's music found at www.mamalisa.com.

[9] Mary McLaughlin, *Sacred Days, Mythic Ways*, Rowan Records, 2012 [Audio].

[10] Hardy, "Popular History," 12.

[11] Angelo De Gubernatis, *Zoological Mythology*, vol. 2 (Edinburgh and London: Ballantvne, 1872), 234.

[12] Hardy, "Popular History," 8.

[13] Hardy, "Popular History," 19.

[14] Hardy, "Popular History," 18.

[15] *Kukulienka, kde si bola*, Slovak folksong, uploaded on Oct. 13, 2010 [Video]. Retrieved from http://www.youtube.com/watch?v=Oc4OnCEjJPg

[16] Hardy, "Popular History," 23.

[17] Hardy, "Popular History," 26.

[18] Hardy, "Popular History," 44.

[19] Nina Matvienko, *Ukrainski Narodni Pisni*, Folklore Ukrainien, 2006 [Audio].

[20] Elias Lönnrot, complier, *Kalevala, the Epic Poem of Finland*, vol. 1, trans. John M. Crawford (New York: John B. Alden, 1888), xxxi.

[21] Hardy, "Popular History," 25.

[22] J. A. Farrer, "Animal Mythology; Or, Stories of Birds and Beasts," *Cornhill Magazine* 47 (1883): 469.

[23] Hardy, "Popular History," 9.

[24] De Gubernatis, *Zoological Mythology*, 236.

[25] Hardy, "Popular History," 9.

[26] Moses Gaster, *Rumanian Birds and Beast Stories* (London: Sidgwick & Jackson, 1915), 284.

[27] Shira Kammen, *Music in a Circle: Medieval, Renaissance & Early Baroque Rounds, Canons, Catches & Other Forms of Musical Imitation* (Richmond, CA: Average Press, 2006).

[28] Lars Svensson and Peter James Grant, *Birds of Europe* (Princeton, NJ: Princeton University Press, 2009), 220.

[29] American Heritage Dictionary (Boston: Houghton Mifflin, 2006).

[30] Malicorne, *Almanach*, Griffin, 1976 [Audio].

[31] Hardy, "Popular History," 25.

[32] De Gubernatis, *Zoological Mythology*, 229.

[33] De Gubernatis, *Zoological Mythology*, 226.

[34] Hardy, *Popular History*, 15.

[35] Farrer, *Animal Mythology*, 469.

[36] Parashqevi Simaku, *Kendo moj qyqe se povjen behari*, Albanian folk song, uploaded on Jun 18, 2009 [Video]. Retrieved from http://www.youtube.com/watch?v=kFWlfBdPZj8

[37] Cecil J. Sharp and Charles L. Marson, *Folk Songs of Somerset*, vol. 3 (London: Athenaeum Press, 1906), 48–50. This variant transcribed from The Pentangle, track 8 on *Basket of Light*, Castle Music, CMRCD 207, 1969, cd.

[38] Hardy, *Popular History*, 23.

[39] W. R. S. Ralston, *The Songs of the Russian People: As Illustrative of Slavonic Mythology and Russian Social Life* (London: Gilbert and Rivington, 1872), 216.

[40] *Birds of North America* (New York: St. Martin's Press, 2001), 172.

[41] De Gubernatis, *Zoological Mythology*, 233.

[42] Clarence Ashley, *American Roots Collection*, Smithsonian Folkways, 1996. [Audio.]

[43] Jean Ritchie, *Mountain Hearth and Home*, Rhino/Elektra, 2004. [Audio.]

[44] Cecil J. Sharp and Maud Karpeles, *Eighty Folk Songs from the Southern Appalachians* (London: Faber and Faber, 1968), 61.

[45] Adriana Ochisanu, *Colo-n frunza codrului*, Romanian folksong, uploaded on Mar 17, 2011. Translated by Stephen Carter. Retrieved from http://www.youtube/watch?v=uOPTEqlE3qo

Originally published in *Kodály Envoy* 40, no. 2 (Winter 2014): 14-20. Reprinted by permission.

SEA SHANTIES: THE HARDY SURVIVORS

Eleanor G. Locke

L'étude du contenu extensif des sons enregistré et imprimé de la bibliothèque du Musée Maritime du San Francisco produit ainsi qu' une douzaine de chansons de bord utilisés uniquement pour les travaux sur les bateaux de voile. Ils étaient parmi les plus favoris qui ont survécu de l'âge d'or des voiles. Ce compte-rendu va leur procurer un emplacement historique avec l'aide de diapositives et des exemples musicaux enregistrés.

The sea shanty, "epitome of worksongs,"[1] which flourished in the golden age of sail (1820–1860), arose with the full-rigged, deep-water vessels that carried on vital international trade along global sea routes.[2] Early in that period American-built clipper ships were supreme, British in full competition, establishing an English-speaking folk tradition among the crews. This presentation has an Anglo-American base, though many other peoples contributed to the molding of the songs. It will be confined to songs that were inseparable from labor. Fo'c'sle songs, the music of the rare leisure time, are not included, nor are shoreside ballads, nor any discussion of sailors' instruments.

The community that made and used the maritime work songs of the nineteenth century was the crew of the deep-water, full-rigged sailing ship of the United States, Canada, the British Isles and Europe. The century saw an explosion of commerce in coal, hides, cotton, tea, silks, lumber, nitrates and so forth, with thousands of emigrants and gold-seekers making crossings in the only transportation available. The whaling trade was too large, and the slave trade too unspeakable, to be brought into this quick survey.

From 1812 until 1860 the new America dominated these races, and races they were. Baltimore builders, with the aid of French design, pioneered the fast ship to elude British blockades. "Clipper captains pressed their luck to the limit, for speed meant passengers, freight, profits, fame."[3] Famous shipyards turned out vessels by the hundreds, mainly from the northeast coast of the United States and Canada. Ship designer Donald MacKay, Scots carpenter from Nova Scotia, who mastered his craft in the Webb Shipyard of New York, built the *Lightning*, the *Flying Cloud*, and forty-five more beauties. The Clydeside in Scotland became noted in the art. The entire story is outside the scope of this brief presentation, but has a bearing on the class of men who sailed before the mast, for the ship was their real home for their working lifetime, and they intimately knew and loved her.

Their countryside was the geography of the sea lanes: the doldrums, the horse latitudes, the "line," as the equator was called, and the fearful encounter with Cape Horn, its sixty-foot graybeards, its savage, unremitting westerlies, hail, sleet, lightning and massive icebergs. Ports of call were their familiar oases, rated by pleasures enjoyed or bitter experience.

Crews generally ran from eighteen to over fifty men, two or three mates, a ship's carpenter, sailmaker, cook and several boy apprentices. The captain was absolute monarch—either benign or sadistic tyrant, or something in between. He was often forgiven, if he knew his ropes and winds. Able-bodied seamen got their training in the Navies and Merchant Marine Schools of their nations of birth.[4] They learned also on family ships from Maine or Wales, and as apprentices. Part of the crew, and sometimes too large a part, were unlucky drifters, runaways, drunks and down-and-outers swept up in portside barrooms. A wicked system of crimps and corrupt boarding houses flourished in all major seaports. They supplied crew at captains' request, using shanghaiing, liquor and promises to fill the complement of departing ships.

Diaries, logs and accounts of voyages indicate that crews were of widely mixed nationality: American, British, German, Scandinavian, Finnish, African-American, Chinese, French, Italian, Kanaka and more.[5] Nevertheless, on the ropes and at the capstan, English-language shanties flourished on vessels under English-speaking command. Toward the end of the century major German and French companies dominated the runs around Cape Horn.[6] The shanty tradition, shown in books from those countries, is full of borrowings from the Anglo stock of songs as well as those of their own rich folklore.[7]

Sailors sang, shouted, yelled, intoned and groaned shanties to put extra energy into the backbreaking labor of hauling tons of yards and canvas up the masts, reefing, furling, bracing sail, heaving on the capstan bars or pump handles. In his battle with the vast power of wind and ocean, in confined group life, suffering a large degree of direct oppression of man by man, seamen became "welded as a family, and their very adversities draw them closer."[8] Crews adopted shanties as part of shipboard routine. Captains and mates demanded the extra edge the singing gave to manpower. There was an *esprit de corps* aboard a well-run vessel that raised all spirits. Like warriors, men gave heroic outpourings of muscle, stamina and soul.

Shantymen came forward from the ranks of the crew because of their talents as leaders in work, their musical ability, their quality of voice and the singing repertoire they brought with them from their homelands. Eyewitness commentary (see Appendix) gives African-Americans rave notices, with Irish and other Brits, Netherlanders and Germans also rating. The shantyman to whom we are most indebted for the continuity of the art is Stan Hugill of Liverpool. After twenty years at sea, four years as prisoner of war during World War II, and a long stint as teacher as the Outward Bound School of Aberdovey, Wales, Stan Hugill is still, in his eighties, devoting his talents to keeping shantying alive in folk festivals and maritime museum programs throughout the world. That he is the authority in the field is clear from his published books and the fact that he was chosen to write the article on the subject in the 1980 edition of Grove's Dictionary of Music.

Sea music for centuries had contributed a ritual of blessing and invocation for God's protection against the hazards of the voyage. The working shanty was no hymn; it was a rough diamond, a pragmatic weapon in the "drive her, captain, drive her" arsenal. But this music, in addition to being part of the work ritual, was also a blessing for a ship.

Passed on orally, the chants and songs came from the vernacular of dance music, patriotic marches, music-hall favorites, spirituals, minstrel-show ditties and traditional ballads, with their varying melodic turns. Tunes were of two or four phrases, with antiphonal interplay

67

between solo and chorus. Form, rhythm, and style were part of the work-bound gesture. Informants insisted that "We al'us knowed 'em."[9]

Texts that have come down to us have been considerably and considerately expurgated. Experts agree that subjects that enthused the crews were the faraway feminine in grosser manifestations, booze, historic stories and heroes, favorite ports and other symbols of home, and the gripes of everyday life. Expression of these gripes was permitted only in song. Choruses were: Way, hay, roll and go; Blow boys, blow; Ranzo me boys, Ranzo; and so on. Short clear forms, strong, mouth-filling vowels and consonants and decisive rhythm give shanties their musical integrity.

From the days before World War I when Cecil Sharp, a colleague of Kodály in the International Folk Music Society, took down the pulling and hauling songs of old John Short and others, and set them with piano accompaniment for English schools,[10] there has been a stream of books, arrangements and recordings. A true archival heritage in the United States was the product of careful collectors in the period from 1920–1950. This material came mainly from the northeast coast of the U.S. and Canada, the singers from the British Isles and Africa.[11] A core repertoire has survived to this day, with little change.

New research for this paper was based on a major collection of books, transcriptions, illustrations, photos, logs and recorded music available in the Library of the National Maritime Museum of San Francisco, California, U.S.A. This most important source of West Coast maritime history contains the lifetime accumulation of John Lyman, eminent maritime historian, who, incidentally for his main work, made a sweepingly eclectic gathering of any and all recordings of music relating to the sea. He managed to include all the public output of Folkways Records, the Archive of Folk Song of the Library of Congress, Washington, D.C., Peter Kennedy's *The Folksongs of Britain, Vol. VI* and commercial discs of all sorts from North European nations.

On these recordings (1935–1960), three hundred and fifteen different songs and shanties are performed. These have been catalogued, song by song, and taped for public access and archival safekeeping, a project I completed as a volunteer, under the supervision of David Hull, principal librarian, with advice from archivists at U.C. Berkeley and Stanford University, and the Recording Division of the Library of Congress, Washington. These sources provide the carefully documented singing of retired seamen.[12] Most of the records simply show, with varying degrees of musical skill, what sea music was popular, and have kept the songs alive.

The community that loves shantying today is found in singing clubs, maritime museum programs and schools. Park rangers and modern day "folk singers," and sometimes teachers, are the new shantymen. The songs link us with a vivid past, and recreate the power of community that made the music what it is: "of all songs in English . . . the noblest, the most vigorous, the most stirring, and the hardest to imitate."[13]

The twelve most often performed in the Lyman record collection, the most often referred to by title in accounts of voyages, the most often notated in published collections are the "top favorites" listed below. Today's singers may have the pleasure and none of the pain that was bound into life at sea. The most melodious and spirited songs may be chosen and enjoyed by everyone in the afterglow of the historic achievements that gave them birth. These are among them:

AWAY RIO (pronounced Rye-o): An outward-bound shanty used for raising anchor; Rio Grande do Sul, on the east coast of Brazil, was a delightful port for seamen.

A-ROVING or THE MAID OF AMSTERDAM: A well-formed melody with longer phrases and sequential motifs, possibly Elizabethan; used at the capstan.

BLOW, BOYS, BLOW: Descriptive of the Yankee-run hell ship; satirized by European veterans of Cape Horners. Often sung on packet ships.

BLOW THE MAN DOWN: Second and third mates were called "blowers and strikers" for the way they carried out discipline with the crews.

BONEY: English sailors took the tune from the French traditional shanty "Jean-François de Nantes." Strained relations between the nationals resulted in English-speaking sources claiming the song as entirely their own, with no reference to its French origin. Napoleon was a popular figure among seamen. (See Appendix.)

GOODBYE, FARE-YE-WELL: Ritually sung on leaving South American nitrate and guano ports for the journey home, accompanying a splendid ceremony in the harbor involving many sailing ships together.[14] Much beloved.

HAUL AWAY, JOE: The Dorian melody is of Irish heritage. Used for tacks and sheets.

HAUL ON THE BO'LINE: Of great antiquity, used for short hauls. In Newfoundland in 1929 it was collected from use to haul granite blocks for the cathedral in St. John's.[15]

REUBEN RANZO: The story of the landlubber aboard ship was all too familiar. The text has a happy ending which is surely satirical. See the appendix for the Sicilian fishermen's song that must be its origin, though I have never seen mention of this.

SANTIANNA: A popular halyard shanty, this Irish melody carries a story that made the vanquished the victor in the Mexican-American War, a feat no doubt close to the heart of exploited tars.

SHENANDOAH: An American shanty with melodic line and poetic imagery strong enough to carry it from deck to concert hall. Tape will offer a West Indian variant.

WHISKEY, JOHNNY: Military march motifs and an obsessive subject made this a prime favorite for long hauls.

APPENDIX: Shipmates Describe Shantymen

PADDY FURLONG (pseudonym), described by a Welsh apprentice, 1905:

A six-foot-two, fifty-year-old Irishman . . . "whose high spirits and courage nothing could quench. He had the right, sailors' way of doing things, as practiced by seamen of the genuine old school. . . always good-tempered and making jokes in his broad brogue to keep his shipmates in good spirits. He was a natural and accepted leader in any company of seamen at work, as his qualities were outstanding. He was always at the head of a line of men, bracing up or squaring in the yards, and providing the sing-song shanty to which all pulling on ropes was done. . . sung in his deep, melodious voice, which made the work seem much easier."[16]

AN ANONYMOUS OLD "SHELLBACK," described by a young seaman:

His voice was a loud, rich baritone. We always looked to him to lead us in a chanty. From him I learned nearly all the chanties I have heard sung, for I was then young and impressionable. Later, as I launched into manhood I heard the same chanties sung by other sailors but they varied somewhat in tune, for not all chantymen sing chanties just alike. [17]

LEMON CURTIS, as described by his ship's captain circa 1905:

Lemon Curtis was an American Negro of superb physique, a superstitious, simple fellow whose voice resounded like the beat of a bass drum. As a shanteyman he was worth his weight in gold. I can see him yet, towering head and shoulders above his shipmates, his head thrown back and the words of an unforgettable halyard shanty "Somebody Wants to Know My Name" soaring to the mastheads. . .[18]

Notes

[1] *The New Grove Dictionary of Music and Musicians* (Oxford: Oxford University Press, 1980).

[2] Joseph Jobé, and Basil W. Bathe, *The Great Age of Sail* (Greenwich, CT: Edita Lausanne, 1967).

[3] Alan Villiers, *Men, Ships and the Sea* (Washington, D.C.: National Geographic Society, 1973), 220.

[4] L. A. Smith: 80,000 North Germans worked at sea in 1880s

[5] Richard Henry Dana, Jr., *Two Years Before the Mast* (New York: Harper and Bros., 1840).

[6] Capt. Armand Hayet, *Chansons de Bord* (Paris: Editions Eos, 1927); Hermann Strobach, ed., *Shanties* (Rostock, Germany: Hinstorff, 1970).

[7] *Le Chant de Marin: Guide du répertoire traditionnel* (Douarnenez, Brittany, France: Le Chasse-Marée, 1989).

[8] Richard Lunt Hale, *The Log of a Forty-niner: Journal of a Voyage from Newbury-port to San Francisco* (Boston: B. J. Brimmer, 1923), 178.

[9] Rex Clements, *Manavilins* (London: Heath Cranton, 1928), 19.

[10] A. L. Lloyd, *Folk Song in England* (New York: International Publisher, 1967), 306.

[11] William Main Doerflinger, *Songs of the Sailor and Lumberman* (New York: MacMillan, 1972), xii.

[12] Duncan Emrich, liner notes for *American Sea Songs and Shanties* (Washington, D.C.: Library of Congress AAFS L26, 1).

[13] Alan Lomax, *Folk Songs of North America* (Garden City, NY: Doubleday, 1960), 37.

[14] A. Basil Lubbock, *Round the Horn Before the Mast* (London: John Murray, 1902), 7.

[15] Elisabeth Bristol Greenleaf, and Grace Yarrow Mansfield, *Ballads and Sea Songs of Newfoundland* (Hatboro, PA: Folklore Associates, 1968), 338.

[16] William H. S. Jones, *The Cape Horn Breed* (New York: Criterion, 1956).

[17] Stanton H. King, *King's Book of Chanties* (Boston: Oliver Ditson, 1918).

[18] Captain James P. Barker, *The Log of a Limejuicer: The Experiences Under Sail of James P. Baker, Master Mariner, As Told to Roland Barker* (London: Putnam, 1934).

Originally published in *Bulletin of the International Kodály Society* 16, no. 2 (1992): 11-15. Reprinted by permission.

MAKING MUSIC AS THE LANGUAGE OF COMMUNITY: TOWARD AN ORGANIZATIONAL FRAMEWORK FOR NORTH AMERICAN FOLKSONG RESEARCH

Jerry L. Jaccard

Introduction

The residents of Oskina, a miniscule village in the Voronezh region of Southern Russia, had heard that the folksong collector was coming. They knew she was curious about the ancient song and dance heritage they had been accumulating for centuries. For many decades these villagers had carefully kept this treasure hidden from the view of the recently dismantled Communist regime that had forbidden the practice of almost all reminders of Old Russia. Outsiders generally believed that the old ways had been forgotten—erased by chaotic decades that had abruptly thrust the Russian people into the industrial age. The villagers had not only preserved their folkways, but had actually been celebrating them on the sly, unseen by the rest of their country as it rushed along to mechanization. Unseen, perhaps, because their village was believed to be so insignificant that they couldn't possibly make a difference. How wrong modernity had been! The folksong collector was coming to see *them*, and *they* were ready. It was the time of the *Rusalka* rituals—Rusalka, the water sprite of ancient lore who blessed the land with water and sun and growth, promising a good planting and a good harvest. As the collector approached, driving around potholes and ruts as big as her small car, she was met by the villagers in full song, full dance, and full regalia. They embraced her and took her into the secret life of their village. They sang for her, and she wept with them as they remembered the old songs and dances that their now-deceased grandparents had taught them.[1] This tiny village, unknown to most of the outside world, is a testament to the indomitable will and unstoppable voice of the universal common man and woman. *This* is music as the language of community![2]

Zoltán Kodály told his doctoral student, Lajos Vargyas, that *"the most illuminating endeavour would be to map a village's entire melody stock, the description of its music life in minute detail, that is, to create a musical monograph of it"* (Vargyas, 2000, p. 7). Through following the counsel of his advisor, Vargyas was able to document living music as the language of a community instead of simply collecting songs. In guiding Vargyas, Kodály posed questions that reveal how deeply Kodály himself was thinking about the natural musical functioning of a community:

The mere registration of tune and text, however precise this may be, reveals nothing of the life and physiology of the tune. It must be explored whether it changes when a singer repeats it in the song, or sings it at a later day; whether this change is deliberate or spontaneous; whether its transmission always entails modification; what are the circumstances, causes, laws of variation. The singers once recorded can be revisited.

Intriguing observations are to be expected: ha[s] the performance of songs changed over the years and decades? When the singers are no longer alive, does the song leave any trace or disappear with the singers? Has musical taste changed with a changed way of living? Has the folksong stock increased or decreased? Why have certain songs been abandoned?

. . . Little is known of the extent to which the tunes have spread: how deep they are rooted in society; how many people know them, whether they can be differentiated within a narrow circle; what are the occasions and customs of singing; whether transmission is solely oral or is also facilitated by printing (handwritten, printed songbooks sold at fairs). Is there a conscious, deliberate component in learning songs, or does it just "stick in mind"? How much does its spread owe to text and how much to tune? Are texts known without tunes and vice versa? Are new words applied deliberately to old tunes? Are there people who claim to be authors of such texts? (p. 81)

Just as in this Hungarian village, just as in the musical life of the Oskina community, we can still find living music all over the world. Sadly, we must also realize that for too many other communities, the traditional process of song genesis and transmission we call folksong has been disrupted, interrupted, and even halted. This paper aims to report on some key aspects of the path Zoltán Kodály took through the complexities of Hungarian folk- and composed music. In so doing, this paper also reflects on the implications of his journey for us today in the Americas concerning our social, musical and educational cultures.[3] I think that once again, we will be surprised and delighted at how accurately Kodály foresaw our current situation.

Because we tend to hold great thinkers like Kodály in such high esteem, we often overlook the fact that their original ideas seldom, if ever, spring from a vacuum—we tend to de-contextualize them. Therefore, in order to really come to grips with Kodály's thinking about folk music, composition, and teaching, it is necessary for us to view him in his context, to understand the musical trends around him, and to examine the activities of some of Kodály's network of peers and contemporaries.

Nationalistic environments

To begin with, it is helpful to remember that until the full flowering of the Renaissance, composition often consisted of putting already existing folk songs, folk dance tunes, chants[4] and chorale melodies[5] into the clothing of new and often experimental composed forms (Sharp 1965, p. 140; see also Dobszay 1992, p. 99). It was only when polyphony began to take on a life of its own that composers became prolific producers of freely composed melodies independent of the oral tradition. This is not intended to be an absolute statement; free composition had been jump-started by the happy coincidence of Guidonian notation and early polyphony within the same century. László Dobszay, Head of the Folk Music Department of the Hungarian Institute for Musicology and Head of Church Music of the Liszt Academy, describes the dynamic balance between folk- and art music elements in the early Renaissance:

From the history of music and from the comparative method of musicology we know that the rich musical life of Europe and its flourishing traditions advanced to a synthesis between the tenth and the sixteenth centuries; art music (composed music) absorbed in various waves the most valuable elements of folk music; the monophonic Gregorian culture amalgamated with the most precious traditions of the folk music of that time and made it firm in a special form which was half folk music and half art music in character. It was integrated into the richness and fullness of the monophonic and polyphonic art music of the Middle Ages and the Renaissance and also contained folk music motifs. In the meantime the vocal repertoire of the troubadours, minstrels (minnesänger), etc., continuously enriched art music on the side of folk music and the situation was reciprocated; thus there was a constant mutual influence on both parts. . . . By the sixteenth century composed music could claim such products, results, and complexities, that it increasingly took precedence over folk music. . . . (Dobzay, 1992, p. 99)

Additionally, Western European folk music merged much earlier with art music than elsewhere in Europe. This enabled composed music to almost overwhelm authentic oral tradition. Before then, "a healthy reciprocity of folk and art music existed" (p. 35).

Thus, we see that by the end of the Renaissance, composed music began to outrun folksong as a source of melodic genesis, although composers of most subsequent stylistic periods continued to dip into the well of folksong for inspiration and musical material. For example, Haydn, Mozart, and Beethoven incorporated local folk melodies into many of their smaller as well as large-scale works. Haydn and Beethoven were also commissioned by English publishers to do various settings of "folksongs" from the British Isles, but very few of these settings actually employ authentic folk tunes and texts from the British Isles (see, for example, the 1970 Kalmus mini-score editions of the Beethoven songs). Most of them reflect the then British ignorance of their own indigenous music. However, they *do* demonstrate that the voice of the people—or at least the essence of it—was never completely lost in the music of the masters.

Almost concurrently with Haydn and Beethoven, Johann Gottfried Herder (1744–1803) was laying the groundwork for making the serious study of folksong an important aspect of German Romanticism, a reaction to imperialism and rigid social stratification. However, in Herder's day, it was common to transcribe folksong text *without* the melody, as evidenced by his own publications. Goethe was much more proactive in noting down tunes *and* texts.[6] We can only wonder how many tunes and their variants passed out of existence before the realization dawned that melody is the more defining element of folksong (Kodály, 1906, p. 1). Nevertheless, Kodály adhered to some of Herder's views on culture and humanities education as an extension of the folk culture of a nation,[7] resulting in Kodály being awarded the Herder Prize by the University of Vienna in 1965 (Kodály, 1966, p. 97). During the late nineteenth and twentieth centuries, there was substantial folklore and folksong collecting activity in many other European countries—often spearheaded by composers—notably in Finland, Bohemia, Norway, and Russia. Some may have been following Germany's early lead in exhibiting interest in their folksong, but in spite of that, a more common motivation seems to have been the need to establish national cultural identity.[8]

Just immediately ahead of Bartók and Kodály was Emile Jaques-Dalcroze, who had begun to realize and write about the educational value of folksong (1930, p. 225). His own work, however, was already far down the path to Eurhythmics, and the types of folksong readily available to him were of the less authentic, more superficial kind, something he did recognize (p. 231). His friend and successor, the composer Frank Martin, was able to dig more deeply into indigenous Swiss music[9] in a way more akin to the academic approaches of Bartók and Kodály.[10]

Béla Bartók and Zoltán Kodály met in college and soon discovered their mutual curiosity about the nature and value of the genuine music of the Magyar people. Up until then, this music had existed just out of reach of citified Hungarians, having been pushed aside for centuries by the dominant German culture. The pure Hungarian language was not even spoken by the general population of Budapest until the beginning of the twentieth century (Kodály, 1966, p. 50). Bartók and Kodály, among other young Hungarians of their generation, yearned to restore Hungary to the Hungarians, but their approach was more artistic and academic than political—an important example, I think, for our own time and place. As musicians, they recognized how true Hungarianness resided in the folk life of the peasantry, the not-so-musically-silent majority of their country. Paying their own way out of their meager student pockets, the two young men spent their summer breaks hiking through remote villages to collect songs. They transcribed most tunes and texts into notebooks on location; only the highly ornamented ones were recorded for later transcription on an Edison wax cylinder gramophone (Kodály, 1966, p. 27). The machine was so cumbersome that they had to take it apart and distribute the pieces between their knapsacks in order to carry it from village to village. Again drawing on their own meager resources, they finished their transcribing and organizing of the melodies while back at school. There is another lesson for us in this, and that is Bartók and Kodály's passion for the work and their willingness to make significant personal sacrifices to achieve it—song collecting was not even required coursework for them.

These young composers' determined fascination with folksong set the stage for the playing out of a series of events that touch us even now. As with all great endeavors, timing is everything, and just as the young Bartók and Kodály were grappling with the realization that they had their hands full of highly significant melodic structures and the responsibility of making sense of them, the tool they needed came from the unexpected direction of Finland. Although Finnish and Hungarian are remotely related languages—not at all mutually intelligible—it is amazing how Ilmari Krohn's analyzed collection of Finnish folksongs (1904–1928) made it all the way to Budapest and into the young composers' hands when it was most needed. However it came into their hands, Krohn's work provided a consistent scientific model and set of processes for classifying the ever-growing numbers of melodic variants that Bartók and Kodály were collecting. Krohn's model provided the tools for a systematic comparison of structural, rhythmic and melodic variants of similar tunes (Erdely, 1965, p. 45). Over the decades since, three main Hungarian folksong classification systems have grown out of Krohn's original one: the Bartók, the Kodály, and the Járdányi.[11] The so-called *universal collection* maintained by the Folk Music Research Group of the Institute for Musicology of the Hungarian Academy of Sciences is organized according to these three systems (Jaccard, 2004, npn).

While the Hungarian effort was just beginning, the English folksong revival was in full bloom. The boundless enthusiasm manifested in the first issue (1899) of the *Journal of the Folk-Song Society* emanates from a veritable Who's Who of English musical greats: Lucy Broadwood, J. Spencer Curwen, Edward Elgar, Lady Alice B. Gomme, Sir Hubert Parry, Sir John Stainer and Charles Villiers Stanford. Within a few years, Gustav Holst, Ralph Vaughan Williams, Percy Grainger and Cecil Sharp are also at the center of the English folksong revival, and it is at this juncture that musical connections between Hungary and the rest of Western Europe get interesting. Vaughan Williams went to Paris and fell under the compositional influences of Ravel and Debussy, especially Ravel, with whom he studied for an extended period.[12] He collaborated with Cecil Sharp and others in the enthronement of English folksong in school music. Vaughan Williams and his close friend, Gustav Holst, began to develop individual folksong-like styles of composition in the same three ways as Bartók and Kodály: 1) direct quotations of existing folksongs; 2) newly-composed folksong-like melodies; and 3) folksong-like elements incorporated into free composition (Vikár in Jaccard, 1993, npn). Yet another connection is Kodály's pronouncement that he greatly admired the English choir school approach to choral sound and the British cultivation of school singing in general (Kodály in Bónis, 1964, p. 121).

We therefore see that early in Kodály's career, the die had been cast for Hungary's contribution to the proliferation of national musical styles, but with a new twist, that of connecting national style to sweeping reform in public education. All along, it seems that Kodály was thinking beyond his role as a composer to being vitally involved in the process of music education. In his most autobiographical work, published the year before his death, he reveals how he had used folksong in his own teaching of theory and composition at the Liszt Academy. He further explained how he identified potentially adept and influential music education majors and purposely invited them into his composition classes (1966, pp. 45–46). He thereby created a working partnership between dozens of composers, theorists, musicologists and educators while forging with them his philosophy, now known as the Kodály Concept of Music Education.[13] All attempts to claim possession of any original "Kodály method" pale in the light of this information. Clearly, Kodály, too, was a music teacher who like the rest of us, was laboring throughout his career to unravel the mysteries of the musical teaching-learning process. For him, the answers were to be found in the music itself and in the students themselves.

Rivers and streams: How folksong research flows into the classroom

Up until now, we have been sitting on our laurels. What I mean is, we have been enjoying the pioneering efforts of the first handful of people and institutions to introduce the Kodály Concept to North America. We should be very grateful to these pioneers, for they have brought us to where we are today. But I am also sure all of them will agree that it is time for us to get *far* beyond our present successes. For us today, what Bartók and Kodály did with their collected and classified melodies is essential to understanding what our next frontier must be. It is a matter of the utmost urgency for us to get *deeply* and *thoroughly* into our song systems. We can take our cue from Kodály's own developmental timeline. The first step he took based on his folksong research was his doctoral dissertation entitled *The Strophic Structure of Hungarian Folk Song* (1906). This served as a template for future decades of analytical, comparative, and compositional work by Bartók, Kodály, and their dozens of associates. Then, there was their ongoing compositional output so solidly founded on the Hungarian musical language. In 1943, the Hungarian Ministry of Education published Kodály and György Kerényi's *School Song Collection*. This is more than a mere list of songs. It groups them by melodic element according to grade level and then provides the specific tune variants intended to be used. This was the foundation for the development of the Hungarian national music curriculum, from which *many* master teachers who had been in Kodály's classes at the Academy gradually worked out a variety of approaches, methodologies, and techniques under Kodály's wise guidance (Jaccard with Ittzés, 2004, npn).

The third publication resulting from Bartók's and Kodály's research deserves special mention here, the mostly posthumous ten volumes of the *Corpus Musicae Popularis Hungaricae*, or "Body of Hungarian Folksong," more of which are still in preparation. The structure of this monumental work is specific to the present topic: Volume One is *Children's Songs*, Volume Two is *Calendar Customs*, Volume Three is *Wedding Songs*, Volume Four is *Courting Songs*, and Volume Five is *Funeral Laments*. After these volumes come various folksong types that do not fall into strict calendar- or social function categories (Bartók and Kodály, 1951–). In the first five volumes, we have Bartók's and Kodály's discovery that many folksongs are associated with specific rituals, customs, ceremonies and life events. In other words, there are categories of how folksongs *function* within communities. Within each of these categories, there exist specific melodic types and forms into which songs can be classified. Without going into detail, suffice it to say for now that unlike the superficial "analysis" we are taught to do in Kodály certification courses, there exists a much deeper type of comparative classification, right down to the level of specific intervals (Erdély, 1965). Through it, Bartók and Kodály observed how large compositional forms are derived from smaller folksong structures. In Hungary, this ongoing effort produces a rich and varied repertoire available for school music curricular use. It is this combination of good materials, profound understanding and flexibility that have helped Hungarian music teaching to develop its quality reputation. According to Ildikó Herboly, "The reason children read music so fluently in Hungary is because they have such good tools in their hands" (Herboly-Kocsár, 1993, p. 1). This *virtuosity of musical materials* is what we in North America must now strive to attain in order to advance and bring to maturity the pedagogical, compositional and societal aims inherent in the Kodály vision we espouse.

If after a hundred years the Hungarians themselves have not yet stopped collecting, sifting and classifying their music, then we would do well to consider how to accelerate and deepen our folk music research.[14] Whereas forty years of research preceded the first folksong-based Hungarian school song curriculum (Kodály and Kerényi, 1943), we in North America had to quickly fuel the startup years of our adaptations with small collections that addressed specific pedagogical issues without seeing the wholeness of our music. These initial collections and analyses were in turn built on the foundation of considerable collecting and archiving that had previously been done without the Kodály-inspired goals or techniques in mind. Most folk materials found in local, state and national collections have not yet been transcribed, much less analyzed and classified in a way useful for our purposes. An essential component of such activity must be to carefully document in such a way that the song-to-source context is preserved so that multiple variants can be compared and classified. The Holy Names University Kodály Center online collection (*kodaly.hnu.edu*) is not only exemplary in this regard, but it is useable at several levels ranging from day-to-day teaching practice to academic research. This collection mostly consists of melodies transcribed by Anne Laskey and Gail Needleman from archival recordings in the Library of Congress. Jill Trinka wrote illuminatingly about singable transcription techniques in Cramer and Panagapka's 1998 book, *Teacher of Teachers: Papers in Honour of Lois Choksy*. A new book by László Vikár and Jeanette Panagapka sets another important precedent for the North American Kodály community, that of transcribing and classifying the repertoire of just one singer (2004). Still other long-term projects are underway but not yet far along enough to bring to publication. Actually, publication need not be the end goal of such activity. If we take care of the research, publications will naturally emerge in their own time.

Another aspect of music as the language of community must be considered here. Not only did Kodály and Bartók raise the bar for comparative folksong musicology in general, they also discovered definite connections between certain folksong forms and larger composed forms that had developed from them. They brought to light the actual reciprocity between folk- and art music mentioned above. This suggests another essential set of research problems for North American adherents to pursue. For László Vikár (1993, npn), the solution to making those connections is found in the multiplicity of variants that define the most beautiful and the most typical song forms. As he explained, folk- and art music are not opposite, but complementary—one illuminates the other. He noted that a healthy musical community generates multiple variants of the same tunes and that researchers need to be "crazy about variants."

Music in Community: Back to Our Future

How to begin? I think it can be shown that there are certain universals in folksong—whether European, or Anglo- or African- or Native American, or Hispanic, or Middle Eastern, or Asian—that hold constant. Since time will not allow us to look at each of these separately, let us look more deeply at one or two of them as we try to grasp how to begin sorting through our rich fund of musical languages.

The Rhythm of the Seasons: Calendar Customs and Life Events

It appears that for millennia, much music-making has been driven by nature's own timetable. Thus, we see in all cultures and in all times and places some universal calendar customs and daily rituals that celebrate planting and cultivating, herding or hunting, making and building, harvesting, storing, and preparing to do all of them again at the proper times of the year. Interlaced with celebrations of these major seasonal turns are individual and community thanksgivings, blessings, and pleas for abundance and protection. These are basic human needs being sung, danced, played, and re-enacted not as performances, but as humankind's unselfconscious and life-sustaining rhythms and melodies. These primal ways of making music are the foundation of music as the language of community. The ancient natural foundations of the English-language musical heritage can be partly understood through the Celtic and Anglo-Saxon names for months of the year (Sermon, 2001, p. 3). Table I presents the Celtic month-name sources closest to modern English:

Table 1:

Celtic name	Source language	Modern name
Eanaír	Irish Gaelic	January
Feabhra	Irish Gaelic	February
Márta	Irish Gaelic	March
Ebrill	Welsh	April
Mai	Welsh	May
Lúil	Irish Gaelic	July
Awst	Welsh	August

Table 2 shows how Anglo-Saxon month names referred to specific calendar functions and activities (p. 4):

Table 2:

Anglo-Saxon	Translation		Modern English Meaning
Æfterra Geola	Later Yule [Yule = Winter Solstice]	January	Midwinter months
Solmonao	Sol-month	February	Mud month, offerings
Hreomonao	Hreth-month	March	A-S goddess Hretha
Eastremonao	Easter-month	April	A-S goddess Eastre
Drimilce	Three-milkings	May	Abundance in nature
Ærra Lióa	Earlier Litha	June	Midsummer months
Æfterra Lióa	Later Litha [Litha = Summer Solstice]	July	Midsummer months
Weodmonao	Weed-month	August	Weeds grow most
Haligmonao	Holy-month	September	Harvest thankful
Winterfylleo	Winter-full	October	First winter full moon
Blotmonao	Blood-month	November	Animals slaughtered
Æerra Geola	Earlier Yule	December	Midwinter months

Table 3 adds to these the Anglo-Saxon names for seasons, solstices and equinoxes to give us a rather complete framework for understanding many Celtic, British and American songs, dances and customs that are celebrations of Nature's calendar (p. 4):

Table 3:

Anglo-Saxon	Translation	Modern English
Lencten	Lent	Spring
Sumor	Summer	Summer
Haerfest	Harvest	Autumn
Winter	Winter	Winter
Efniht	Even-night	Spring Equinox
Middansumor	Midsummer	Summer Solstice
Efniht	Even-night	Autumn Equinox
Middanwinter	Midwinter	Winter Solstice

Originally, many English language songs and customs were tied to specific times of the year. I also suspect that similar but culturally specific calendar templates will be found in the various African and African-American, Hispanic, Native American and other traditions around the world.

In addition to the calendar customs governed by nature, there is another major engine driving human music-making. Woven around and through the fixed cycles of Mother Nature are the variable but often occurring major life events of marriage, birth, work, the joys and sorrows of life, and death. Some of these are the songs of community, others are personal and private expressions. Still others are both. I will never forget being present at a traditional burial of a member of the White Mountain Apache Tribe in Arizona: each individual woman's wailing lament was added to another, until the community of women were individually improvising on the same theme of grief, but all at the same time and in an incredibly responsive and interactive way to each other. Then there are songs of personal expression such as the deeply private romance "Black Is the Color of My True Love's Hair," or the old Irish "Shule Agra" and its American descendent, "Johnny Has Gone for a Soldier." Categories unique to the African-American tradition include spirituals, Underground Railroad melodies, and certain improvisational song forms. Additionally, Bartók, Kodály and many others have demonstrated how there is a separate music of childhood, so distinctly different from, yet such a remarkable commentary on adult life (Erdely, 1965, p. 21).[15]

Toward an Organizational Scheme for North American Folksong Research

It is apparent that in the Americas, we must view ourselves as a *community of communities*, each with ancient musical languages that often come together at important junctions, such as the calendar and life events discussed above. Without being ethno-specific, we can name many folksong functional types likely to occur in our communities. Table 4 is by no means complete and is only meant to help us get started on the vast number of tasks needing attention—it is truly a jigsaw puzzle with many pieces still missing:

Table 4

Calendar Customs	Life Events	Personal Expressions
Preparing to Plant	*Work*	*Laments*
•plowing songs	•street cries	*Lullabies*
•blessing songs	•waulking[16] songs	*Riddle Songs*
•fruit tree wassailing	•building songs	*Love songs*
•corn pollen songs	•weaving songs	*Narrative Songs*
	•spinning songs	*War Songs*
Planting and Growing	•sea shanties	Long Walk songs
•May Day carols	•military songs	"walking-out" songs
•well-dressing songs	•food preparation songs	
•ploughboy songs	-milking, churning	
	-milling, grinding	
Harvest and Thanksgiving	•herding songs	
•songs of thanksgiving	•trail-riding songs	
•harvesting songs	•cattle-calming songs	
•songs of supplication	•hunting songs	
	•railroad songs	
Holiday [Holy Day] Songs	*Marriage Songs*	
•carols [songs that are danced]	•courting songs	
•re-enactment songs [*Las Posadas*]	•partner-choosing songs	
•songs of supplication	•teasing songs	
•songs of adoration	•warning songs	
•ceremonial songs	•forfeit songs	

Each of these functions generates tune-families with specific melodic and rhythmic structures. These tune families are rich in variants that can serve to increase our teaching, composing and arranging possibilities. These possibilities are *contextual*, not pedagogical. What I mean is that if we will teach music as the language of community, the pedagogy will automatically flow from it in a natural, non-artificial way. Kodály was not interested in simply preserving folksong. Rather, he was vitally committed to *perpetuating* it and bringing into the schools the *context* in which folksong thrives. It is not uncommon to see music-related folk customs being re-enacted in Hungarian music lessons or performances. One such example is the village teacher-welcoming ceremony, with the aim of enticing teachers to stay longer (Forrai, 1985, npn). This ritual also exemplifies why we must get beyond the "every-song-must-have-a-game" mentality. The natural context we have been describing will allow music to become interesting to children on its own terms; sometimes it will be a game, other times a custom or ritual, sometimes a traditional dance, other times a beautiful song being sung simply because it is beautiful. I witnessed another fine example of perpetuating folk context in December, 2002, during a winter concert by the Hungarian Radio-Television Children's Choir. In this concert, the Junior Choir came onto the stage of the Liszt Academy of Music in folk costume: some dressed as angels, some dressed as the Holy Family, some dressed as peasant folk. They sang, acted, and danced the traditional Hungarian Christmas re-enactment. It was authentic, it was reverent, it was full of good cheer and sometimes intentional humor. It was musical, and above all, it was a natural, unforced, child-centered celebration full of joy!

In one particular school where I was a music specialist, I volunteered for as much playground and after-school bus duty as possible. This allowed me to figure out which children in the school were the chief culture-bearers and who had the largest repertoires. Every once in a while, such a child would come up with a magnificent singing game. After collecting and transcribing their songs, games, and dances, I found that I could simply put these children in charge of sharing them with their own classmates during a portion of our music classes. Validating the natural musical life of childhood is motivating to children; they will invest hard work in it to learn it well, and it functions well beyond "just making kids like music." This is one aspect of children's "musicking" so aptly captured in Patricia Shehan Campbell's 1998 book entitled *Songs in Their Heads: Music and its Meaning in Children's Lives*.

I have often heard the criticism that what Bartók and Kodály accomplished in Hungary cannot be done in the English-speaking world because we do not have enough song material, or our melodies are not as beautiful, or our songs are too simple or that American Kodály educators are unable to relate to the depth of the Hungarian experience. As just one example of why these criticisms are unfounded, we can follow the voyage of an English folksong through Ralph Vaughan Williams' hands. He and some colleagues collected several variants of "Divers[sic] and Lazarus" around the turn of the twentieth century (Vaughan Williams, 1905, pp. 118–119). As the editor of the 1906 edition of the Anglican hymnal (Heffer, 2000, p. 28), Vaughan Williams harmonized one of the *Lazarus* variant tunes for use as a hymn. Sometime after, he combined two halves of two other variants of the tune for use in his *English Folksong Suite* (1923) for military band. His student, Gordon Jacob, later transcribed this same work for full orchestra. Still later (1939), Vaughan Williams arranged several versions of the tune for string orchestra, known as *5 Variants of Dives and Lazarus*. So, again we have a viable and useful English parallel to what Bartók and Kodály were doing in Hungary. Many more such examples could be cited, but more to the point, we have only begun to scratch the surface of the vast treasury of folk melodies in the Americas and their current or potential influences on teaching and composed music.

Another exemplary practice of Bartók and Kodály concerns multicultural music education. It is the arrogance of our time to suppose that our generation is the first and only one to have thought of such a thing. Bartók and Kodály divided their research among themselves in such a way that Bartók specialized in collecting and processing the music of non-related peoples, beginning with Hungary's bordering neighbors and working outward from them, like ripples emanating from a pebble dropped in a pond (Erdely, 1965, pp. 98–99 and Bartók, 1936). I once observed a remarkably illustrative multicultural seventh grade lesson taught by László Nemes. The class sang and danced Bulgarian folksongs in changing asymmetric meters. Then, they discovered how Bartók had used the same tunes and meters in his *Allegro Barbaro* for solo piano. These two activities were only a buildup to the main task of the lesson: to move to, take down by dictation, and analyze a section of Stravinsky's *Rite of Spring* in order to discover the composer's use of shifting asymmetric meters in his unique twentieth-century idiom (Jaccard, 1998, npn).

Kodály's focus, however, was on collecting and processing the music of peoples closely related to Hungarians. This is how he came to discover the existence in the Ural Mountains of Russia of some of the same tunes that he had collected in Hungary. He then sent László Vikár and Gábor Bereczki to do thorough research among the related Mari-Cheremis, Chuvash, Votyak and Tatar tribes living there (Vikár and Bereczki, 1971, 1979, 1989, and 1999). The Folk Music Research Group of the Institute for Musicology of the Hungarian Academy of Sciences is still actively engaged in folksong collecting. One example among many is János Sipos, a staff ethnomusicologist who has collected songs in Turkey, Kazakhstan, and similar peoples who have linguistic connections to the Hungarians (see Sipos, 2001 and 2004). So, once again in Bartók, Kodály and the corps of researchers coming after them, we find inspiration for what we should be doing. It is a matter of balance, not of either-or. We have the opportunity to embrace multicultural music in a holistic way that makes sense, not just to be politically correct. What are the universal elements among the music of various cultures? How do they interrelate or even overlap? When and where should they occur in the overall curriculum because they *do* interrelate and illuminate each other? We can only answer these tough questions the more deeply we investigate our own extant musical cultures in the Americas. We will never answer them if we continue to pick and choose according to whim, convenience, and opportunities for commercial gain.

Conclusions

In summary, I see several tasks for us to address in researching and making pedagogical use of the folk music of the Americas:

1. Find the most ancient layers of the musical cultures of the Americas.
2. Identify the actual *substance* of our musical languages.
3. Get beyond analysis into comparative classification.
4. Organize for efficiency, open communication, and sharing.
5. Open up (and keep open) a direct line of interchange between all those engaged in both the worldwide Kodály movement and in serious folk music research.
6. Organize and engage in peer-reviewed scholarly discourse and publication about folksong research that measures up to principles and standards of Hungarian ethnomusicology as well as being engaged with the best of international

ethnomusicological scholarship.

7. Continually publish our work-in-progress as we arrive at significant points of understanding and insight about the music we research.

In many ways, the North American Kodály movement has become a victim of its own success. We have so often recycled teaching songs and techniques that they are now frequently borrowed, even altered, by proponents of so-called "eclectic" music education (who was more "eclectic" than Zoltán Kodály?). The noble, holistic, and inclusive Kodály Concept is too often reduced to a mere "method" that can be bought and sold for its commercial possibilities or conveniently inserted piecemeal into school music programs ("I'm doing some 'Kodály' this week") rather than requiring some sort of moral and intellectual commitment to its principles. Although imitation is the sincerest form of flattery, we ourselves must move upward from where we are now. Having superior and comprehensive musical materials for teaching and performing will actually increase teacher- and student individuality and musicianship. We will see that increasing our treasury of folksong will profoundly influence our individual teaching techniques. The better we know our own musics, the better we will be able to recognize the universals in other musics in order to understand how to combine them in our curricula. It will also allow us to be more sensitive to the cultural composition of individual schools and communities. Let each community know itself musically, then share itself, then interconnect in a global community of simultaneous uniqueness and oneness. An excellent example is the ongoing research by Dr. Miriam Factora, whose collection of children's songs from the Philippines is revealing how so many languages and cultures (thirty-nine ethno-linguistic communities) co-existing in one country can generate unique yet recognizable combinations of musical elements that can be combined into a single curriculum (Factora, 2003 and 2004). Could this be an aspect of the "great Harmony" Kodály had in mind? (in Szabó, 1969, p. 34).

This presentation began with a glimpse of the musical life of a small Russian village. Let us end with a commitment to discover, reconstruct when necessary, and engage our students in as many aspects of our rich, natural musical communities as possible.[17]

REFERENCES

Amann, J-P. (1983). *Zoltán Kodály, suivi de huit lettres á Ernest Ansermet et de La «Méthode» de Kodály*. Lausanne, Switzerland: Editions de l'Aire.

Bartók, B., and Kodály, Z., eds. (1951–) *Corpus Musicae Popularis Hungaricae* [Body of Hungarian Folksong], Volumes 1–8. Budapest, Hungary: Akadémiai Kiadó.

Beethoven, L. van (1970). *25 Irish songs with piano, violin and cello and 20 Irish songs with piano, violin and cello*. New York: Edwin F. Kalmus.

Beethoven, L. van (1970). *25 Scottish songs with piano, violin and cello and Irish Songs with piano, violin and cello*. New York: Edwin F. Kalmus.

Beethoven, L. van (1970). *26 Welsh songs for piano, violin and cello*. New York: Edwin F. Kalmus.

Bónis, F., ed. (1964). *The Selected Writings of Zoltán Kodály*. New York: Boosey & Hawkes, Inc.

Campbell, P. S. (1998). *Songs in their Heads: Music and Its Meaning in Children's Lives*. New York: Oxford University Press.

Dobszay, L. (1992). *After Kodály: Reflections on Music Education*. Kecskemét, Hungary: Zoltán Kodály Pedagogical Institute of Music.

Eösze, L. (1962). *Zoltán Kodály: His Life and Work*. Boston: Crescendo Publishing Company.

Erdely, S. (1965). *Methods and Principles of Hungarian Ethnomusicology*. Indiana University Uralic and Altaic Series, Monograph 52. Bloomington, IN: Indiana University.

Erdely, S. (1987). "Complementary Aspects of Bartók's and Kodály's Folk Song Researches." In Ranki, G. ed. *Bartók and Kodály Revisited: Indiana University Studies on Hungary 2*. Budapest: Akadémiai Kiadó.

Factora, M. (2003). *Philippine children's songs, spoken rhymes and games for teaching–Book One* (Mga likas na pambatang awitin, tugmaan at laro sa Pilipinas: Gamit sa pagtuturo). Manila, The Philippines: Miriam Factora [self-published].

Factora, M. (2004). *Philippine children's songs, spoken rhymes and games for teaching–Book Two* (Mga likas na pambatang awitin, tugmaan at larosa Pilipinas: Gamit sa pagtuturo). Manila, The Philippines: Miriam Factora [self-published].

Factora, M. (2011). *The musical heritage of the Ilocanos* [Aweng ti Kailokuan]. San Juan City, The Philippines: Dr. Miriam Factora and Kannawidan Foundation Inc.

Forrai, K. (1985). *Music belongs to everyone: Kodály's pedagogical legacy, Grades K–8*. Videocassette, Budapest.

Heffer, S. (2000). *Vaughan Williams*. London: Weidenfeld & Nicolson.

Herboly-Kocsár, I. (1993). *Solfège and solfège pedagogy*. Pre-conference lecture notes transcribed by Jerry L. Jaccard. 1993 National/International Conference of the   Organization of American Kodály Educators and the International Kodály Society,   August 1993, West Hartford, Connecticut. Unpublished document.

Herder, J.G. (1778). *Stimmen der Völker in Liedern* [The people's voice in song]. Leipzig, Germany: P. Reclam.

Jaccard, J. L. (1993). Interview with László Vikár on 13 August 1993, West Hartford, Connecticut. Unpublished document.

Jaccard, J.L. Observation field notes for 3 May 1998. Unpublished document.

Jaccard, J.L. "Water from the Well: Deep Folksong Research and Musical Education." *Kodály Envoy* 26, no. 4 (Summer 2000): 7–13.

Jaccard, J.L. Conversation with Mihály Ittzés on 15 March 2004, Kecskemét, Hungary.

Jaccard, J.L. Observation field notes for 16 March 2004. Unpublished document.

Jaccard, J.L. Personal correspondence with Mary MacLain of the *Commun An Cliath Clis Milling Society*, Cape Breton, Nova Scotia, Canada, during April, May and June, 2004.

Jaques-Dalcroze, E. (1930), *Eurhythmics, art and education*. Translated by F. Rothwell. New York: A.S. Barnes & Co.

Kodály, Z. (1906). *A magyar népdal strófa-szerkezete* [The strophic structure of Hungarian folksong]. Doctoral dissertation, Eötvös Lorand University, Budapest, Hungary.

Kodály, Z. (1966). *Mein Weg zur Musik—Fünf Gespräche mit Lutz Besch* [My path through music—Five interviews with Lutz Besch]. English translation by Jerry L. Jaccard, publication pending. Zürich, Switzerland: Peter Schifferli Verlags AG «Die Arche».

Kodály, Z. and Kerényi, G. (1943). *Iskolai énekgyütemény I-II* (School song collection I-II). Budapest: National Board of Public Education.

Krohn, I. (1904-1928). *Suomen kansan sävelmiä* [Finnish song collection], Volumes II-IV. Helsinki, Finland.

Martin, F. (1965). "Les sources du rythme musical." *Deuxième Congrès International du Rythme et de la Rythmique*. Geneva: Institut Jaques-Dalcroze.

Marshall, R.L. "Chorale," in Stanley Sadie, ed., (1980). *The New Grove Dictionary of Music and Musicians*, Volume 4. London: Macmillan Publishers Limited.

O'Grady, W., Dobrovolsky, M., and Aronoff, M. (1989). *Contemporary Linguistics: An Introduction*. New York: St. Martin's Press.

Pratsika, C. (1965). "La rythmique en Grèce." In *Deuxième Congrès International du Rythme et de la Rythmique*. Geneva: Institut Jaques-Dalcroze.

Sermon, R. "The Celtic Calendar and the English Year." *English Dance and Song*. Spring 2001, pp. 3–4. London: English Folk Dance and Song Society.

Sharp, C.J. (1965). *English Folk-Song: Some Conclusions*. 4th edition, prepared by Maud Karpeles. Belmont CA: Wadsworth Publishing Company Inc.

Sipos, J. (2001). *Kazakh folksongs: From the two ends of the Steppe*. Book with audio CD. Budapest, Hungary: Akadémiai Kiadó.

Sipos, J. (2004). *Azeri folksongs: At the fountainhead of music*. Book with audio CD Budapest, Hungary: Akadémiai Kiadó.

Szabó, H. (1969). *The Kodály Concept of Music Education*. New York: Boosey & Hawkes, Inc.

Vargyas, L. (2000). *Egy felvidéki falu zenei világa—Áj, 1940* [The musical world of a Hungarian village—Áj, 1940]. Budapest, Hungary: Planétás Kiadó and the Institute for European Folklore.

Vaughan Williams, R. (1912). *Folk-Songs for Schools, Set 6*. London: Novello.

Vaughan Williams. "Come All Ye Faithful Christians: Variants of the Tune Noted by R. Vaughan Williams." *Journal of the Folk-Song Society* 2, no. 7: 118–119.

Vikár, L. (1969). *Folk music and music education*. Paper presented at the Dana School of Music Teacher Training Workshop, Boston, MA.

Vikár, L. and Bereczki, G. (1971). *Cheremis folksongs*. Budapest: Akadémiai Kiadó.

Vikár, L. and Bereczki, G. (1979). *Chuvash folksongs*. Budapest: Akadémiai Kiadó.

Vikár, L. and Bereczki, G. (1989). *Votyak folksongs*. Budapest: Akadémiai Kiadó.

Vikár, L. and Bereczki, G. (1999). *Tatar folksongs*. Budapest: Akadémiai Kiadó.

[1] This paragraph describes excerpts from a film documentary viewed in the original session where this paper was presented, now summarized here in text. Cressman, T. and Paulsen, D. (1995). *Russia: Hidden Memory*. Videocassette. Provo, Utah: Brigham Young University.

[2] Although terms like "folk music" and "folksong" will be hereafter employed in this article, the author's intent is to convey the sense of wholeness contained in the Greek term *orchesis*, which anciently implied the indivisible unity of melody, rhythm, dance, drama, ritual and ceremony (Pratsika, 1965, pp. 43–44). Indeed, Cecil Sharp reported having collected many English folksongs that were danced or dramatized by the singers—or said to have been danced or dramatized—when they were younger. He regarded this as a remnant of ancient times before these "*sister arts*" went their separate ways (Sharp, 1965, p. 134).

[3] The plural term "Americas" is intentional. English, African-American, French, Hispanic and Native American musical cultures, to name a few, developed according to ethno-linguistic dynamics rather than along politically imposed boundaries and frontiers. Once cannot fully study or understand any of the musical cultures extant in the United States without also tracing their extra-territorial connections. English-language American folksong belongs to a larger community of English expression, including Australia, Canada, New Zealand, the United Kingdom and still others. There is clear evidence of cross-transmission of tune and text among these geographically separated regions. The same paradigm can be applied to the Hispanic and African-American/Caribbean cultural-linguistic spheres as well as to the several major Native American language families. One of the largest, the Na-Dene Language Family, stretches southward from the Arctic Circle through Canada to the Arizona-Mexico border and comprises some 47 tribal groups, including the Navajo and Apache peoples. Another of the largest, the Uto-Aztecan, stretches northward from deep down in Central America to near the US-Canadian border (O'Grady et al, 1989, pp. 246–248), and includes the Aztec, Ute, Paiute and Comanche peoples, among others. These two large families collide in the middle of their ranges in the Four Corners region (Arizona, Colorado, New Mexico and Utah) where distinctly different cultures and song types exist alongside each other with only slight and subtle influences on one another. One might be tempted to view the entire American musical situation as too complex, but this author suggests that it may actually present opportunities with immensely beneficial potential for music education.

[4] Gregorian chant is nothing more than the "*unsurpassable treasury . . . of the folk music of the Mediterranean, in which the Jewish psalm melodies, the Greek hymns, [and] the songs of the people once inhabiting Asia Minor and Egypt are still living and pulsating . . .*" (Vikár, 1969, p. 5).

[5] Chorale melodies derive from multiple sources, chief among them being pre-existing liturgical chant from the Catholic tradition [which was strongly rooted in folksong], specifically composed tunes, and folksong (Marshall in Sadie, 1980, pp. 313–315).

[6] Herder himself apparently only transcribed one melody, while Goethe amassed a considerable collection that provided an early impetus to the growth of the German folksong collecting movement, according to my search of archival records and conversations with the staff of the *Deutches Volkslied Archiv* (German National Folksong Archive) on 21 May 2005, in Freiburg, Germany.

[7] For instance, Kodály wrote that *"once a composer intended, as did Herder, to hear and then somehow amplify the voice of the nations—also the voice of his own people—then first he had to get to know these voices"* (Kodály, 1966, pp. 25).

[8] Unfortunately, neither the scope of this paper nor publication space allows for an inclusive list of composers engaged in this period of folksong collection. There were very many, and indeed, it could be said that because of so many composers being involved, folksong played a prominent role in the transition out of the Romantic Period into the modern era of composition.

[9] I have come to this conclusion by comparing the folksong examples used in Jaques-Dalcroze's folksong-based compositions and those used by Martin in his analyses. My 1996 and 2000 conversations with his widow, Mrs. Maria Martin, reinforced this conclusion.

[10] For example, Frank Martin, like Kodály, saw folksong as the natural place where the two rhythmic systems of language and melody *"are mutually born from each other"* yet *"for when the two are combined, the whole is greater than the sum of its parts"* (Martin, 1965, pp. 20–21).

[11] Hungarian ethnomusicology and its analytic-comparative methods are numerous and complex in their interrelationships, and several volumes have been written about them. Briefly, then, the Kodály (*lexicographical*) system is a "modified dictionary" arrangement with melodic cadences as the deciding feature for classification. Bartók's system *"developed alongside Kodály's. . . the two researchers unselfishly placed the materials and results they collected at each other's disposal."* The Bartók (*grammatical*) system is more focused on the rhythmic characteristics of the phrases of a melody, such as but not limited to *isosyllabic* or *heterosyllabic* textures. Note, however, that such a view of rhythmic structure is also closely tied to melodic structure. Pál Járdányi's synthesis of the separate-but-related Kodály and Bartók catalogues was to gather as many melodic variants together as would fit into well-defined *tune-types* regardless of text, cadential or rhythmic differences and then to rank them in ascending order of complexity. Bartók and Kodály recognized early on that a set of cross-referenced indexes would be needed to link all of the song material and the various approaches to its classification (summarized from Dobszay and Szendrei, 1992, pp. 14–19; Erdely in Ranki, 1987, p. 86; and Eösze, 1962, p. 51).

[12] Bartók and Kodály had also visited Paris, each at separate times (Eösze, 1962, p. 17). *"Bartók and Kodály were deeply motivated by Debussy's use of pentatonic melodies, which provide opportunities for more subtle and complex harmonization than the tonic-dominant to which we are accustomed in Western composed music. Hungarian folksong is primarily pentatonic"* (Amann, 1983, p. 20). This pivotal English-French-Hungarian commonality further unifies the English folksong revival with the rise of Hungarian musical nationalism through the initiatives of Bartók and Kodály.

[13] Representative of them were Jenö Ádám, Lajos Bárdos, Mátyás Seiber, and Antal Doráti (Eösze, 1982, p. 64) and later, Katalin Forrai, Erzsébet Szönyi and Klára Kokas (personal knowledge).

[14] This paragraph has been added to update this paper since it was presented at the 2004 OAKE National Conference in San Francisco.

[15] In proper Hungarian usage, this surname would be written with an accent as Erdély. The actual source cited omits the accent in all instances where the author's name appears, therefore the spelling used in this article reflects that practice.

[16] *Waulking* is a Scottish [mostly in the Hebrides Islands] and Nova Scotian [mainly in the Cape Breton area] combined social and work gathering similar to an American quilting bee or barn-

raising. During a *waulking* session, independent weavers bring their bolts of woolen cloth to be softened by community members sitting at long tables and turning and stretching the unrolled cloth in a beat-related motion that continually moves the cloth from one person's hands to the next person sitting adjacent. Such communities sing and transmit a variety of special waulking songs, usually improvisatory in form and often teasingly mentioning names of individuals sitting around the waulking table. Other waulking song forms recount ancient local legends and events (McLain in Jaccard, 2004, npn). Waulking songs should not be confused with *walking* songs, which take many forms ranging from Germanic mountain hiking songs, through English "walking-out" songs, to Native American forced migration songs such as the Navajo Long Walk genre.

[17] The author extends an open invitation for teachers and researchers to contact him via email at *jerry_jaccard@byu.edu* if they are interested in collaborating on the kind of long-term, in-depth folksong research described in this article.

Paper presented at the 30th Organization of American Kodály Educators National Conference in March 2004, San Francisco, California. Originally published in *Kodály Envoy* 32, no. 3 (Spring 2006): 5–12. Reprinted by permission.

THE MUSIC EDUCATOR AS A FIELDWORKER:
DISCOVERIES IN THE FIELD
Miriam B. Factora

In the latter part of 1998, I started a project in cooperation with the Kodály Society of the Philippines. I conducted in-depth research on the country's present state of music education and the available vocal materials for classroom use.

As a result of my interviews and observations, it became apparent that the Philippine educational system needs to address the issue of more relevant music education. Music teachers have explicitly stated three main issues:

1) Music education is not given importance in the curriculum. To cite an example, music as an independent subject to be taught in grades one, two and three has been excluded from the curriculum by the Department of Education.

2) A pedagogical mismatch exists between learner and content. There is no concrete pedagogical framework for teaching music as a literacy with a related body of literature;

3) A cultural mismatch exists between learner and content. Most of the materials used are still foreign songs. There are not enough Philippine materials for use in the classroom. In light of Filipinos' continuous search for a stronger national identity, there is a need to indigenize and localize the music curriculum.

The historical and political dynamics of the current Philippine situation are similar to those that provided the impetus for Kodály's vision for Hungarian music education. The Kodály Concept has proven to be effective in the development of literate musicianship and cultural consciousness in students. Hence, it has been used as the guiding framework of this study. One of the immediate goals of the project was to design a sequence that would present rhythmic and melodic elements and concepts to enhance the teaching of literate musicianship in a literature-based curriculum utilizing systematized Philippine vocal materials.

To arrive at a plausible teaching sequence to be used in the context of Philippine culture, I followed a process of systematization which was grouped into five major components: 1) collection and gathering of Philippine children's folk songs, spoken rhymes and musical folk games; 2) transcription; 3) translation of the materials into English and translation of selected materials into Filipino, the national language (for clarification, "Filipino" refers to both the national language and citizens of the Philippines); 4) analysis; and 5) classification and systematization of the materials. Systematization resulted in the development of a sequential music teaching model utilizing Philippine vocal materials. I discussed this model in more detail during my presentation at the IKS Symposium in England in 2005.[1]

The Music Educator as a Fieldworker

When I was a student in Hungary, I was impressed by the close collaboration of ethnomusicologists and music educators. The former provided the latter with the materials to deliver to schoolchildren. For example, Kodály's publications of his folk song collections have been valuable for pedagogical use. Kodály's doctoral dissertation, *A magyar népdal strófa-szerkezete* [The Strophic Structure of Hungarian Folksong], was enriched by his collection of folk songs in the region where he lived during his childhood. The Hungarian Ministry of Education published Kodály's and Kerényi's *Iskolai Énekgyûjtemény I-II* [School Song Collection I-II][2], which served as the foundation for the development of the Hungarian national music curriculum, and from which many master teachers who had been in Kodály's college classes worked out a variety of approaches, methodologies and techniques. The publications resulting from Bartók's and Kodály's research are the ten mostly posthumous volumes of the *Corpus Musicae Popularis Hungaricae*. In Hungary, these publications provide a rich collection for curricular use, and these varied repertoires have helped Hungarian music teaching to develop its quality reputation. Herboly-Kocsár states, "The reason children read music so fluently in Hungary is because they have such good tools in their hands."[3]

I found myself wishing this situation were the same in the Philippines. After my studies in Hungary in 1987, I went back to the Philippines with the hope of establishing a closer collaboration with ethnomusicologists. Instead, I was challenged by Dr. Jose Maceda, a reputable Filipino ethnomusicologist, to engage myself in fieldwork research. A music teacher doing fieldwork? Shouldn't that be left to ethnomusicologists?

For quite a while, Filipino music educators have had to avail themselves with whatever teaching materials existed, due to the unavailability of funds for more thorough research and fieldwork. However, I had always advised the Kodály Society of the Philippines that it could not justify its existence if its members kept using foreign songs translated into Filipino. Moreover, Filipino teachers could not continue composing songs just to accommodate the teaching sequence of other countries. While it is true that several Filipino music educators have undertaken folk song research with the purpose of making a study of the songs' possible uses in the classroom, many of the folk song collections consist of beautiful songs that are difficult for young learners to sing, and even more difficult to use to learn simple concepts. Having spent my childhood in the Philippines, I knew that there were more appropriate materials through which children could learn concepts—spoken rhymes, games and other children's songs that had not been collected. I definitely knew what I needed to find. Fieldwork was imminent.

Alan Lomax stresses that it is only through extended and serious contact with living folk tradition that the true essence of folk song can be understood. He states, "A song expert without field experience is like a Marine botanist who never observed life under the surface of the sea."[4] It is through collecting and sorting through materials that one determines their authenticity. In the process, one has to delve deeply into the natural musical functioning of a community. J. S. Kofi Gbolonyo, an African music educator/ethnomusicologist, shared in a jazz course that I attended last summer:

It is wrong to say that a music teacher should not do the work of an ethnomusicologist. . . . The ethnomusicologist goes to the village and collects music, writes from his own perspective . . . and as we read, we don't get the context of it. . . . When a music teacher collects and goes to the classroom to teach, he can put this knowledge that is not in the book into practice. . . .The music teacher can only interpret what the ethnomusicologist has written but not what he [the ethnomusicologist] has seen. As a music teacher [in Africa], you are a researcher, a composer, a performer.[5]

Ethnomusicologist Jeff Todd Titon could not have expressed it any better when he wrote, "The world is not like a text to be read but like a musical performance to be experienced."[6] Kristina Benitez—a distinguished Filipino composer, educator and ethnomusicologist— further clarifies that it is not fieldwork research per se that should be the undertaking of music teachers, but the understanding of the music and music-making. Fieldwork is one of the many ways through which music can be contextualized and more fully understood, and as such is highly recommended in the training of music teachers, especially in developing countries where music instruction programs are often underdeveloped and relevant materials for teaching are limited or unavailable.[7]

Cultural Diversity

Kodály's discovery of the value of authentic folk song in the historical development of national musical culture led him to focus on literature-based musical education as a national priority. His indomitable vision of perpetuating culture through music education, coupled to his educational innovations for addressing issues of literate musicianship and overall musical development, has led other countries to pursue Kodály's vision in their own countries. Despite socio-political structural changes that call for flexibility in methodological approaches, the principles underlying Kodály's vision remain immutable. It is recognized by music pedagogues all over the world that the basic pillar of Zoltán Kodály's educational concept is the premise that school music should begin by making each nation acquainted with its own "musical mother tongue," with each nation continuing to value its own folklore traditions as representing national identity.[8] However, with the existence of diverse ethno-linguistic groups in many countries, and of course in the Philippines, the question could be posed whether the Kodály Concept can truly be successful in schools where students come from diverse cultural backgrounds.

As I began this research, I was caught in a dilemma as to which direction I was going to pursue with regard to the language issue. The Philippines has more than seventy-five ethnic groups with more than a hundred dialects, which are derivatives that fall under major languages because they are so distinct from one another. These languages belong to the Austronesian family of languages, which includes the languages of Oceania, Indonesia, Madagascar, Malaysia, Taiwan and some scattered ones in Vietnam, Thailand, Cambodia and

Laos.[9] Many of the languages have also assimilated words from the Indian, Arabic, Chinese, Spanish, and English languages.[10] I had to make a decision whether to use a national, regional or provincial approach. In a national approach, there is an effort to include most of the country's ethno-linguistic groups in the selection of teaching materials. However, this would put the "mother tongue" issue in question because of the number of languages spoken. This raises the question as to which language should be used for the musical materials school children are going to initially perform. Because of this complexity, regional, provincial or more localized approaches were also considered. However, these directions also pose similar concerns: for while it is true that a more limited geographical scope narrows the number of languages spoken, it still does not solve the problem of which language is to be used initially. It is surprising to note that places like Cotabato City in the southern Philippines alone, for example, have about eight different ethno-linguistic groups. This prerogative language issue finally led me to consider a national approach to unify and give a concrete structure to the national music education system.

The premise of this study is for children to start music education using materials in their mother tongue or vernacular. Considering that Filipino is the national language in the Philippines, this usually becomes the second language of the children. They are expected to gain a certain level of proficiency, and it is studied formally as an independent subject; its integration across the curriculum is encouraged. Therefore, it becomes logical that the majority of the materials for this study were translated into this national language. I propose that students sing the translated version with the premise that they sing the original language if they speak that language. Moreover, depending on the readiness of the students, especially as they get older, they can be given the option to sing the original language regardless of their ethnic background. The Department of Education mandates one and the same curriculum for all schools in the Philippines. The results of this research are to be proposed to this office as a meaningful and relevant contribution to this curriculum; hence, such a unified approach is highly desirable.

Multiculturalism

The "mother tongue" issue gets even more complex as we look at the world at large. Multicultural, multilingual communities are increasingly the norm in today's world. Teachers are increasingly challenged to identify single "mother tongue" music to teach when there are multiple expressions evident. Patricia Campbell raises questions as to the validity of a mono-cultural approach to our teaching and our students' learning, and suggests that it becomes complicated, if not even a moral dilemma, to teach the repertoire of only a single dominant culture.[11]

I advocate a music education program that respects diversity, and hence encourages multiple perspectives in designing curriculum, through multicultural education. In the process of my research, I communicated with educators of other countries to find out what they were doing in this direction.

The United States of America, for example, has become a melting pot of diverse cultures from all over the world; hence, a multicultural approach would be the most logical. This heterogeneity of the nation's populace is being dealt with among American Kodály educators with a spirit of pro-activity and inclusiveness. Jerry L. Jaccard was the first to begin developing a dual English-Navajo music education curriculum. Moreover, he and his colleagues are now developing a dual English-Spanish music curriculum.[12]

In Jaccard's presentation for the Organization of American Kodály Educators in San Francisco in March 2004, he called it the "arrogance of our time to suppose that this generation is the first and only one to have thought of multicultural music education."[13] Bartók and Kodály divided their research in such a way that Bartók specialized in collecting and processing the music of non-related peoples, beginning with Hungary's bordering neighbors and working outward from them.[14] Kodály's focus was on collecting and processing the music of peoples closely related to Hungarians. Through this, he discovered the existence of some of the same tunes in the Ural Mountains of Russia that he had collected in Hungary. He then sent László Vikár and Gábor Bereczki to do thorough research among the related Mari-Cheremis, Chuvash, Votyak and Tatar tribes living there.[15] (Vikár & Bereczki 1971, 1979, 1989, 1999). The Folk Music Research Group of the Institute for Musicology of the Hungarian Academy of Sciences is still actively engaged in folk song collecting. Jaccard concludes that Bartók, Kodály and the researchers after them should be an inspiration for Americans to embrace multicultural music in a holistic way that makes sense and not just to be politically correct.[16]

Universality of Music

In the midst of musical pluralism as a result of the diverse ethno-linguistic groups in the Philippines, one of the most amazing discoveries that has been presented to me is the constant emergence of songs and games that are either variants or versions of the same musical ideas. These commonalities and similarities were observed in different corners of the archipelago. One concrete example is the game, "Pen, Pen de Sarapen." Below are examples of variants from the three main islands of Luzon, Visayas and Mindanao.

Pen Pen de Sarapen (Iriga)

Source: Collected by Miriam B. Factora
Informant: Helen V. Largo, 55, Teacher, Iriga City, Camarines Sur (Luzon)
Language: Tagalog

Pen pen de Sarapen de kut - sil - yo de al - ma - sen

Aw aw de ca - ra - bao ba - tu - ten

Ku - la - sing, ku - la - sing Na - nay ku - ting

Pan - yong pu - la i - sang pe - ra

Pan - yong pu - ti i - sang sa - la - pi

Bog bog ka - la - bog mang - gang hi - nog.

Pen Pen de Sarapen (Surigao)

Source: Collected by Miriam B. Factora

Informant: Segundina Abude, 57, Farmer, Brgy. Sukailang, Surigao City, Surigao del Norte (Mindanao)

Language: Cebuano

Pen pen de Sa - ra - pen de kut - sil - yo de al - ma - sen

Haw haw de ca - ra - bao de ba - tu - ten

Sa - yang pu - la i - sang pe - ra

Sa - yang pu - ti i - sang sa - la - pi

Bug - no, as - wang, pi - ang.

Pen Pen de Sarapen (Tolosa)

Source: Collected by Miriam B. Factora

Informants: Grade Five Pupils, Daniel Z. Romualdez Memorial Elementary School, Tolosa, Leyte (Visayas)

Language: Waray, translation by Miriam Factora

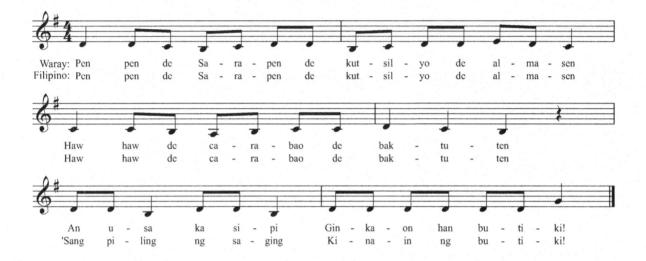

Waray: Pen pen de Sa - ra - pen de kut - sil - yo de al - ma - sen
Filipino: Pen pen de Sa - ra - pen de kut - sil - yo de al - ma - sen

Haw haw de ca - ra - bao de bak - tu - ten
Haw haw de ca - ra - bao de bak - tu - ten

An u - sa ka si - pi Gin - ka - on han bu - ti - ki!
'Sang pi - ling ng sa - ging Ki - na - in ng bu - ti - ki!

Game Directions:

Formation: cluster **Number of players:** two or more

1. Players gather together and put their forefingers on a designated flat surface.

2. One of the players acts as the leader. As the song starts, the leader touches each player's forefinger, including his or her own, with his or her other forefinger on the beat moving in either a clockwise or counter-clockwise direction. The leader should decide which direction, clockwise or counter-clockwise, he or she will follow throughout the game.

3. Whoever is touched at the last word of the song will be out of the game.

4. The song begins again and the leader starts touching the forefinger of the person next to the player who was eliminated.

5. The game goes on until one player is left to be the winner.

* * *

"Music is the universal language of mankind," Longfellow has written. Belief and interest in universal traits of music, characteristic of nineteenth-century scholarship, resurfaced in the late 1960s. Discussions about what ties humans together were devoted to the subject, and some of the leading scholars of the field[17] had significant things to say about it. In contrast, comparative musicologists and the anthropologists who supported them from the early twentieth century on were opposed to this unified view of world culture. They claimed that diversity in human culture is paramount, which includes the many sounds, systems, and uses of music developed by humans. Later, it became important to find ways in which the various musics of the world are alike, and ethnomusicology returned to seeing the world's musics as part of a single whole. There has been an argument, for millennia, that human societies have some kind of direct and indirect contact with each other, and that there is a single world of music, rather like a single language superfamily that has generated many variants.[18]

Significantly, before one spoke explicitly of universals, and before one used the expression "musics" of the world rather than speaking of the "music" of the world, ethnomusicologist George Herzog—advocating the view that one should study the music of each society in its own terms and learn it individually—referred to "music's dialects" rather than "music's languages."[19] Musical systems do exist as separable units but they are connected with each other. Bruno Nettl concludes that despite the enormous variety of musics, the ways in which people everywhere have chosen to sing and play are more alike than the boundaries of the imaginable might suggest.[20] With this in mind, the "Pen Pen de Sarapen" phenomenon has ignited my curiosity to continue looking. I have been encouraged to expand my fieldwork research in the school community where I work at the Osaka International School, Japan. To my amazement, my students from Japan, Korea, Philippines, Thailand, China, Belarus, Bulgaria, Turkey, Hungary, France, Germany, Spain, United States of America, Costa Rica and Brazil have their own versions of the popular musical game, "Rock, Paper, Scissors." Below are some examples;

JAPAN (Fukuoka Area)
Chiho Yanagi, School Nurse

Gu cho - ki   pa   da - shi mon ku - na - shi!

98

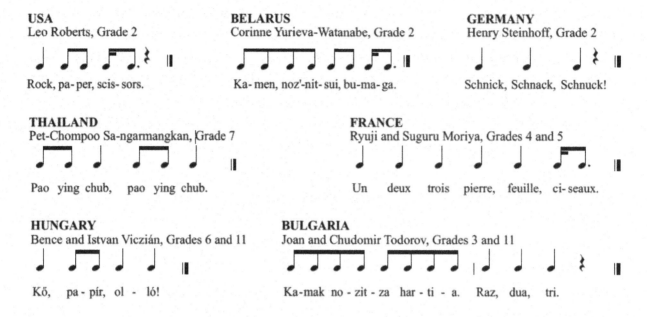

USA
Leo Roberts, Grade 2

Rock, pa- per, scis- sors.

BELARUS
Corinne Yurieva-Watanabe, Grade 2

Ka- men, noz'-nit- sui, bu-ma- ga.

GERMANY
Henry Steinhoff, Grade 2

Schnick, Schnack, Schnuck!

THAILAND
Pet-Chompoo Sa-ngarmangkan, Grade 7

Pao ying chub, pao ying chub.

FRANCE
Ryuji and Suguru Moriya, Grades 4 and 5

Un deux trois pierre, feuille, ci- seaux.

HUNGARY
Bence and Istvan Viczián, Grades 6 and 11

Kő, pa- pír, ol - ló!

BULGARIA
Joan and Chudomir Todorov, Grades 3 and 11

Ka- mak no - zit - za har - ti - a. Raz, dua, tri.

Indeed, we can find commonalities of musical culture all over the world. One could argue that we are living in a single, globalized musical culture with different kinds of music relating and influencing each other in many ways.

Conclusion

A total of 1,500 songs, chants and rhymes were recorded from the fieldwork that I conducted from 1998–2001. As part of the project, a teaching sequence to present rhythmic and melodic concepts has been designed for use by Filipino music educators. Future teachers are welcome to include other rhythmic and melodic elements and concepts not presented herein as more materials not included in this study are added. This sequence is not fixed and may change according to availability and choice of materials.

There is no single way to do fieldwork, nor is there a single interpretive voice. An authoritative interpretation of a culture is not possible. As ethnomusicologist William Noll concludes, "No book, no study is written forever, and it would be foolish to believe otherwise."[21] Since music is always in a state of change, what I found to be true in my trips might still be true for another researcher later on, or it may be quite different. Indeed, a journey is a person in itself; no two are alike.[22] One of Bartók's and Kodály's great strengths was that they involved dozens of other researchers in their research, encouraging each of them to develop their specialties. Thus the Hungarian model was created as a plurality of perspectives and not as a single perspective.

I strongly recommend that music educators establish a close collaboration with ethnomusicologists. However, I also advocate that music educators involve themselves in fieldwork, as they are in the best position to select the most appropriate and valuable musical literature to be utilized in the pedagogical process. My fieldwork experience has crystallized my awareness of the children's present musical world, and this awareness can serve as a binding force for me to connect to the real issues pertaining to the selection of musical literature and pedagogical practices.

Filipino music educators should make their best efforts to propagate Philippine musical culture and encourage students to learn more about the music of ethno-linguistic groups within the Philippines. From here, they can branch out to the music of the neighboring Asian countries and then ultimately music of the world. However, the treatment of Philippine musical culture in music education should respect all the influences that comprise the Filipino as he/she is today. I advocate that the music curriculum should aim to perpetuate and preserve a Philippine musical culture that is united, respective of diversity, and dynamically reflective of a history that has undergone changes due to the circumstances of the times. Moreover, the effects of urbanization, globalization and industrialization cannot be avoided. These phenomena are pervasive global issues that need to be reconciled with educational trends. Educators, therefore, have to approach the curriculum in a more global context. Although the infusion of world music in the curriculum is still in its infancy, I advocate that we, as music teachers, make our best efforts to be inclusive of all the voices of the world. In this way, we shall let all the world in every corner sing. And I would like to go a step further by inviting you to join me in my quest, as I continue to discover this one song that connects all these voices together, that there could be universality and unity in diversity. This could be a way to realize Zoltán Kodály's vision towards universal harmony of mankind, as he put it in the preface of his *Bicinia Hungarica*: "We must look forward to the time when all people in all lands are brought together through singing."[23]

Notes

[1] Miriam B. Factora, "A Model of Sequential Music Teaching Utilizing Philippine Vocal Materials" (paper presented to the IKS Symposium, Leicestershire, England, August 20, 2005).

[2] Zoltán Kodály and György Kerényi, *Iskolai Énekgyûjtemény [School Song Collection] I- II* (Budapest: Hungarian National Board of Public Education, 1943.)

[3] Ildikó Herboly-Kocsár, "Solfège and solfège pedagogy," pre-conference coursework notes transcribed by Jerry L. Jaccard in attendance at the National/International Conference of the Organization of American Kodály Educators and the International Kodály Society, August 1993, West Hartford, Connecticut.

[4] Alan Lomax, *Cantometrics: An Approach to the Anthropology of Music* (Berkeley, CA: University of California Extension Media Center, 1976).

[5] J. S. Kofi Gbolonyo, lecture notes taken by Miriam B. Factora in the Jazz Course with Doug Goodkin, San Francisco, CA, July 28, 2006.

[6] Jeff Todd Titon, "Knowing Fieldwork," in G. F. Barz and T. J. Cooley, eds., *Shadows in the Field: New Perspectives for Ethnomusicology* (Oxford: Oxford University Press, 1997), 91.

[7] Kristina Benitez, email correspondence with author, May 12, 2007.

[8] Ildikó Herboly-Kocsár, *Teaching of Polyphony, Harmony and Form in Elementary School* (Kecskemét, Hungary: Zoltán Kodály Pedagogical Institute of Music, 1984).

[9] Isidore Dyen, 'The Austronesian Languages and Proto-Austronesian," in T.A. Sebeok, ed., *Current Trends in Linguistics*, vol. 8, *Linguistics in Oceania* (The Hague: Monten, 1971): 5.

[10] Virginia Mitchell, *Welcome to the History of the Philippines: Pearl of the Orient Seas*, accessed December 1, 2001, <http://www.ualberta.ca/~vmitchel/>.

[11] Patricia S. Campbell, "For the World's Children: Teaching Music with a Capital 'M'" (keynote speech presented to the 16th International Kodály Symposium, Ourimbah, New South Wales Australia, July 10, 2003).

[12] Jerry L. Jaccard, email correspondence with author, November 28, 2004.

[13] Jerry L. Jaccard, "Making Music as the Language of Community: Toward an Organizational Framework for North American Folksong Research" (paper presented to the OAKE National Conference, San Francisco, California, March 27, 2004).

[14] Stephen Erdély, *Methods and Principles of Hungarian Ethnomusicology*, vol. 52 of Indiana University Uralic and Altaic Series (Bloomington, IN: Indiana University Publications, 1965); Bela Bartók, "La musique populaire des Hongrois et des peuples voisins" [Folk Music of the Hungarians and Neighboring Peoples], in *Archivum Europae Centro Orientalis* 2, nos. 3-4 (1936): 197-232.

[15] László Vikár and Gábor Bereczki, *Cheremis Folksongs* (Budapest: Akadémiai Kiadó, 1971); *Chuvash Folksongs* (Budapest: Akadémiai Kiadó, 1979); *Votyak Folksongs* (Budapest: Akadémiai Kiadó, 1989); *Tatar Folksongs* (Budapest: Akadémiai Kiadó, 1999).

[16] Jaccard, "Making Music," 2004.

[17] John Blacking, "Can Musical Universals Be Heard?" *The World of Music* 19, no. 1/2 (1977b): 14-22; Frank Harrison, "Universals in Music: Towards a Methodology of Comparative Research," *The World of Music* 19, no. 1/2 (1977): pp. 30-36; Dane L. Harwood, "Universals in Music: A Perspective from Cognitive Psychology," *Ethnomusicology* 20, no. 3 (September 1976): 521-33; Mantle Hood, "Universal Attributes of Music," *The World of Music* 19, no. 1/2 (1977): 63-69; David P. McAllester, "Some Thoughts on 'Universals' in World Music," *Ethnomusicology* 15, no. 3 (September 1971): 379-80; Charles Seeger "Reflections Upon a Given Topic: Music in Universal Perspective," *Ethnomusicology* 15, no. 3 (September 1971): 385-98; Klaus Wachsmann, "Universal Perspectives in Music," *Ethnomusicology* 15, no. 3 (September 1971b): 381-84.

[18] John Lyons, *Noam Chomsky*, rev. ed. (New York: Penguin Books, 1977), 145.

[19] George Herzog, "Music's Dialects: A Non-Universal Language," *Independent Journal of Columbia University* 6, no. 10 (1939): 1-2.

[20] Bruno Nettl, "Come Back and See Me Next Tuesday: Essentials of Fieldwork," in *The Study of Ethnomusicology: Thirty-one Issues and Concepts* (Urbana and Chicago: University of Illinois Press, 2005), 133-148.

[21] William Noll, "Selecting Partners: Questions of Personal Choice and Problems of History in Fieldwork and Its Interpretation" in Gregory F. Barz and Timothy J. Cooley, eds. *Shadows in the Field: New Perspectives for Ethnomusicology* (Oxford: Oxford University Press, 1997), 171.

[22] John Steinbeck, 'Travels with Charley in Search of America," in Gregory F. Barz and Timothy J.

Cooley, eds. *Shadows in the Field: New Perspectives for Ethnomusicology* (Oxford: Oxford University Press, 1997), 63.

[23] Zoltán Kodály, *Bicinia Hungarica 2* (New York: Boosey & Hawkes, 1937).

Keynote address presented at the 18th International Kodály Symposium in August 2007, Columbus, Ohio. Originally published in *Bulletin of the International Kodály Society* 33, no. 2 (1998): 3–12. Reprinted by permission.

SWEET BETSY FROM SMITHFIELD?

Judith Johnson

"The national culture of music of every people rests on a healthy relationship between folk music and composed music. Only the music which has sprung from the ancient musical traditions of a people can reach the masses of that people."[1]

This is only one of the many comments Kodály made about folk music. He further stated: "It is a fact that the folk song is the musical mother tongue of us all. And music instruction must begin with the folk song with which we have been brought up from birth and learned from our mother."[2]

And here is the problem. I know few mothers in Australia, or few teachers for that matter, who know any folk songs. For many, once the first verse of "Waltzing Matilda" has been sung, the other verses remain a mystery. If we feel it is important to reintroduce our children to this genre of music, and if we want to use the folk song as an effective part of music instruction in Australia, there is much to be done.

Again let me quote Kodály. "Each nation has a rich variety of folk songs, very suitable for teaching purposes. Selected gradually, they furnish the best material to introduce musical elements and make the children conscious of them."[3]

Here is the crux of the matter: "selected gradually."

In his article in the Autumn 1997 edition of the Bulletin of the International Kodály Society, Dr. Ramon Santos reminded us:

In looking closely at the method one cannot but conclude that Kodály, together with the pioneering individuals who contributed to its development and crystallization, went through painstaking efforts to study and analyze the folk music repertoire, its nature and its potential as a basic tool in achieving the ultimate objective of effecting music literacy among the students.[4]

This, I believe, is what has not been done in Australia. There has been a token attempt to use Australian folk music in music programs but without the depth of understanding needed to select the very best songs or, in many cases, to even know what exists.

There is a misconception that our roots, like those of American and parts of Canada, are mainly from England, Scotland and Ireland and therefore the work has already been done.

When I first became interested in this movement, our bible was *150 American Folk Songs*, plus the songs in *The Kodály Method*, by Lois Choksy. In fairness, the work in Australia would never have begun or developed without these texts, but to our detriment, we mostly did not follow on from there.

As a student at Holy Names College I, along with my classmates, diligently did my part in transcribing folk song recordings from the Library of Congress. In our methodology classes we applied much of what we had found to the teaching of musical elements. One of the songs I learned in order to teach 3-meter was "Sweet Betsy from Pike."

I always loved the melody of that song; however, on returning to Australia, "prairies," "yaller dogs" and "spotted hogs" did nothing to help Australian children learn 3-meter. The students were more than a little rude about what they called the "stupid" words. They should have said the "stupid teacher" who gave it to them in the first place.

I had to go back to Lois Choksy to be reminded that Kodály's views regarding the folk music used in music education programs were:

1. That children's songs and folk songs should come from authentic sources;
2. That folk music is important because it is living music;
3. That folk music was not contrived for pedagogical purposes; and
4. That children should learn their musical mother tongue before other music.[5]

So "Sweet Betsy from Pike" was relegated to the back of the filing cabinet, never to see the light of day, I thought—until about eighteen months ago, when I came across this:

Sweet Betsy from Smithfield

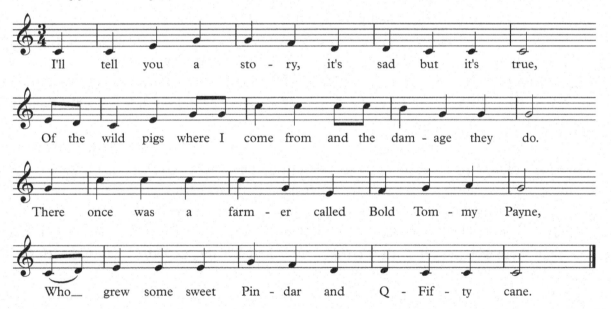

It was late in the evening an old boar he came,
And he started a-dining on Bold Tommy's cane,
So up stepped Bold Tommy, the fire in his eye,
He cursed and he swore that the old boar must die.

He reached for his rifle that stood by the door,
And he called for his pig dogs, and they came by the score,
Then down to the cane fields, all dressed for the fray
In waistcoat and trousers, Bold Tom made his way.

As he stood on the headland and gazed all around
He heard the cane crackling, and he heard a strange sound,
As the big boar came charging straight for Bold Tom,
The dogs were all barking and the battle was on.

Up stepped Old Tommy, six feet in the air,
As he straddled the porker he heard his pants tear,
Well, you should have heard the language and the words of Bold Tom,
When he found to his sorrow his trousers were gone!

Now out in old Smithfield where the Pindar it grows,
The folks tell the story and they ought to know,
How up on Black Mountain that old boar resides,
And they say that he's still wearing Bold Tommy's strides!

Same melody, but even today, farmers in the North Queensland cane fields have trouble with the wild pigs. The irony is that the Smithfield referred to in the song is now a suburb of the northern city of Cairns. When I used this folk song with children in Mackay they left the room laughing—but singing the words.

"Bold Tommy Payne" and "Sweet Betsy from Pike" both use the old English tune commonly known as "Villikins and his Dinah," a parody of the folk ballad "William and Dinah," which became a popular music hall song in the Victorian era. In its early days the music hall relied heavily on folk songs and their tunes, and many early performers made a specialty of folk song parodies—some of which have lasted better than the originals. There were fewer folk song tunes than there were sets of words, so the tunes were used and reused, sometimes with small variations.

"Villikins and his Dinah" started life as a music hall burlesque, but a new generation of Queensland children are beginning to sing "Bold Tommy Payne" to this tune because of the relevance of the words. If a by-product is also the teaching of 3-meter then so be it, but the greatest joy is to hear the children singing a true Australian folk tale with enthusiasm and enjoyment.

All of this raises what seems to be the everlasting question: What is a folk song?

In her book, *An Introduction to English Folk Song*, Maud Karpeles reports that Johann Wolfgang van Goethe was not only a famous German poet but also a competent collector of folk music. She reports that he once said: "We are always invoking the name of folk song without knowing quite clearly what we mean by it."[6]

As Alexander Ringer reported in his address at the 10th International Kodály Symposium in Calgary, Zoltán Kodály asked rhetorically, at the outset of his seminal study *Folk Music of Hungary*, "What is folk song?"—only to admit that "nobody has yet found a satisfactory answer."[7]

In 1964 Bill Scott, who was one of the major folk song collectors in Australia until his death in 2006, wrote in *Australian Folk Lore*:

What is a folksong anyway? I once heard them described as a song everyone knew a bit of, and the endless variations described as the result of a lot of blokes with bad memories singing to one another. I think the main thing is that the good songs will be remembered and the bad ones die.[8]

Kodály remarked: "The musical mother tongue of a nation is a combination of the treasures of musical expressions and forms and in fact this is the distinguishing difference between each nation's musical heritage. It can only belong to that Nation and its close relatives."[9]

All of this simply reinforces Goethe's comments that we just don't clearly know what a folk song is. So I am back to "Sweet Betsy from Pike." If we believe that Australian children should be exposed to songs of their "folk," and if we believe that one way to do that is to include them in music education programs, then we really do have a great deal of work to do.

We should first acknowledge that our desire to use folk song differs in many ways from the early ideals of Kodály. He was devastated by the disappearing sense of national character in his homeland: by the fact that many Hungarian children and adults knew little of their folk song heritage and that gradually this was being supplanted by other Middle European cultures. The use of Hungarian folk songs in the music education programs, whilst providing excellent teaching materials, also provided a way to establish a Hungarian basis for music education.

In Australia, whilst we mostly do not suffer from a sense of the loss of national character, the influence of the worldwide media does affect almost every aspect of life. The thinking of our children cannot help but be permutated by events in other parts of the world. The multicultural mix of our population makes it increasingly difficult to decide just what is the music of the "folk."

For us, the folk songs of our colonial past are a way to make history more realistic to those whose ancestry stems from those times, and also to make it clear to the many "new Australians" who have made their new homes on our shores. If, carefully chosen, these folk songs also offer a way to music performance and music literacy, then their value is incalculable.

There are many anthologies of Australian folk song on bookshelves. Some are well researched and provide good information; others are nothing more than commercial enterprises to try to sell books.

A.B. (Banjo) Paterson began collecting bush songs as early as 1898 and folk ballads and bush songs continue to be performed by soloists and groups.

Many of the printed folk song collections come to us from "broadside" sheets. In nineteenth-century England a favorite pastime was the singing of the ballads on broadsides which told the stories of events and scandals and politics of the day.

Broadsides contained only words; the melodies of the songs had to be already known. Many of the early Australian ballads were sung to popular tunes such as "Villikins and his Dinah," mentioned previously. These tunes were often brought from England or Ireland. There were many hundreds of broadsides written on aspects of Australian life—not always in complimentary terms. The great Australian poet John Manifold, in his introduction to *The Penguin Australian Song Book,* commented:

> The first white men to settle in Australia were London pickpockets, Irish rick-burners, and poachers from the Midlands, already the inheritors of a long tradition of folk-music. . . The boys from the country found colonial conditions little harder than those they had left behind, and were prepared to go on singing in their ancestral way.[10]

The early broadsides eloquently describe such men. The broadsides also provided a medium for expressing grievances at harsh treatment and often expressed the humor which became part of the Australian character. They provide a cameo of life in Australia—from the transportation of convicts, to life on the gold fields, to the development of pastoral life with its shearers, bullockies, cane cutters and swagmen: a history told in song.

The largest collection of broadsides was made by Ron Edwards, from Kuranda in Northern Queensland. There are small collections of broadsides in the Mitchell and National Libraries in Australia, but Edwards believed that the major British libraries might have larger collections, seeing that most of the material originated there. In 1985 the Australian Folk Trust awarded him their Research Fellowship, which allowed him to search broadside collections in such places as Liverpool, Dublin, Sheffield, Glasgow and the British Museum. His sole interest was in trying to discover broadsides which related in some way to Australia. His research resulted in thirteen volumes of broadsides which will now be included in our analysis project.

I believe that it is the history contained in this material which will reignite an interest in folk music for our young people. In the study of the folk song "On a Queensland Railway Line," children discover that many of the railway stations named in the song no longer exist; they have disappeared with the march of time and progress. The children need to find a very old atlas to discover the location of many of these towns.

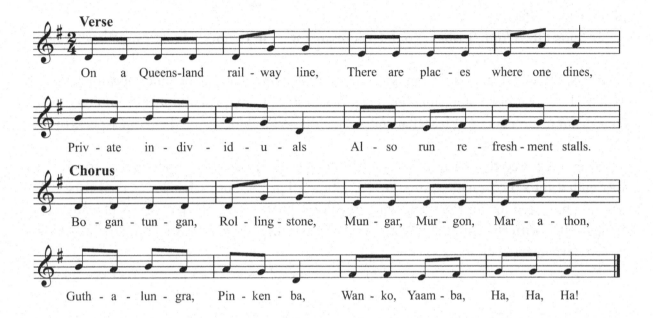

On a Queens-land rail-way line, There are plac-es where one dines,

Priv-ate in-div-id-u-als Al-so run re-fresh-ment stalls.

Chorus

Bo-gan-tun-gan, Rol-ling-stone, Mun-gar, Mur-gon, Mar-a-thon,

Guth-a-lun-gra, Pin-ken-ba, Wan-ko, Yaam-ba, Ha, Ha, Ha!

2. Pies and coffee, baths and showers
   Are supplied at Charters Towers
   At Mackay the rule prevails
   Of restricting showers to males!

3. Males and females, high and dry,
   Hang around at Durikai,
   Boora-Mugga, Djarawong,
   Giligulgul, Wonglepong.

4. Iron rations come in handy
   On the way to Dirranbandi
   Passengers have died of hunger
   During halts at Garradunga.

5. Let us toast, before we part,
   Those who travel, stout of heart,
   Drunk or sober, rain or shine
   On a Queensland railway line.

The conditions of train travel described in this song are completely foreign to children of the twenty-first century. The use of this song has allowed the teacher to suggest that children ask their grandparents what rail travel was like; and they often report, with surprise, that the folk song echoes the tales told by their grandfather or grandmother.

In an effort to gauge what work had been done in analyzing and categorizing collected songs, I contacted every university in Australia and a number of folk song organizations. There is no doubt that collecting continues. Even now, the National Library in Canberra has people in the field throughout the year. In addition, there are a number of groups whose main interest is the performance of collected songs. But it was disturbing to discover that other than a minute amount of work undertaken by the University of Queensland and to a lesser extent the University of Western Australia, there are no collections which have been studied and analyzed anywhere in Australia.

If we want to efficiently use Australian folk song as a sequential tool in music education, we have to start at the beginning and ensure that the analysis of collected material allows us to choose what effective teaching material is available.

In 2005 I flew from Brisbane to the National Library in Canberra to investigate what might need to be done. In Canberra I first met Dr. Edgar Waters, who acts as the folk song consultant to the National Library, and then with Hugh Anderson, who has been a collector for many years. These two elder statesmen are enthusiastic if not fanatical about their interest in folk music, but it soon became clear that collection and performance were the main aspects of their scholarship.

They suggested that perhaps I would like to view the Australian collection, so together we descended into the basement area of the Library. I'm not sure what I expected to see, but nothing prepared me for the scene when the doors to the vault opened. It was like an aircraft hangar filled with shelf after shelf after shelf of recordings from all parts of Australia—most of which have never been transcribed.

László Vikár described the goals of ethnomusicology as collection, notation, analysis/systematization and edition of folk music.[11] It seemed to me that to all intents and purposes only the first of these goals, collection, has been realized and perhaps a little of the second, notation. I felt like I was looking at a treasure chest but that someone had lost the key and it had never been opened.

Over lunch I described to Dr. Waters and Mr. Anderson my interest in folk music and its possibilities for music education, but after seeing this immense collection I just didn't know where to start. Edgar Waters said, "Oh, if I were you, I would begin with the Bob Michell Collection in the Fryer Library." I was astounded. The Fryer Library is a library in the University of Queensland—my own University—and no one in the School of Music knew that this collection existed.

So back on the plane, back to Brisbane, and the search began. At first no one knew where the collection was, but after much investigation and perseverance it was finally located. It was housed in four large boxes—thirty tapes of collected songs, stories and recollections and many papers and letters from the now defunct Queensland Folklore Society—including letters from Hugh Anderson, whom I had met in Canberra. Among the many figures in this Society were Stan Arthur, Bill Scott and Rob Michell, the Secretary, whose family had donated his collection to the University after his death. Bill Scott was living in Warwick in Queensland and, although old and frail, he graciously allowed me to spend a whole morning with him as he reminisced. He filled in many of the gaps about the Queensland Folklore Society and the role of Rob Michell in particular.

Work has now begun on copying notated songs and transcribing tapes in the Michell collection. It is a large task and it is being accomplished through the help of students in Queensland who are completing the second and third level of the Australian Kodály Certificate. It will take time and we may find nothing new—or we may find our own treasure chest. It is a beginning, and in conjunction with this project, students have also begun work on analyzing the collection of Ron Edwards broadsides. In time we hope to be able to report on the results.

In the meantime, teachers continue to become more interested in using folk songs as part of their teaching material. More and more we come to understand that this genre of music is not old-fashioned or out-of-date. Yes, it does contain the history of our nation, from the terrible fate of transportation, to the immigration of English and Irish settlers, to the days of the gold rush, to the development of a pastoral industry and the beginning of a railway system; but in surprising ways it is still relevant to the students of today. For many years the main penitentiary in Queensland was called Boggo Road Jail and was situated in the Brisbane suburb of Annerley. It opened in 1883 and was decommissioned in 1989. Many children in the primary school who live in Brisbane and nearby country areas no longer remember that it even existed, although the buildings are still there—until they learn our final folk song. History, for them, becomes a living thing: a true history in song.

When Dad Comes Out of Gaol

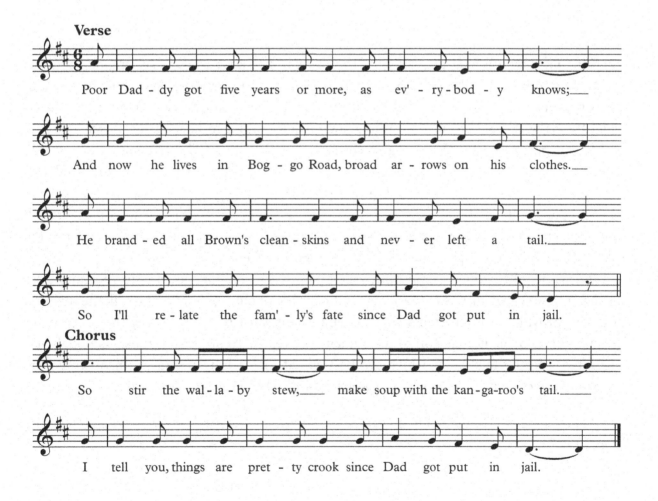

110

Our sheep all died a month ago, not rot, but flaming fluke,
Our cow was boozed last Christmas Day by my big brother, Luke,
And Mother has a shearer cove forever within hail,
The family will have grown a bit when Dad gets out of jail.
(Chorus)

Our Bess got shook upon a bloke, he's gone, we don't know where,
He used to act around the sheds, but he ain't acted square.
I've sold the buggy on my own, the place is up for sale,
That isn't all that won't be junked when Dad gets out of jail.
(Chorus)

They let Dad out before his time to give us a surprise.
He came and looked around the place, and gently damned our eyes.
He shook hands with the shearer cove, and said he thought things stale,
So he left him there to shepherd us, and battled back to jail.
(Chorus)

This folk song was first published in *The Bulletin* magazine in 1897. Its original title was "When Dad Comes Out of Gaol." It is thought to be sung to the tune of "According to the Act." The song tells the story of the vicissitudes of a family of no-hopers who simply go to pieces when the father is jailed for cattle-duffing and ends up in Boggo Road. The subject matter is perhaps inappropriate for the youngest children, but this song tells a true story of a family living as best it could, through a difficult time, and so is very appropriate for the older students.

It is told in the rascally humor so typical of the early bush settlers, but again gives students an insight into a life vastly different from their own. If they enjoy singing the song, and through that their knowledge of 6/8 meter increases, then who are we to argue? What is important is that the musical knowledge comes AFTER the singing and enjoyment of the song.

The history of a nation is a most important part of the life of its people. How fortunate are musicians if we can continue to study and enjoy the life of our forefathers through the medium of music, providing we remember that the enjoyment must be tempered by the necessity of passing this valuable heritage on to the students we teach. To do this we must, as Kodály has suggested, use the folk songs which are best suited to teaching purposes. In Australia the process of selecting has just begun. We look forward to bringing you further developments.

Notes

[1] Zoltán Kodály, "Introduction to the Performance of the 'Peacock Variations,'" in *The Selected Writings of Zoltán Kodály*, ed. Ferenc Bónis (Budapest: Corvina Press, 1974), 222.

[2] Zoltán Kodály, "The Role of Authentic Folk Song in Music Education," *Bulletin of the International Kodály Society* 10, no. 1 (1985): 15.

[3] Kodály, "Role of Authentic Folk Song," 17.

[4] Ramon P. Santos, "Universalism and Particulars in Folk Musics: Views on the Significance of Kodály on System and Practice, Method and Pedagogy," *Bulletin of the International Kodály Society* 22, no. 2 (Autumn 1997): 30.

[5] Lois Choksy, *The Kodály Method: Comprehensive Music Education from Infant to Adult*, 2nd ed. (Englewood Cliffs, N.J.: Prentice Hall, 1988), 4.

[6] Maud Karpeles, *An Introduction to English Folk Song* (London: Oxford University Press, 1973), 1.

[7] Alexander Ringer, "Folk Music in Hungary," *Bulletin of the International Kodály Society* 17, no. 1 (Spring 1992): 3.

[8] Bill Scott, *The Complete Book of Australian Folk Lore* (Brookvale, NSW, Australia: Child & Henry, 1986), 92.

[9] Zoltán Kodály, "Collection of Songs for Schools" (1943), *Visszatekintés*, ed. Ferenc Bónis (Budapest: Zeneműkiadó, 1964), 1:131-135.

[10] John Manifold, *The Penguin Australian Song Book* (Ringwood, VIC, Australia: Penguin, 1985), ix.

[11] László Vikár, "Kodály, The Musicologist," *Bulletin of the International Kodály Society* 20, no. 2 (Autumn 1995): 21.

Presented at the 18th International Kodály Symposium in August 2007, Columbus, Ohio. Originally published in *Bulletin of the International Kodály Society* 33, no. 2 (2008): 32–40. Reprinted by permission.

CULTURE, IDENTITY AND PLACE IN THE KODÁLY CONCEPT
Frank A. York

Although the concept of cultural identity is not specifically enunciated in so many words in Kodály's writings, it is implicitly addressed in his approach to music education and in the methodologies and techniques of his advocates. It is not that Kodály was disinterested in matters of identity. His writings are riddled with references to "the spirit" and "the soul" of the Hungarian people. Additionally, discussion of what is genuinely Hungarian and what is not plays a large part in the definition of his philosophy. There is little doubt that these terms and references refer to a Hungarian identity.[1] Kodály simply addressed the notion of identity in different words: in terms more common to the discourse of his age.

In this article I will indicate some elements that help construct identity and show the ways in which they are used to negotiate and affirm cultural identity. I will demonstrate how the support of cultural identity underpins many aspects of the Kodály concept. In order to illustrate this, reference will be made to several different societies, including North American and Anglo-Celtic Australian (white Australian) societies, but particularly those of the Hungarians and Torres Strait Islanders (indigenous Australian). I will give examples of how identity is negotiated and expressed in Islander culture, indicate how music and dance are especially used to construct their identity, and show how this relates to the Kodály philosophy. The examples will not only illuminate important features of Islander culture, but also demonstrate how broadly Kodály's philosophy applies to the various cultures of our earth. I will also illustrate the importance of formal education—schooling—in identity formation, and indicate how closely Aboriginal and Torres Strait Islander people's ideas regarding cultural maintenance and preservation in schools relate to Kodály's.

The Torres Strait Islands

The Torres Strait Islands are located approximately 9–10° latitude (S) and 142–144° longitude (E). They lie between the northern tip of the Cape York Peninsula on Australia's eastern edge and the southern coast of Papua New Guinea (see map next page). The approximately 6700 indigenous inhabitants of the islands are black Australians whose oral history attributes their origins to the north, in Papua New Guinea, rather than to the south on mainland Australia.[2] Islanders therefore have different ancestry and few physical and cultural characteristics in common with their more widely known Aboriginal neighbors to the south.[3] Their music and dance are equally distinct.

Aspects of Identity

Simply stated, identity may be defined as knowing who one is[4] and, simultaneously, who one is not.[5] In a social context, this means an awareness of which group(s) we belong to, and which group(s) we are not part of. The duality of our similarity to those in our group(s) and our difference from others is inseparable. To establish and/or confirm our identity we must not only know what makes us like the members of our group, but also what distinguishes us from those who are not part of our group. The "boundaries" created in establishing this inclusivity and exclusivity both define and maintain social identity.[6]

To the Western mind, concepts of identity reside initially in the ascription of blood relationship, "the fact of shared biogenic substance. To be otherwise is unnatural, artificial."[7] Immediate biological relationships are important, but do not sustain the same primacy in Torres Strait Islander society as in many other societies. Islanders regularly utilize extended family networks in ways that are different from Eurocentric systems.

Torres Strait Islands

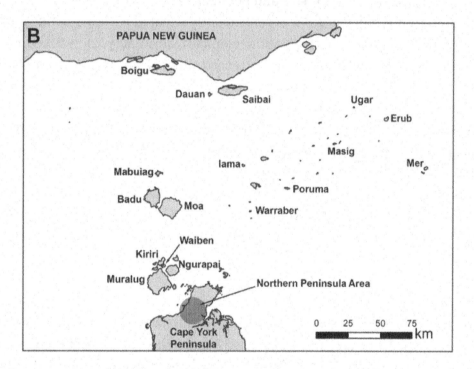

For example, the responsibility for raising Islander children is not always as biologically direct as in Western society. An Islander child's maternal uncle has more authority than the child's biological father.[8] Similarly, Islander children are commonly fostered by brothers, sisters, grandparents, or other cognates, a process which is not seen as an abrogation of parental responsibility but as a positive method of strengthening kinship ties.[9]

Islander identity is broadly conceived socially and culturally, with its basis as much in shared experience as in genealogical connections.[10] Indeed, Australian scholar Deirdre F. Jordan describes identity predominantly in terms of social interaction, defined by experience and supported by cultural heritage.[11] Musically, this is achieved within a powerful shared experience of music production. The characteristics of Islander singing and dance both reflect and shape the collective spirit. There are no solo Island songs or dances, or solos within these forms: Islander singing is choral, and Island dance is performed in parallel rows to common movements.[12] In Torres Strait society, many behavioral conventions are suspended during dance performances, including normally strict restrictions on conduct between cross-sex affines (brother-in-law and sister-in-law).[13] In-laws who are otherwise strictly not permitted to touch or address each other verbally may do so during performances, creating unique opportunities for the negotiation of identity by everyone present.

Anthropologist Jeremy R. Beckett proposes social identity as a product of human imagination, an "imagined community"[14]—i.e., self ascribed. He maintains that "nationalism, ethnicity and Aboriginality remain some of the most passionately felt forms of identity throughout the world,"[15] founded on the pride of being unique. It is through a sense of communal uniqueness that the awareness and acknowledgment of difference is keenly felt, and is most critical in establishing the image and boundaries of communal self.

For Kodály, the common culture was conveniently situated within a national enclave. For him, "the Nation meant common inspiration, common spirituality. He worked in this belief, from the beginning, on the shaping and strengthening of an awareness of national self-knowledge and identity, free from nationalism"[16]—i.e., of a common Hungarian cultural identity, defined primarily through the linguistic and musical mother-tongues.

For Torres Strait Islanders, identity is negotiated and reinforced more through distinctive modes of dance and singing than perhaps through any other means. This is why Gausa Dau of Boigu Island proclaims music "a social event [through which] we celebrate our culture together,"[17] and why Darnley Island cultural custodian James Thaiday posits that "our whole identity, our culture and tradition revolve around music."[18] In the same spirit, Kodály called Hungarian folk music "a living music in which all Hungarians meet and understand one another."[19]

Cultural Emblems and Identity

"Culture" is merely a term used to encapsulate the myriad but characteristic ways in which people live and act. According to psychiatrist Allen Wheelis,[20] it is not possible to view individuals apart from culture, as it is through culture that identity is codified. All people are shaped throughout their lives by complex intersecting social and cultural matrices. As members of a particular culture, they share a common set of values central to their perceptions of the world,[21] as well as sharing common cultural forms (behaviors, customs, and the like). Within this cultural framework, identity depends upon symbols and symbolic reference points that enable a person to mark and remember who she or he is.[22] Kodály called them "those elements in which [people] explicitly or implicitly recognize themselves."[23]

Links with the historical aspects of one's culture can occur through artifacts and through objects and sounds associated with traditional contexts. One good example in Islander society is the *bu* (pronounced "boo") or conch shell trumpet, which was not only used for general signaling purposes but also to announce the return of warriors from battle, as well as herald victory dances after warfare.[24] The aura of this association is evoked today when *bu* are used to announce the arrival of dancers, such as in the Yam Island war dance couplet Gub Nakabu and Awayalag Gulaibui. The call of the instrument generates a stimulating preliminary atmosphere on the dancing ground. The audience is alerted to the dancers' arrival and is emotionally stirred by the power of the shell's sound. The dancers identify with and enter into the character of the warriors they celebrate through their dance. Patrick Thaiday attests to this: "When we do a ceremonial dance, a warrior dance, we start off with the blowing of the *bu* before entering the dancing area. By doing that, you feel very nice when you go in. It's just like you're dancing with the warriors."[25] The dancers become their ancestors. The *bu* and its sound become symbols of Islander identity, bringing the past into the present and projecting the quality of the past association into the future.[26] Past, present and timeless future become one.

Cultures commonly use emblems or "badges" to signify their identity.[27] Easily identified visual symbols may include the constellation called the Southern Cross (Australia), the maple leaf (Canada) and the *dheri*, a native feathered headdress (Torres Strait); see stylized examples, below. Notably, these symbols are found on the flags representing these groups.

Language and music are among the most important and representative emblematic expressions of identity. Different languages clearly distinguish between people. In his novel *Shame*, Salman Rushdie asserts, "Outsider! We know you with your foreign language wrapped around you like a flag."[28] Particular use of vocabulary, characteristic grammar, or a specific dialect acts as a marker of difference (a cultural boundary), and may even be consciously cultivated. Importantly, a specific language or dialect transparently signifies membership within a particular group or culture as much as it signals the "other."

As a linguist, Kodály recognized how crucial language is to identity formation, and this is why he fought so tirelessly for the use of the Hungarian mother-tongue, which he called "the first subconscious keystone of Hungarian-ness."[29] The "nourishing medium of the mother-tongue [is significant] both psychologically, for the feeling of belonging somewhere [see the discussion of "place," below], and musically, as a determinant of the rhythm" of songs.[30] This is why Kodály was adamant that Hungarian folk song, the musical mother-tongue which represents "the other subconscious keystone of Hungarian-ness,"[31] should become the foundation of the child's musical experience, as folk songs use language in its most natural way.[32] If we truly believe that "A person can have only one mother-tongue—musically, too,"[33]

116

then we must make serious efforts to base music education on the music of the culture, at least in the initial stages. Folk songs are "the mirror of the spirit [i.e., identity] of the people."[34]

The association with place is another vitally important element in the establishment of identity. Kodály alludes to it constantly by reference to specific geographic locations in his writings. Geographically, place is a space with a sense of locality and identity—i.e., it is both a physical location and a recognized territory of symbols that tells you who you are: either I belong here or I am an outsider.[35] Stories and folk tales often locate themselves geographically, and many songs similarly refer to places and objects with which we associate ourselves.

"Himnusz," the Hungarian national anthem, references the Tisza and Duna (Danube) rivers, Kunság plains, Tokaj vineyards and other specific places with which the Magyars relate. As one hears the anthem, the mind travels around the country, conjuring up mental pictures of the locations mentioned and stirring memories. Many other anthems and patriotic songs are more general in their content, but still create the image of place in the mind's eye. In fact, it is a strength that America, with its "amber waves of grain," "purple mountains' majesty," etc., allows each individual to situate herself or himself in a location specific to personal experience, as does "Advance Australia Fair" with its sweeping references to "home... girt by sea... and boundless plains... beneath our radiant Southern Cross."

Torres Strait Islanders have no culture-specific national anthem or patriotic songs, per se, but place still plays a strong part in the majority of their songs. "Most of the [Islander] song texts . . . describe . . . the sea, the waves, the wind, the clouds, the course of [a] boat, places which are passed or headed for . . . the movements of the stars and other natural phenomena."[36] Since these topics create an envelope of well-known places, conditions and situations, they allow Islanders to situate themselves comfortably within a physical environment personally familiar to them. Because the songs are so definitive of the environment and its characteristics, the songs are directly supportive of Islander identity.

But place is not only geographic; it is also a construct of the imagination. In Simon Schama's words, "Before it can ever be a repose for the senses, landscape [i.e., place] is a work of the mind. Its scenery is built up as much from strata of memory as from layers of rock."[37] Sidhansan, on Yam Island, is not only a striking rock formation; it is also where the massive footprint of the legendary character Sidah was left as he surveyed the territory of the Central Torres Strait Islands on his journey eastward[38]—a footprint four or five times that of a normal being. The hill, footprint and legend have become one.

Through stories and songs, landscape is assimilated into narrative, and constitutes, says anthropologist Fred R. Myers, a "process by which space becomes 'country,' by which a story gets attached to an object, is part of [a] habit of mind that looks behind objects and events and sees in objects a sign of something else."[39] In other words, through songs and stories, geographic locations become cultural symbols. Even just a song reference to Tura (a location on Yam Island), indicating the direction from which the wind is blowing, will evoke associations with a shrine situated there which was formerly connected with increase rites, and will spark memories of the rituals which consequently occurred at the site. Rich images emerge from a single word indicating a single location. Similarly, Yorke Islanders cannot mention or pass near Sau (a beach location) without thinking of Igawa, a former chieftain, who confronted *markai* (spirits/ghosts) there. The legend, its companion song or the location itself will (singly or collectively) send a shiver of fear up the spine, lest the *markai* return. Places cited in songs are frequently associated with myths, historical events and occasions—which enrich them with meaning and make them far more than simply a physical location. Relating one's self to them creates a sense of "being there" and consequently reinforces one's identity.

Cultural Preservation and Maintenance

Kodály was concerned with what he saw as an erosion of Hungarian national culture by foreign influences, particularly what he perceived as efforts to "Germanize Hungary."[40] He saw formal education—schooling—as potentially the most effective social medium through which to counteract these influences. In Australia, the Indigenous population is also concerned with the perpetuation and protection of its cultures from undue outside (Eurasian) influences. Islanders also see formal education as a means to help sustain their culture. This is demonstrated in both policy and practice, from the local through the national levels. The Torres Strait Islander Regional Education Consultative (TSIREC) Committee's Education Policy for Torres Strait indicates the need to "link education and culture," "enrich and protect our culture," and "acknowledge our history and heritage."[41] The National Aboriginal [and Torres Strait Islander] Education Policy insists that "the most challenging issue of all is to ensure education is available to all Aboriginal [and Torres Strait Islander] people in a manner that reinforces rather than suppresses their unique cultural identity."[42]

In a policy statement by Aboriginals and Islanders for Aboriginals and Islanders, the Queensland Aboriginal and Torres Strait Islander Consultative Committee's (QATSICC) Peninsula Education Policy commences: "Education is the means by which we develop opportunities and choices of lifestyle. In a time of cultural change, no matter how that change is caused, the focus of the schooling process must maintain our children's identity and our children's continuity with the culture of the parents."[43]

This policy is particularly important in three ways: First, it acknowledges the pivotal nature not only of education (which can occur at any time in any number of ways), but specifically of formal schooling in contemporary Torres Strait Islander society. Second, it links education and culture, specifically "the culture of the parents." Third, it affirms maintenance of Torres Strait Islander identity as a major goal, and notes a direct link between education and identity. How reminiscent this is of Kodály's thinking!

The elements of the QATSICC policy statement validate efforts to preserve and maintain culture within the school framework, with curricula devised to implement policy. Subsequent curricular documents further reflect the relationship between culture, identity and education. The *National Principles and Guidelines for Aboriginal Studies and Torres Strait Islander Studies K-12* urges the development of a stronger cultural identity for Indigenous children in its Rationale.[44] The *P-12 Guidelines and Framework for the Teaching of Aboriginal and Torres Strait*

Islander Studies in Queensland Schools notes the relevance of Torres Strait Islander studies in supporting cultural identity.[45]

At the chalkface, both Indigenous and non-Indigenous teachers increasingly ensure that Aboriginal and Torres Strait Islander cultures are represented in their classrooms for the same reasons that Kodály encouraged Hungarian teachers to ensure folk traditions were presented to all Hungarian children: "to establish closer links with the ancient culture. . . . To sink roots in the Hungarian soil and not to toss with a feeling of not belonging anywhere!"[46] All Australians are assisted by both the national document *The Arts—A Curriculum Profile for Australian Schools* (1994)[47] and the *Queensland Education Department's Music Syllabus and Guidelines* (1996). Both encourage the learning of and about Indigenous music by Aboriginal and Torres Strait Islander children, and also—to help promote understanding and reconciliation between different cultures—by Australia's non-Indigenous population.

Although the QATSICC Peninsula Education Policy targets "the culture of the parents" for maintenance and preservation, it recognizes that "elder people in the community hold the knowledge and skills of the past and are a link between the past and the present. The elders hold an important place as protectors of our culture."[48] Significantly, the Queensland Education Department's *P-12 Guidelines and Framework for the Teaching of Aboriginal and Torres Strait Islander Studies in Queensland Schools* (1994) devotes a whole section to "Elders/Community Leaders," notably under the heading Social Structures. Even more significantly, Social Structures is the location in this document where dance, singing style, musical instruments, etc., are listed,[49] recognizing a seamless connection between people, community structures, music, and musical characteristics. In fact, although it indicates "grandparents and relatives" as those whose particular role it is to pass on cultural heritage, the Peninsula Education Policy recognizes that responsibility for cultural maintenance extends throughout the entire social network.[50] As previously noted, it is this expansive social network in its entirety which is the fountainhead of Islander identity.

Education Systems and Identity

In contrast to an explicit emphasis on culture, identity and elders, one of the more recent local educational documents of its type, the *Report on Education and Schooling Practice in the Torres Strait and Northern Peninsula Areas*,[51] presents academic achievement, channels of communication, service delivery and a concern with systems as its major considerations. It asserts, "Educational attainment to Islanders has been and always will be the crucial issue."[52] Although cultural matters barely fill one of the Report's twenty-one pages, this apparently does not signal a critical shift of emphasis at the Torres Strait level from identity and culture to formal academic achievement—which could affect the status of culture studies in schools, music included. Rather, it is a reaction to a lack of progress in the systematization of educational practice (including studies of culture) and a response to ad hoc culture studies courses formulated on a school-by-school basis, often by well-meaning but inadequately trained volunteers. There are clear similarities between these circumstances and those discussed in all of Kodály's articles on education, from "Children's Choirs" (1929) through "Music in the Kindergarten" (1941/1957).

But when cultural studies is accounted for in the TSIREC report as a positive innovation of the National Aboriginal and Torres Strait Islander Education Policy, it is identified "as vital to the cause of increasing attainment levels"[53] rather than for its own sake. We can only hope that current preoccupation in all areas of education with exit levels of achievement based on Western educational principles will not be detrimental to the maintenance of Islander musical culture, and consequently of Islander identity.

The National Federation of Aboriginal and Torres Strait Islander Education Consultative Groups believes that more effective schooling practices should be developed if Aboriginal and Torres Strait Islander children are to achieve their educational potential. In order for this to happen, state and territory governments and non-government education systems must develop, promote and implement a pedagogy that is mindful of indigenous approaches to education, knowledge, learning and teaching practices.[54]

They are not alone in this call. Even the Australian Royal Commission into Aboriginal Deaths in Custody insists that "it is essential that Aboriginal viewpoints, interests, perceptions and expectations are reflected in curricula, teaching and administration of schools."[55]

Islander culture can be and is being sustained within the framework of Western schooling practice. Local developments continue to occur in response to the Education Policy for Torres Strait recommendation that "curriculum and locally relevant teaching materials be produced in Torres Strait by Torres Strait Islanders whenever possible."[56] Accomplishments such as the Torres Strait Music Program[57] make considerable strides in presenting Indigenous perspectives and compiling Indigenous repertoire from across the Torres Strait. Such resources nurture Islander identity admirably. However, while they document and maintain aspects of Islander culture, they are not yet sufficiently comprehensive in their approach. There is much more work to be done.

Cooperative projects have also been established to help broaden the scope of music education in island schools. Cognizant of Kodály's warning, "the greatest deficiency in our culture is that it is built from above,"[58] these projects include an "inverted curriculum"[59]— essentially, a curriculum which springs from the cultural foundations of the user group and which is guided by acknowledged custodians of the culture, rather than a top-down curriculum which is imposed from the outside. This assures that a music curriculum in accord with the Kodály philosophy is also in tune with Islander culture, and consequently supportive of Islander identity. Its objectives can be summed up through a paraphrase of Kodály's "A Hundred Year Plan,"[60] which we hope will take far less than that amount of time in the Torres Strait:

The aim: sustenance of Torres Strait Islander musical culture. The means: making the performance and contextual learning of Indigenous music general throughout island schools; at the same time, encouraging an Indigenous approach in the education of both performer and audience; supporting the maintenance of Torres Strait Islander taste in music, and a continual progress towards what is better and more authentically Indigenous. To make the masterpieces of Islander literature public property; to convey them to people of every kind and rank. The total of all of these will sustain the Islander cultural identity which is glimmering before us.

Notes

[1] László Eõsze, "Formative Years in Kodály's Career and Stylistic Development," *Bulletin of the International Kodály Society* 12, no. 1 (1987): 18-21.

[2] Wolfgang Laade, "The Torres Strait Islanders' Own Traditions about Their Origin," *Ethnos* 3, no.3 (1968): 141-158. See also Alfred C. Haddon, *Reports of the Cambridge Anthropological Expedition to Torres Straits*, vol. 1 of *General Ethnography* (Cambridge: Cambridge University Press, 1935); Jeremy Beckett, *Torres Strait Islanders: Custom and Colonialism* (Cambridge: Cambridge University Press, 1987); John Singe, *The Torres Strait: People and History*, 2nd ed. (St. Lucia: Queensland University Press, 1989); Maureen Majella Fuary, "In So Many Words: An Ethnography of Life and Identity on Yam Island, Torres Strait" (PhD diss., James Cook University, Townsville, Australia, 1991).

[3] Singe, *The Torres Strait*, 2.

[4] Henri Tajfel, ed., *Social Identity and Intergroup Relations* (Cambridge: Cambridge University Press, 1982), 16; Orrin E. Klapp, *Collective Search for Identity* (New York: Holt, Rinehart and Winston, 1969), 5; Andrew Brennan, *Conditions of Identity* (Oxford: Clarendon Press, 1988), 7.

[5] Walter J. Lonner and Roy S. Malpass, eds., *Psychology and Culture* (Boston: Allyn and Bacon, 1994), 13; Herbert W. Harris, "Introduction," in *Racial and Ethnic Identity: Psychological Development and Creative Expression*, ed. H. W. Harris, H. C. Blue and E. E. H. Griffith (New York: Routledge, 1995), 1.

[6] Fredrik Barth, *Social Groups and Boundaries: The Social Organization of Culture Difference* (Oslo: Universitetsforlaget, 1969); Martin Stokes, ed., *Ethnicity, Identity and Music: The Musical Construction of Place* (Oxford: Berg, 1994); John W. Bennett, ed., *The New Ethnicity: Perspectives from Ethnology* (St. Paul, MN: West, 1975).

[7] David M. Schneider, *American Kinship: A Cultural Account* (Englewood Cliffs, NJ: Prentice-Hall, 1968), 107.

[8] Fuary, "In So Many Words," 240; W.H.R. Rivers, (1971). "Kinship," in *Reports of the Cambridge Anthropological Expedition to Torres Strait*, vol. 5: *Sociology, Magic and Religion of the Western Islanders*, ed. A. C. Haddon (Cambridge: Cambridge University Press, 1904), 129-153; W. H. R. Rivers, *Social Organization* (London: Kegan Paul, 1924); see also Gunnar Landtman, *The Kiwai Papuans of British New Guinea: A Nature-born Instance of Rousseau's Ideal Community* (London: Macmillan, 1927), 176-177.

[9] Jeremy R. Beckett, "An Historical Survey of Marriage in Three Torres Strait Island Societies" (unpublished manuscript, Australian Institute of Aboriginal Studies, Canberra, 1961).

[10] Fuary, "In So Many Words," 6; see also Steven Feld, "Sound Structure as Social Structure," *Ethnomusicology* 28, no. 3 (1984): 393, 400, 403.

[11] Deirdre F. Jordan, "Aboriginal Identity: Uses of the Past, Problems for the Future?" in *Past and Present: The Construction of Aboriginality*, ed. J. R. Beckett (Canberra: Aboriginal Studies Press, 1988), 109.

[12] Frank A. York, *Children's Songs of the Torres Strait Islands* (Bateman's Bay, NSW, Australia: Owen Martin, 1990); Jeremy Beckett, *Modern Music of Torres Strait* (Canberra: Australian Institute of Aboriginal and Torres Strait Islander Studies, 1981).

[13] Fuary, "In So Many Words," 271-274.

[14] Benedict Anderson, *Imagined Communities* (New York: Verso Press, 1983); see also Tajfel, *Social Identity*, 21.

[15] Beckett, *Past and Present*, 2.

[16] Eõsze, "Formative years," 21.

[17] Personal communication with author, 1994.

[18] Personal communication with author, 1994.

[19] Zoltán Kodály, *The Selected Writings of Zoltán Kodály* (London: Boosey and Hawkes, 1974), 30; see also 130.

[20] Allen Wheelis, *The Quest for Identity* (New York: W. W. Norton, 1958).

[21] Gerardo Marín, "The Experience of Being a Hispanic in the United States," in *Psychology and Culture*, ed. W. J. Lonner and R. S. Malpass (Boston: Allyn and Bacon, 1982), 24.

[22] Klapp, *Collective Search*, 23.

[23] Kodály, *Selected Writings*, 36.

[24] Haddon, *Cambridge Anthropological Expedition*, 301; John Singe, personal communication, 1993; see also Landtman, *The Kiwai Papuans*, 162, 423.

[25] Personal communication with author, 1994.

[26] Basil Sansome, "The Past is a Doctrine of Person," in *Past and Present: The Construction of Aboriginality*, ed. J. Beckett (Canberra: Aboriginal Studies Press, 1988), 157.

[27] Barth, *Social Groups*, 14; John Bailey, "The Role of Music in the Creation of an Afghan National Identity" in *Ethnicity, Identity and Music: The Musical Construction of Place*, ed. Martin Stokes, (Oxford: Berg, 1994), 48; Christopher Alan Waterman, *Jújù: A Social History and Ethnography of an African Popular Music* (Chicago: Chicago University Press, 1990), 6.

[28] Salman Rushdie, *Shame* (London: Cape, 1983), 28.

[29] Kodály, *Selected Writings*, 130.

[30] Mihály Ittzés, "Kodály and Liszt," *Bulletin of the International Kodály Society* 13, no. 1 (1988): 23.

[31] Kodály, *Selected Writings*, 130.

[32] Kodály, *Selected Writings*, 124-125; also 153.

[33] Kodály, *Selected Writings*, 131.

[34] Kodály, *Selected Writings*, 24; see also Lois Choksy et al., *Teaching Music in the Twentieth Century* (Englewood Cliffs: Prentice-Hall, 1986), 71.

[35] Klapp, *Collective Search*, 28; see also Anthony Giddens, *The Consequences of Modernity* (Cambridge: Polity Press, 1990), 18.

[36] Laade, "Torres Strait Islanders," 18.

[37] Simon Schama, *Landscape and Memory* (London: Harper Collins, 1995), 6-7.

[38] Travis Teske and Lizzy Lui, *Yam: Island of Torres Strait.* (Thursday Island: Queensland Education Department, Far Northern Schools Development Unit, 1987); Fuary, "In So Many Words," 116.

[39] Fred R. Myers, *Pintupi Country, Pintupi Self: Sentiment, Place and Politics among Western Desert Aborigines* (Washington, DC: Smithsonian Institution, 1986), 67.

[40] Kodály, *Selected Writings*, 132.

[41] Torres Strait Islander Regional Education Consultative Committee, *Ngampula yawadhan ziawali: Educational Policy for Torres Strait* (Cairns: Queensland Education Department, 1992), 1.

[42] Department of Employment, Education and Training [DEET], *National Aboriginal and Torres Strait Islander Education Policy* (Canberra: DEET, 1989), 7.

[43] Queensland Aboriginal and Torres Strait Islander Consultative Committee [QATSICC], *Peninsula QATSICC Education Policy* (Balmain: Aboriginal Training and Culture Institute, 1988), 4.

[44] National Aboriginal and Torres Strait Islander Studies Project [NAATSIS], *National Principles and Guidelines for Aboriginal Studies and Torres Strait Islander Studies, K-12* (Canberra: National Federation of Aboriginal and Torres Strait Islander Consultative Groups, 1993), 6.

[45] Queensland Education Department, *P-12 Guidelines and Framework for the Teaching of Aboriginal and Torres Strait Islander Studies in Queensland schools* (Brisbane: Queensland Education Department, 1994), 3.

[46] Kodály, *Selected Writings*, 147.

[47] Australian Education Council, *The Arts: A Curriculum Profile for Australian Schools* (Carlton, VIC, Australia: Curriculum Corporation, 1994).

[48] QATSICC, *Education Policy*, 20.

[49] Queensland Education Department, *P-12 Guidelines*, 29.

[50] QATSICC, *Education Policy*, 10-11.

[51] Torres Strait Islander Regional Education Committee, *Report on Education and Schooling Practice in the Torres Strait and Northern Peninsula Areas* (Townsville, QLD: James Cook University, 1994).

[52] Torres Strait Islander Regional Education Committee, *Report on Education*, 1.

[53] Torres Strait Islander Regional Education Committee, *Report on Education*, 2.

[54] NAATSIS, *National Principles*, 1.

[55] Elliott Johnston, *Royal Commission into Aboriginal Deaths in Custody National Report: Overview and Recommendations* (Canberra: Australian Government Publishing Service, 1991), 95.

[56] Torres Strait Islander Regional Education Consultative Committee. *Ngampula yawadhan ziawali*, 3.

[57] Stephanie Savage, ed., *Torres Strait Music Program* (Cairns: Education Queensland, 1992).

[58] Kodály, *Selected Writings*, 127.

[59] Raewyn Connell, "Curriculum, Politics, Hegemony and Strategies for Social Change," in *Popular Culture, Schooling and Everyday Life*, ed. H. Giroux and R. Simons (Boston: Bergin and Garvey, 1989), 117-129.

[60] Kodály, *Selected Writings*, 160.

Originally published in Bulletin of the International Kodály Society 27, no. 1 (2002): 28-38. Reprinted by permission.

THE KODÁLY CONCEPT FINDS EAGER STUDENTS IN MALAWI

Andrea Matthews

During 2002 and the summer of 2003, while in Malawi, Africa, I visited some local primary schools. As an elementary music teacher, I wanted to see how music was taught in Malawi. I was surprised to find that in many of the schools, English folk songs were taught rather than Malawian songs. And though syllabi for a literacy-based music curriculum existed in the schools, none of those teaching music had any knowledge of music literacy.

I subsequently met teachers and other adults who expressed a desire to become musically literate. I called upon my Kodály training to teach them to read music, but I had only a smattering of children's songs with which to teach. The challenges I faced and the knowledge I acquired of Malawi led to three main discoveries:

a) My Kodály training was effective;
b) I found only four educated music teachers in a country with a population of nearly eleven million;
c) No one has collected the folk music of Malawi, and there is clear evidence that the people are becoming increasingly disconnected from their traditional songs.

Ethnomusicology should not be only for scholars; it—or at least parts of it—should also be for people of developing countries too small and too recently developing for anyone to be able to devote the time necessary for full scholarly training in it.[1]

In January of 2002, I went to Malawi with my husband, who had received a Fulbright grant to teach at a university in Mzuzu, the main city in the north of the country. I knew that I would have to find a way to occupy my time for the seven months that my school had allowed for my leave. As an elementary music teacher, my first thought was to hear children sing. Since my neighbor was a teacher at a primary school nearby, I went to school with her.

The early morning assembly took place outside at 7:00 a.m. After singing the national anthem ("Oh, God Bless Our Land of Malawi") and hearing some announcements, the children began to sing a lengthy medley of songs beginning with "We are marching two by two . . ." and coursing through "We are marching in the light of God . . ." among other songs, all to the lively beat of a battered old drum played by a boy who was hardly bigger than the drum itself. As the children sang, they marched from the outside assembly area to their classrooms.

Next, I was invited to teach music with one of the teachers. When I entered her classroom, she introduced me, after which the children gave their slow, unison (and ubiquitous) reply, "Good morning, Madame, how ala [sic] you?" The teacher said she had to go get something, but would be right back, then left. She did not return: I was on my own. This was my first challenge:

What could an American music teacher do with forty-five children who understood very little of what was said?

I sang two songs from the African American tradition: "Swing Low, Sweet Chariot" and "All Night, All Day." I taught them by rote, as I would teach a new song to my own children. The children were delighted, and they responded in much the same way as my own students, though I was very conscious of how differently we pronounced some words.

This experience led me to check out some of the other local elementary schools to see what they did when they had music classes. At a large elementary school that had multiple classes of the same grade level, I entered a classroom of 180 students all seated on the floor. I was ushered to the only seat in the room to hear the children sing. They sang some Malawian songs and some from the English primer. At a private elementary school, which I visited often, I found that the songs they sang were always in English and were mostly "Bible songs." This school prided itself on teaching the students to speak English well, so they used every available opportunity to reinforce the language. These same students, however, did not know some of the Malawian folk songs that I later taught to them.

A fourth school connection was made at a small day school in a nearby village. The school has a strong church connection. At this school the children sang noticeably better in tune than at the other public schools, and the songs that they sang sounded more traditional, though they, too, sang some "Bible songs." The deputy headmistress, Mrs. Patricia Mkandawire, taught many varied and interesting kinds of Malawian songs. The younger children sang in tune and the older children were able to sing in four-part harmony, with students leading the call-and-response songs. She led most of the music classes that I attended and gradually became one of my most important informants on Malawian songs.

Meanwhile, as I met more local people and students, they asked what I was doing while my husband was busy at the university. I would tell them that I taught music, which often elicited the response "I love music. I want to know more about it. Please teach me how to read music!" The most compelling example of this occurred when we were trying to get a telephone installed in our house. Our neighbor had been trying to get a phone for the past six months, and everyone we talked to about it sarcastically wished us good lock in the endeavor. We filed our application and were told that they would let us know when we were to pay for it. Then we waited. One week passed, nothing. Two weeks, then a month passed, and still nothing. My husband finally decided that he would apply some polite pressure. He began to visit the telephone office every two or three days. This continued for another two weeks. Still, no telephone.

Finally, my husband began to visit every morning. At this point, the lesser officials were getting tired of having to tell him that the installation was still not scheduled, so they sent him up to the "first" (what we know as the second) floor to talk to the assistant manager. After a few days of this, the assistant manager sent him up to the "second" floor to see the manager,

Mr. Mose Nyirenda. Mr. Nyirenda was delighted to chat with my husband, and inquired about the wife at home. When he heard that I was a music teacher, he immediately wanted me to teach him how to read music. My husband told him that I was in the early stages of organizing a class and that I would love to call to tell him when it was to start, but our phone was not yet installed. He immediately took my husband out to his car and drove to our house to inspect it to see what was needed to install the phone. He said that the phone was to be installed two days later.

I stopped by at his office to see him the next day. He immediately began talking, not about the telephone, but about music, and how he sang in a church choir, and how much he loved music, and when did I think I would start my music class. I told him it would be easier to keep him informed about it with a telephone, so we got back to business. He assured me that the installation would be done the next day, and even allowed me to select the number. The technicians did indeed show up the next day to work on the phone. It took two more days to complete the job, as the outside lines needed some repairs, but by the end of the week, Mr. Nyirenda called to verify personally that our phone was working with the assigned number.

I use this story to illustrate how merely the promise of an opportunity to learn how to read music motivated Mr. Nyirenda. I did call him about the starting date of the class, and it was he who arranged for the meeting place for the class. He became one of three Malawians who attended the entire series of music classes. He, with the others, could sight-sing at a basic level by the end of the course, which met weekly from March to July.

My willingness to teach a class of adults created a new challenge:

Should a Kodály-educated teacher, knowing that the music of the culture of the people is a necessary tool, presume to teach Malawians how to read music without knowing many of their folk songs?

I had only a handful of songs from the children at school, though several of them had clear examples of various melodic elements.

For example:

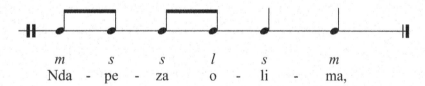

Translation: *I have found a boy . . .*

And this example:

m   s   m   s   s   s   d'   l   s   s   s
Ga - lu - yu ngwan-da - ni___   wad - ya ma-tem- ba?

Translation: *Is this the dog/hyena that stole my matemba* [a kind of fish]?

When I first sang a children's song to my adult class ("Galuyu Ngwandani"), they were amused that a *mzungu* (white person) would learn such a silly little song. But when I explained to them why I was using it—that their song was a unique expression of the Malawian culture, and that it could serve as an example of how to remember correctly the way the written music elements should sound—they were excited to realize that the songs from their childhood had some value other than to entertain children.

Listen to all folksongs attentively, for they are the treasure trove of the most beautiful melodies and through them you can get to know the character of peoples.[2]

They shared more songs with me, knowing that they would be put to good use. Suspecting that this might be the only opportunity they would ever have to learn any music skills, I decided that responding to the Malawians' desire to learn to read music with music from their own culture was important. This gave rise to my next challenge:

How could a corpus of songs be built?

I continued to go to the schools, especially Lupaso School, where my friend, Mrs. Mkandawire, taught fine traditional songs to the children. There I found the occasional song that had some possible pedagogic use in my teaching.

A visit to the Malawian National Archives in Zomba, the former capital city in the southern region, yielded some startling information: there were no books of Malawian songs, and only about 120 old gramophone recordings of folk songs made in the 1940s or 1950s—the curator was not sure when. My library search has turned up a reference to a song recording project done in that part of Africa (though Malawi was not specified) by Hugh Tracey in the late 1950s.[3] It would be interesting to see if this is the source of those unidentified gramophone recordings. There were also four or five CDs of traditional music by local bands, and some audiocassettes that were dubbed by a nongovernmental organization (NGO) monitoring the radio during the presidential elections in 1999. The NGO recorded how broadcasters commented on music, both local and foreign, and showed how that music was used for political purposes. Some videocassettes of interviews from villages made at the time of land reforms may also have some traditional music on them. These song material sources are yet to be studied, as there were several obstacles to their access: no working cassette player, no VCR, monitor, or CD player, and no time to spend on the project. It was apparent that the traditional folk songs of Malawi had not been collected into any usable form. I faced yet another challenge:

With what could that small body of songs be supplemented?

My series of music classes began in March 2002 and lasted for 15 weeks, ending in July 2002. After using the initial group of Malawian children's songs, I began to draw from song literature with which they might have some familiarity, such as "Kumbayah." I also sang to them Beethoven's "Ode to Joy," but was greeted with blank stares; clearly the classic Western literature was unknown. This meant that early on I had to teach them foreign songs in order to have the necessary musical examples to continue with the sequence. Fortunately, I had found a school songbook in a used bookshop that gave me some good folk song examples, since I had not imagined that I would need any of my teaching materials in Africa. I also wrote down a series of sacred canons gleaned from a songbook that I had with me, thinking that these might be useful in their churches. Since most of the music in their churches was transplanted British and American hymnody, I didn't feel that these songs were out of line. Gradually, another challenge emerged:

Simple rhythm examples were needed, but most of the songs had more complex rhythms.

I used and reused the songs with simple rhythms that I had found, in lieu of changing the rhythms of any of the songs just to have more material. I then began to teach foreign songs with rhythms at the next level. With so little song material to choose from, I knew that if I had been teaching my children at home, they would quickly have been bored with them. My adult Malawian students assured me, however, that they were not at all bored; in fact, they often seemed to appreciate the simplicity of having few songs when they were being asked to assimilate so much new information so quickly.

This rhythm problem, however, continues to haunt me. Most African songs use complex rhythms, and my Malawian students were certainly capable of singing, clapping, and performing complex rhythms. I, however, am familiar with only the European-derived way of thinking about those rhythms. While doing research related to this paper, I came across an article by Jay Rahn that discusses this very issue and proposes a solution: "Rather than depicting syncopated rhythms merely as deviations from a four-square metrical hierarchy, I try to show how they can be portrayed as highly integrated wholes in their own right."[4] This is an area that deserves further study that is beyond the scope of this paper.

Was it possible to teach enough sight-singing skills for the students to be self-sufficient after the instruction ended?

The Malawian adults are good singers and so excited to learn that they seem as open and eager as children, but with the focus and intellect of adults. It was abundantly clear that they knew that this was a once-in-a-lifetime opportunity to learn music-reading skills. We covered nearly the entire list of "first grade" elements in the first lesson! They wanted to see how the little pieces fit together to look like written music. The pace was very fast, with little time spent on preparation of elements, and only a short time on review at the beginning of each class. They were given assignments to practice at home, and the more serious students did them each week.

A small core of the group was diligent in preparing for each lesson, and soon a leader of that core group emerged: Joseph Sibande. Joseph, in his mid-thirties, was a church choir director at the local Presbyterian church (CCAP). He had participated in some music-reading workshops in past years that had been sponsored by and/or paid for by his church. He was employed as a low-level bank manager, but it was clear that music was a strong avocation for him.

Joseph was a quick learner and was vocal in his appreciation of the clear sequence in which the concepts were presented. His earlier training had been neither as comprehensive nor as comprehensible as what he was getting from my class, but it had clearly provided a foundation upon which the new information was building. I gradually began to realize that in him lay a potential partial answer to the problem of continuing instruction.

When I approached him about teaching the material to a new class of students after I was gone, Joseph agreed, with one caveat: I must write it all down as a guide. This was more than reasonable, considering the daunting request I had made of him, so I set about my task as quickly as was possible. This brought me to another challenge:

A lesson guide with musical examples was needed that was clear enough to be used independently by a relative beginner.

I wanted my guide to be as readable and look as nice as possible, because I believed that it would ultimately find its way into many hands. Malawi is a place where no one ever gives away information for free, except for this music knowledge that the *msunga* (white woman) was making available.

I wrote the lessons in Microsoft Word on our laptop computer, adding more information, writing exercises, more song material, and more singing exercises that came to mind as I worked. For many weeks I didn't seem to move forward in the writing process, because I was charting totally new waters in my own thinking about how to outline all the steps necessary to be able to look at a piece of music and decode it well enough to be able to sight-sing it. My total teaching experience up to that time had been at the elementary school level. The shortest path to the goal is not often the best path with young children, but in Malawi, the shortest path was the only one that there was time to traverse. By the time I had to leave Malawi in August 2002, I had completed ten lessons, and had the outline for about fifteen more.

My parting from Malawi in August 2002 was somewhat sad. I had made friends in the schools and in my music class. This was the first time in my life that I felt that all of my skills were used and needed. My Malawian students who completed the series of lessons had succeeded at learning to sight-sing at a basic level. The Kodály-inspired pedagogy worked well in the most demanding situation I could ever have imagined. My music class was important to a number of Malawians as a one-of-a-kind phenomenon in Mzuzu, and possibly all of Malawi. Word had spread about what we were doing, and more and more Malawians were asking me if they might join the class.

It was on this note that I said my goodbyes. When they offered their thanks for the opportunity to learn so much, I could only respond with my own gratitude that I had been asked to teach such a wonderful group. It is inspiring to work with adults who know that they might never again have such an opportunity to learn something they had always wanted to learn. They had driven me to learn my subject matter far better than I had known it at the outset of the class.

Once back in the U.S., I continued working on the music lessons for Joseph. I regularly talked to my husband (who had remained in Malawi) about the music classes, and found out that Joseph was doing very well. He quickly had a larger group of students than had attended my classes. Joseph met with them nearly every week, asking for no pay. He knew that teaching the subject would help improve his understanding of music, and so was happy to instruct others. He had my husband as a sounding board whenever he was uncertain. I did answer a few questions, but by and large, the written lessons seemed to be clear and adequate. When my husband came home just before Thanksgiving 2002, Joseph was still teaching his class two or three times a month, typically spending several weeks on each lesson.

In March 2003, my husband returned to Malawi for three weeks and took with him six more lessons. Joseph's class was nearly ready for them, so the timing was good. By this time, I was making plans to return to Malawi in early July, after my school was finished. I took with me several more lessons and finished the rest while in Malawi.

The day after I arrived, I attended Joseph's class. He was delighted to see me, and all his students treated me respectfully, since I was their teacher's teacher. I had ample opportunity in my five-week visit to see how well Joseph was doing at conveying the basics to his students, though it was clear to me that the version they were getting from him was more elementary than what I was able to provide. Joseph is really not much more than a beginner himself, though a very competent one. Another challenge:

Joseph had to find a way to augment his musical knowledge.

Joseph informed me that the class I had presented in 2002 was the best class he had ever attended. It had also provided a foundation for better understanding a church music workshop that he had attended in July 2003. As he had already looked for and attended all the music workshops that he could find (only one or two are available a year), he needed an ongoing way to augment his knowledge. An interesting connection was made that helped address this problem.

One of my husband's colleagues has two teenage boys, Tiwonge and Khumbo, who started a band several years ago. The band grew out of the boys' love of music that was fostered by a family friend. After receiving a keyboard from the friend, they taught themselves to play it and began to write and perform their own songs, in a kind of Malawian gospel style. Gradually they found others to join them and together they created Tikhu Vibrations.

By the time I returned to Malawi in July 2003, Tikhu Vibrations had won a contest among bands in the entire southeastern region of Africa in late 2002, and was preparing to collect their prize: a six-week concert tour of Sweden in October 2003. This tour also included school workshops in conjunction with the scheduled concerts. They had no idea what to do with the schoolchildren, so they asked me to help them create a workshop. I met with them weekly to help them figure out how to present a Malawian musical experience for the children, which could then be included in their concerts, thus assuring them of a full audience wherever they went.

I enlisted Joseph to help me with the band. They needed instruction in how to use a mixing board, and Joseph had once worked in a recording studio. While we were working with the band, they mentioned that they had an unused keyboard. The family already knew Joseph, so it wasn't hard to get them to loan it to him. He was delighted to receive a basic introduction to the keyboard and to have the use of one. He was able to practice with a keyboard theory book I had brought from the U.S. (I later sent him a proper adult piano methodology series of books.) It didn't take Joseph long to begin to employ information from the theory book to augment his music lessons in the areas where he found his students' reading to be weak, primarily in the area of rhythm. Finally, in November, after the band returned from its concert tour, Joseph began teaching them to read music.

More Malawian folk songs were needed.

I again went to Lupaso School. This time I was able to bring a digital video camera to record the children and Mrs. Mkandawire's songs, thus solving the problem of missing the steps and motions that went with the singing. The adults in Joseph's class allowed me to record a session of songs from their childhood, some of which I had heard in the schools and some of which were new. Tikhu Vibrations was also kind enough to allow me to videotape all the traditional songs they could remember from their childhoods. In this manner, I nearly doubled the number of songs that I had collected the year before.

After deciding that my investigation into the traditional music of Malawi would not be complete without a visit to the "experts," I traveled to Chancellor College (in the southern region), the only place that offered music instruction in Malawi. My main reason for interviewing two of the "three or four" (in their words) fully educated music teachers in the country (and the only ones teaching in a program with a major in music) was to find the answer to this question:

Did Kodály's philosophy of music education fit the Malawian vision of the way music should be taught?

I spent an hour and a half interviewing Robert Chanunkah and Grant Ntala, the two music teachers at Chancellor College. Together they teach about sixty students working at four different levels in the music department.

Dr. Chanunkah had just returned from the Pan African Symposium on Music and Arts in Education (PASMAE) in Nairobi, Kenya, at which, he informed me, the group had decided that they must use their own indigenous music for teaching music literacy. Dr. Chanunkah explained that during the colonial period in Malawi, all things "Western" were accepted as being "better" and "more civilized" than the indigenous ways. Once the British were thrown out, however, the Malawians who came into positions of educational oversight began to criticize the use of Western music, saying that the people who were educated in that manner understood very little of it and were not effective. Consequently, music education itself is not well regarded by the Ministry of Education and by school headmasters (principals).

During the course of the interview, Dr. Chanunkah informed me that there has been a recent trend of trying to "go back" to the musical structures, principles, and philosophies that have long been practiced in the villages. What he described sounded very much as though they were trying to apply the principles that Kodály has outlined as necessary for effectively teaching music. When asked directly, he admitted to having studied Kodály's philosophy. Further, ". . . we are trying to use the same philosophy. Let's start from here, and then use the Western concepts, yes, just to enrich our understanding."[5]

My inquiries of Dr. Chanunkah at Chancellor College led me to the conclusion that the teaching I had begun in Mzuzu was, indeed, conducted in a manner that was in alignment with the Malawian music educators' vision of how music should be taught in their country and in that region of Africa.

In Summary

Of the three Malawians who finished my course, one was skillful enough to be encouraged to teach what he had learned. When I left Malawi in August 2003, Joseph was about to begin his third iteration of the same material. At that time, however, the class was to be led by Joseph's apprentice, Johnathan Tembo, with Joseph acting in a supporting role. Joseph was deliberately using the teaching to build his own sight-singing skills and was helping Johnathan to do the same.

I collected (transcribed) about fifteen folk songs the first year, which, in the second year, grew to about twenty, with nearly that many more on audio and videotape. Many of these songs are anhemitonic pentatonic, which lends itself well to Kodály pedagogy.

Teachers who are required to teach music presently do not understand the school music syllabus, indicating that music education is needed in order to implement the syllabus. Among the faculty of six teacher training colleges and two universities in Malawi, there are only four fully educated music teachers. Only at Chancellor College is there a full music curriculum. The rest of the teaching colleges provide only a single music course for teachers, and this course is taught by an educated music teacher in only one location.

The music professors at Chancellor wish to use their own folk music to teach music literacy, but they have collected and transcribed only a few songs. Their jobs would be much easier if the Malawian songs were properly collected, analyzed, and catalogued. To do this job well, a trained Malawian must be involved to help with the languages and musical analyses. Even though the music professors at Chancellor College have read about and agree with the Kodály concept, they are neither in a position to actually implement it, nor do they have the education to do so.

There are still unresolved problems in need of help.

The issue of how to teach rhythm from an African perspective, rather than a European perspective, must be addressed.

The task of collecting the folk music of a country is a daunting one, in need of the efforts of as many people as possible. Parts of Malawi are, at times, not accessible except on foot. Many of the best informants speak only tribal languages, of which there are several hundred.

The transcription process is very difficult outside of Malawi. I don't speak Chitumbuka or Chichewa (two of the main languages), so a translator is necessary to understand the words and meaning of the songs.

A Malawian educated in music and folk song analytical procedure would be able to help determine some of the cultural questions, as well as various musical questions, such as: Are the singers singing out of tune, or is there some kind of different tonal system in use in Malawi?

More Malawians need to be educated to play active roles in music education in Malawi. Government and school policymakers are just beginning to recognize that music has value in the education of children. However, only if the music teaching is of the highest quality will these policymakers feel that time and money spent on music instruction is justified.

Three Malawian Folk Songs

The words are in Chichewa, the
official tribal language of Malawi.

1. *Ndapeza Olima* (I have found a hard-working boy)

Nda - pe - za o - li - ma, o - li - ma nya - ma - ta.

O - li - ma yo, yo, yo, o - li - ma nya - ma - ta.

2. *Tikafike Kwa Mandala* (Let's go to Mandala. Aye, Mama!)

Ti - ka - fi - ke kwa Man - da - la. Ti - ka - fi - ke kwa Man - da - la, ti - ka - fi -

ke kwa Man - da - la, a - ye,___ Ma - ma. Ti - ka - fi - ke kwa Man - da - la, a - ye,___ Ma - ma.

3. *Galayu Ngwandani* (What dog/hyena is this who ate my fish (*matemba*)? Let's cut him open to see if it is inside!)

Ga - lu - yu ngwan - da - ni,___ Wa - dya ma - tem - ba?___

Tim - che - ke pa - mim - ba,___ nga - ti wa - dya ma - tem - ba___ Wa - dya ma - tem - ba.

Last time, repeat to fade out.

135

Notes

[1] Barbara Barnard Smith, "Variability, Change, and the Learning of Music," *Ethnomusicology* 31, no. 2 (Spring-Summer 1987).

[2] Zoltán Kodály, "Who Is a Good Musician?" in *The Selected Writings of Zoltán Kodály* (London: Boosey and Hawkes, 1974), 190.

[3] Cynthia Schmidt, review of *African Guitar: Solo Fingerstyle Guitar Music from Uganda, Congo/Zaire, Central African Republic, Malawi, Namibia, and Zambia*, directed by Gerhard Kubik and Wolfgang Bachschwell, *Ethnomusicology* 41, no. 3 (Autumn 1997): 582-85.

[4] Jay Rahn, "Turning the Analysis Around: Africa-Derived Rhythms and Europe-Derived Music Theory," *Black Music Research Journal* 16, no. 1 (Spring 1996): 71-89.

[5] Robert Chanunkah, personal interview at Chancellor College, Zomba, Malawi, August 2003.

Originally published as "The Kodály Concept Finds Eager Students in Malawi, Africa," *Kodály Envoy* 32, no. 1 (2005): 12–16. Reprinted by permission.

Postscript:

In 2015, a book of Malawi children's songs for teachers was published by the Teacher Training Improvement Partnership Malawi-Switzerland. Available as a free download, Songbook for Primary School Children in Malawi, by Davie Kaambankadzanja and Marc Wagner, includes 12 songs, including "Galuyu ngwandani," one of the songs featured in this article. Songs include scores (some multi-part), original texts and English translations, background information and game directions. Interestingly, the scores also include sol-fa syllables written underneath the notes. As it turns out, Malawi was an early center for the spread of tonic sol-fa in central Africa, due to the work of nineteenth-century Scottish missionaries who came to the country, then known as the Nyasaland Protectorate, to help end the slave trade.

From Andrea: Malawi's society is very tribal in nature, with about 126 different languages--the main two being Chitumbuku and Chichewa. The songs and the culture in the south (where Chancellor College is located) is Chichewa. Chitumbuku is the main one in the north, in the region where I was located in Mzuzu. Those in the south rarely speak Tumbuku, but those in the north more frequently speak Chichewa, since it was declared to be a national language, along with English, by the long-time dictator, Hastings Kamuzu Banda, from 1966-1994.

I actually interviewed Dr. Robert Chanunkah when I was there in 2006. He headed up the music program at Chancellor College in Blantyre. He had already collected a few songs, but his workload was so great that it was very slow. He also had a very uphill battle just getting students educated--the courses were all electives and students who were training to be teachers had almost no time for electives.

I always intended to follow up on this, but was unable to find funding. Then my parents, one by one, died, then a brother as well. I guess I just got totally derailed by all of it.

I have video footage of children in the context of school, with nothing arranged, and with the children accompanying themselves. I also have footage of adults singing children's songs remembered from their childhood. Those were the main sources for the songs I used in my lessons.

"WEGWEISER": A 'GUIDEPOST' TO UNDERSTANDING THE HARMONIC LANGUAGE OF SCHUBERT

by Edward Bolkovac

One of the many advantages of using the relative movable-do solfège system for analysis and teaching within a Kodály-inspired approach is the clarity with which it is possible to define harmonic phenomena from various historical periods or composers. Through a careful harmonic and stylistic analysis of music by a particular composer, it is possible to learn the specific techniques and harmonic practices which combine to form the rhetorical language of that composer in a particular genre or time period. Through the use of solfège syllables in the analysis process, tonal relationships and standard modulations can be made clear, and—most importantly—provide a practical and necessary means of engaging the ear through singing. In addition, the use of solfège syllables is especially expedient to clarify the various resolutions of "enharmonic" chords.

Winterreise (1827), based on poems by Wilhelm Müller, is a rich storehouse of some of Schubert's most inventive harmonic writing. Among the many inventive songs in *Winterreise*, the powerful setting of "Wegweiser" is an excellent paradigm to illustrate many of Schubert's harmonic practices with the assistance of solfège. Although it can be said that Schubert's harmonic language moves in the direction of Romanticism, he never really abandons the syntax and functional relationships of Viennese Classicism. It is this "clinging to tradition" combined with an expansion of harmonic resolutions that makes the music of Schubert so pedagogically expedient. This article will describe some idiomatic features of Schubert's harmonic language in "Wegweiser" as well as provide a reference list of other examples of Schubert's harmonic practices in some of the other songs from *Winterreise*.

1) Modulating from parallel minor to major

The first and third stanzas of "Wegweiser" are based primarily in G minor, while the second stanza shifts to the key of G major via a pedal point on G. The shift from parallel minor to major (or parallel major to minor) in Schubert's art songs is an important and essential element of his rhetorical language. Although Schubert does sometimes modulate or turn towards the relative major or minor key in his art songs, the most regular and predominant tendency is the turn to the parallel minor or major key. These changes to the parallel key frequently involve much more than a simplistic change from sad to happy, and often express a subtle or sudden turn of emotion and psychology. The transformation from parallel minor to major in "Wegweiser" moves from the anger and self-doubt of the text in G minor to the poignant expression in G major of the wanderer's vulnerability and self-pity on the words "Habe ja doch nichts begangen, Dass ich Menschen sollte scheun" (I have done nothing to make me avoid people). This modulation can be expressed by a change in solmization on the pedal point (*la-do*). In the case

140

of "Wegweiser" the parallel minor and major tonalities are clearly delineated in sections based on the different stanzas of the poem. In many other Schubert songs, however, the lines are much less clearly delineated and a shift to the parallel key can happen instantly and with little or no preparation. In some circumstances particular pieces appear to be written simultaneously in major and minor to create an unsettling effect (see "Letzte Hoffnung" from *Winterreise*).

2) Neapolitan and Augmented 6th chords (in traditional and non-traditional inversions)

Schubert's settings of dramatic texts can be particularly rife with Neapolitan 6th chords and Augmented 6th chords in their traditional inversions. Three examples from "Wegweiser" are shown below:

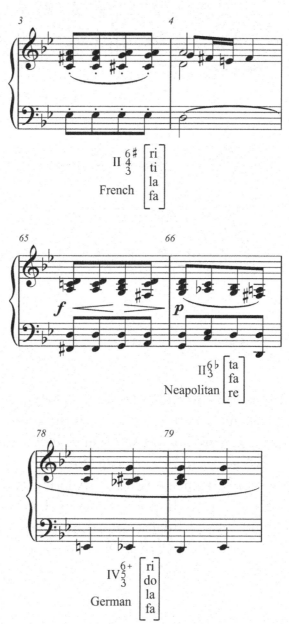

In such traditional contexts the use of "6th" in the name of these structures agrees not only with a figured bass analysis, but highlights the characteristic interval a 6th above the bass which bears the chromatic alteration (Neapolitan in minor: *re-ta*; Augmented 6th in minor: *fa-ri*). Although Schubert never abandons the functionality of these chords, he sometimes uses them in other inversions as passing structures:

When referring to these other inversions, the term "6th" in the name can be misleading because there is no longer a 6th above the bass which is the altered note. The examples cited above in bars 11–14 and 71–72 may well be the result of voice leading, but their "coloration" is unmistakable. Describing these structures as having "Neapolitan coloring" (containing *ta*, *re*, *fa* in minor), or "Italian, German or French Augmented coloring" (containing *fa* and *ri* in minor) makes it possible to relate them to the more traditional inversions, while avoiding the misapplication of the term 6th. The chordal structure in bar 71 has no "6th," but describing it as a IV chord with "Italian Augmented coloring" allows the appropriate reference to be made back to the traditional IV6#.

3) Sequential modulations of short fragments of musical material

Bars 11–14 not only contain the Neapolitan coloring mentioned above, but also demonstrate Schubert's propensity to modulate sequentially short fragments of musical material:

4) Changing the quality of a chordal structure to facilitate modulation

To facilitate modulation Schubert sometimes makes an immediate and unexpected change to the quality of a chordal structure, from major to minor, as in bar 16:

By changing the C major chord [V in F minor) to C minor [iv in G minor] the modulation process is quick and fluid. Another similar change of chordal quality occurs in bars 34–35.

5) Pedal point

Schubert makes extensive use of tonic and dominant pedal points in his art songs to sustain a particular mood, heighten the dramatic tension or facilitate modulation. *Winterreise* has abundant examples of Schubert's ingenious use of pedal points and "Wegweiser" is no exception. In bars 20–21 a tonic pedal point on G is used as a modulatory link between the parallel keys of G minor and G major, allowing a seamless tonal and psychological transition. Another tonic pedal point in bars 69–74 acts as a tonal anchor for the two chromatic lines in contrary motion. The frequent use of pedal points on G may represent the "unverrückt" (immovable/fixed) nature of the guidepost as it points unerringly to a foreboding fate:

6) Deceptive resolution of secondary dominant (V^7/vi)

The term deceptive cadence or interrupted cadence is used to describe the motion of V→VI. Schubert sometimes uses this relationship of V→VI in the context of resolving a secondary dominant (V^7 of vi), as in bars 27–28:

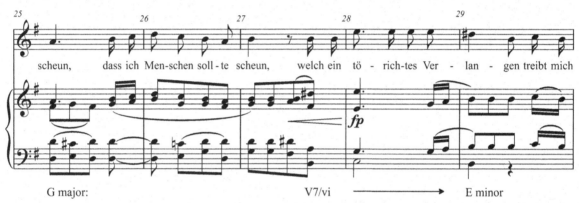

The V^7 of vi (*mi-si-ti-re*) sets up the expectation of a resolution/modulation to E minor (*la-do-mi*). The unexpected resolution to a C major chord, however, imitates the relationship of V^7→VI (*mi-si-ti-re-fa-la-do*) in the transitional context of E minor. This sudden appearance of a C major chord on the word "thörichtes" (stupid/foolish) gives added rhetorical emphasis to the protagonist's bitter self-mockery.

7) Linking triads a major third apart

In bars 33–39 Schubert modulates from a V chord in an implied E minor tonality back to G minor. The text before this modulatory interlude, "treibt mich in die Wüstenei'n" (drives me into the wilderness), conveys simultaneously the meaning of "wilderness" as well as the "emotional chaos" of the wanderer. Schubert sometimes links chords or key areas a third apart for the sonic effect with little or no apparent functional reason, as in bars 36–37 (B minor chord to G minor chord). By the ingenious use of the chord progression B major→ B minor→ G minor→ German Augmented 6th, Schubert deliberately conveys a sense of emotional confusion; the tonality seems lost in the "wilderness" due to the quality change from B major to B minor as well as linking of the B minor and G minor triads:

in die Wü-ste- nein?

Bars 55–66 represent the emotional climax not only of "Wegweiser" but arguably of *Winterreise* itself—Müller's ill-fated and rejected wanderer finally confronts and comes to terms with his stark destiny and embarks upon a path of no return, "eine Strasse muss ich gehe" (I must travel a road):

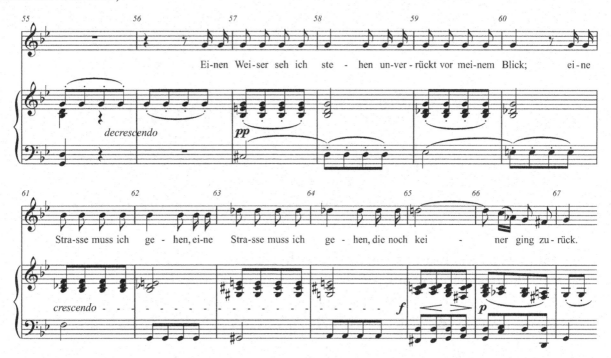

Ei-nen Wei-ser seh ich ste - hen un-ver-rückt vor mei-nem Blick; ei-ne

Stra-sse muss ich ge - hen, ei-ne Stra-sse muss ich ge - hen, die noch kei - ner ging zu-rück.

To understand this emotionally charged passage, it is necessary to observe Schubert's use of 6/4 structures as well as his unharnessing of the enharmonic potential of the fully-diminished 7th chord and the German Augmented 6th chord.

8) 6/4 substitute resolution of secondary dominant

In bars 57–58 the vii°7/V secondary dominant resolves to a i6/4 chord as a substitute for V in G minor. This resolution to a i6/4 chord is not unusual in Viennese Classicism, but in bars 54–66 it becomes the paradigm for establishing a sequence of quick tonal centers. Because the i6/4 chord is such a strong cadential structure, it often acts as the indicator of a temporary tonal center even when a complete cadence never fully materializes:

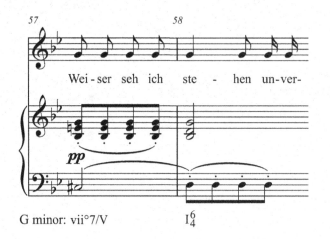

G minor: vii°7/V $\qquad$ I$^6_4$

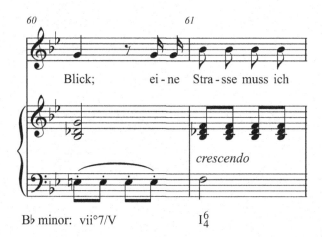

B♭ minor: vii°7/V $\qquad$ I$^6_4$

9) Enharmonic resolution of fully-diminished chord

Fully-diminished 7th chords always sound the same in every inversion:

It is only their resolutions which help us to determine aurally what inversion is being used. Some typical resolutions are shown below:

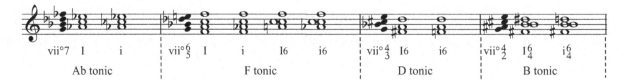

146

A fully-diminished 7th chord in root position often resolves to a root position tonic chord in a major or minor key, while a first inversion fully-diminished 6/5 resolves down to a 5/3 tonic triad or up to a 6/3 tonic triad.

The fully-diminished 6/5 structure in bar 62, based on its written form, should resolve down to an F triad in root position (or its 6/4 substitute) or up to a 6/3 triad:

Clearly this is not the case! The C# minor 6/4 structure in bar 63 is an indicator of the temporary key of C# minor, thus the fully-diminished chord in bar 62 can only resolve onward to it via an enharmonic resolution. This fully-diminished 6/5 relates back to Bb minor as written, but resolves forward as a fully-diminished chord in root position. The enharmonic relationship is as follows:

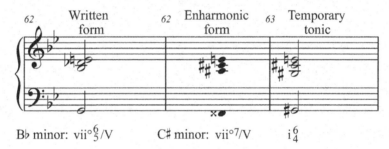

Thus, Schubert uses the pattern of vii°7N →i6/4 to pass through three tonal areas each a third apart: G minor, Bb minor and C# (Db) minor respectively. The pseudo-pedal point notes in the voice part outline these three tonal areas. The enharmonic resolution of the structure in bar 62 allows the ascent by minor thirds to progress unimpeded.

10) Enharmonic use of the German Augmented 6th

The sound of a German Augmented 6th chord is the same as a V^7, although its resolution is quite different:

The resolutions of such an "enharmonic structure" can lead to keys that are a half step apart, forming a link between a key and its Neapolitan key (G minor→ Ab major). A similar enharmonic potential is first utilized in bar 59. The structure sounds like a German Augmented 6th (Eb, G, Bb, C#) in the key of G minor, but resolves onward in the direction of Ab major in its written form (Eb, G, Bb, Db), and eventually to a triad built on F after the E natural enters in bar 60:

The same phenomenon occurs in bar 64—the chord sounds like a German Augmented 6th (A, C#, E, F𝄪) in the key of C# minor, but leads on to a D major chord in its written form (A, C#, E, G):

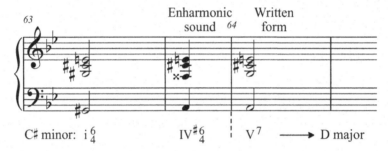

The entire passage from bars 57–64 is a wonderful paradigm to view how Schubert expanded the potentiality of harmonic resolutions, and consequently the possibilities of modulation through the use of enharmonic chords. Solmization can help clarify the tonal momentum and enharmonic phenomena:

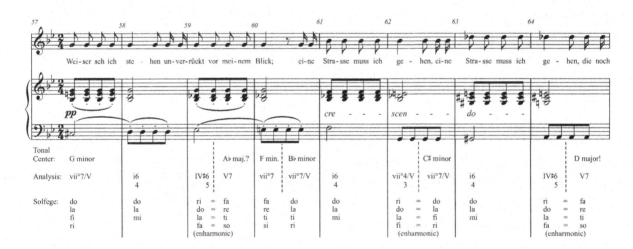

11) Inconsistencies/limitations of written notation

Bars 62–64 highlight most clearly the notational anomalies between the voice and piano parts. There is really no "correct" way to write out these bars, because the relationships are based on sound and function—not on the limitations of notational convention! It is easy to imagine Schubert improvising such passages at the piano unconcerned with the way they will eventually look on the printed page. Pianists know how easy it can be to play through various keys at the keyboard without being concerned or aware of the exact spelling of chords (e.g. B# or C, F$\times$ or G, etc.). Schubert followed his inner hearing during the compositional process—writing out the notation was secondary. Such inconsistencies in the written notation are signs that Schubert was beginning to push the boundaries of Viennese Classicism.

Other songs from *Winterreise* can provide valuable study of typical Schubertian harmonic practices exemplified in his more dramatic settings. The following list compiled from *Winterreise* contains the harmonic practices described above and a few additional ones. The list is not meant to be comprehensive.

1) Modulating from parallel major to minor (or minor to major)

I.	Gute Nacht (bars 70–71, minor to major via V)
V.	Der Lindenbaum (bars 24–25, abruptly from major to minor: I→i)
XIV.	Der greise Kopf (bars 35–36, minor to major: i to I^6)

2) Neapolitan and Augmented 6th chords (in traditional and non-traditional inversions)

III.	Gefror'ne Tränen (bars 22 and 26, Italian and German Augmented 6th chords)
X.	Rast (bars 26–29, Italian, German and French Augmented 6th chords on submediant pedal point)
XIV.	Der greise Kopf (bar 21, Italian IV$^{6\#}$ in major)
XVII.	Im Dorfe (bar 42, German Augmented 6th in major)
XI.	Frühlingstraum (bars 16–20, 22 and 24, French Augmented coloring, root position)
XV.	Die Krähe (bar 3, traditional Neapolitan 6th and Neapolitan coloring, root position)
XIX.	Täuschung (bar 26, French Augmented coloring, root position)

3) Sequential modulations of short fragments of musical material

VII.	Auf dem Flusse (bars 54–57, 62–65)
X.	Rast (bars 17–20, descending by diatonic step)
XI.	Frühlingstraum (bars 16–20, ascending minor third, E minor to G minor)
XII.	Einsamkeit (bars 36–39, ascending by diatonic step)
XV.	Die Krähe (bars 16–22)

4) Changing the quality of a chordal structure to facilitate modulation

    XXI.   Das Wirtshaus (bar 6 and 12, C major→minor chord; bar 28, F major→minor chord)

    XXIII. Die Nebensonnen (bar 19, E major→minor chord)

5) Pedal point

    X.   Rast (bars 25–29, submediant pedal point)

    XI.   Frühlingstraum (bars 32–36, dominant pedal point)

    XII.   Einsamkeit (bars 1–14, tonic pedal point)

    XVII. Im Dorfe (bars 18–26, modulation on D pedal point: D minor→G major)

    XXIV. Der Leiermann (entire piece written on tonic pedal point)

6) Deceptive resolution of secondary dominant (V⁷/vi)

    VII.   Auf dem Flusse (bars 27–28, V6/of vi→IV6)

    XI.   Frühlingstraum (bars 2–3, V⁷/vi→IV)

    XII.   Einsamkeit (bars 28–29, V⁷/vi)

7) Linking triads a major third apart

    VII.   Auf dem Flusse (bars 55–56 D# major→B major; bars 63–64, B major→G major) See category 3, above.

    XXII. Muth (bars 32–33, E major→C major). For a more startling example see *Schwanengesang*, Der Atlas (bars 35–36, E minor→G minor)

8) 6/4 substitute resolution of secondary dominant

    XXI.   Das Wirtshaus (bar 24, V⁷/V→i6/4)

    VIII. Rückblick (bars 40–41, enharmonic vii°7/V→I6/4)

9) Enharmonic resolution of fully-diminished chords

    III.   Gefror'ne Tränen (bars 34–35, fully-diminished 6/5 = fully-diminished 7)

    VIII. Rückblick (bars 40–41, fully-diminished 6/5 = fully-diminished 7)

10) Enharmonic use of the German Augmented 6th

    III.   Gefror'ne Tränen (bar 37 and 47, V⁷ in Gb major [Neapolitan key] = IV6#-5 in F minor)

    IX.   Irrlicht (bars 32 and 36, IV6#/5 in B minor = V⁷ in C major [Neapolitan key])

    XII.   Einsamkeit (bars 32 and 44, V⁷ in Eb major [Neapolitan key] = IV6#/5 in D minor)

11) Inconsistencies/limitations of written notation: see 9 and 10 above.

12) Elision

    VII.   Auf dem Flusse (bars 65–66, *so* 4/2→*mi* 7)

    VIII. Rückblick (bars 39–40, *so* 4-2→*mi* 7)

    XII.   Einsamkeit (bar 28, *so* 4/2→ *mi* 7)

XXI.   Das Wirthshaus (bar 5, *mi* 5/3→*so* 7)
XXIII. Die Nebensonnen (bar 14, *mi* 6/5→*so* 7)

13) Minor coloring in major (*loo* and *ma*)

XXI.   Das Wirthshaus (bars 8, 14, 20, 21)
XVII.   Im Dorfe

14) Parallel major and minor as the same key—constant shifting between the two

XVI.   Letzte Hoffnung
XVII.   Im Dorfe

Originally published in *Bulletin of the International Kodály Society* 22, no. 2 (1997): 49-57. Reprinted by permission.

BRITTEN'S *NOYE'S FLUDDE*

Betty Bertaux

Debussy, Stravinsky, Bartok, Schoenberg and Varèse are all composers whose works reflect bold and innovative departures from traditions, establishing a tradition of their own which has been nurtured and developed by their contemporaries and successors. In examining their works, or the works of any composer for that matter, there is a tendency to select instrumental pieces for study. It is, also, of interest to take note of how effectively a composer uses his craft in vocal works. Especially is this true in the realm of the technically, aurally, and intellectually challenging music of the twentieth century. It would appear that the practices of this period would be unsuitable for singers except for a limited, gifted few.

The question comes to mind: Can twentieth century compositional techniques be used on as wide a scale and as effectively in the vocal music of today as were the compositional techniques of past periods? It was Schoenberg's dream to have his music whistled with the same familiarity and fondness as Tchaikovsky's—an almost absurd concept to the average ear. It would seem that the fulfillment of that dream could approach reality without the delay of generations or centuries, knowing that it is primarily through the conditioning of children that new traditions are established. We hope that the challenge of that fulfillment will not be too great for the fine craftspersons of our time, for one might wonder: How effectively can twentieth century elements be incorporated by those craftspersons into vocal music which can be performed by children? For without suitable materials, our future audiences are left to be bred on old, often tired Romantic sonorities. Eric Roseberry has said,

> It is unfortunate for the future of music that the great majority of music written especially for the young still tends to cling to an outworn style which insidiously builds up resistances to what is already an accomplished fact in the significant music of our time; what Schoenberg called 'the emancipation of the dissonance.' It is, one feels, important to expose the comparatively unprejudiced and receptive ears of the young to sound and rhythmical asymmetries which, while having passed and won acceptance with an advanced musical public today, are still resisted by a large section of the so-called serious musical public.[1]

The logical action at this point is to explore material which has been written by distinguished composers of this century for performance by children. What elements have they employed? How successfully have they worked within the unique limitations imposed by writing for children? Or have their works been condescending and simplistic in their attempt to write down to children? A prevalent practice appears to be that many of those who write for children seem to hold the position that the often insipid music they compose is for the feeble-minded, not just technically immature individuals.

There are many distinguished composers of the twentieth century who have written more or less effectively for children. One, however, emerges as having demonstrated an outstanding sensitivity and ability in providing artistic music to fill the void. Benjamin Britten, by 1970, had written eleven operas, thirteen song cycles, ten cantatas, many songs, choruses, and other free vocal forms. Of these compositions, the following catalogued works are for children's performance:

Operas: *The Little Sweep* and *Noye's Fludde*;

Choral works: *A Ceremony of Carols, Fancie, Friday Afternoons, Missa Brevis in D, Psalm 150* and *Three Two-Part Songs.*

Britten's works were almost always composed with specific artists and events in mind. This fact, coupled with his knowledge and appreciation of literature and his interest in children, quite logically produced the work selected for this article. *Noye's Fludde*, the Chester miracle play, was written for the Aldeburgh Festival in England in 1958. The work can easily be performed by children of any age, incorporating professional or at least trained musicians as well.

Of the cast, three performers are adults; the Voice of God (spoken), Noye (bass-baritone), and Mrs. Noye (contralto). Noye's sons, Sem, Ham, and Jaffett, their wives, Mrs. Sem, Mrs. Ham and Mrs. Jaffett, Mrs. Noye's Gossips, and the Animal Chorus are all children. The Raven and the Dove, danced, are also children. Britten additionally treats the audience as part of the cast, assigning to them the function of the congregation, whose participation is required in the hymns and a final canon.

The orchestra has at its core a string quintet made up of professional musicians. Additionally, trained performers are required for solo recorder, piano duet, timpani, and organ. The ripieno orchestra is composed of children with varying technical abilities, specified in the introduction to the score. Other instrumental parts to be taken by children include recorders, bugles, percussion and handbells. Generally, the music calls more for cool rhythmical heads than for correct notes.

The opera opens with a congregational hymn, the first phrase of which Britten uses later as the Flood Theme. During this hymn, Noye makes his way through the congregation to the front of the church. The Voice of God then calls to him above the ominous support of the timpani, expressing His annoyance with Man and commanding Noye to build the Ark.

Having been given the exact specifications, Noye, his sons, and their wives begin work. As the work progresses, Britten employs the ripieno strings and recorders in clever and appropriate ostinati, a device he uses in other works. The effect created is one of industry as the Ark is finally assembled. Mrs. Noye, however, refuses to have anything to do with it. She and her drunken Gossips spend their energies scoffing and drinking ale.

Seeing that the Ark is finished, God orders Noye to bring the animals aboard. Britten has captured the Medieval logic involved by having the animals process chanting "Kyrie, kyrie, kyrie eleison." The fact that the story of Noah is one from the Old Testament is no reason to avoid inserting appropriate New Testament liturgy! In fact, this section closes with a very definite, but brief, chant-like treatment of the Kyrie, typical of Britten.

Each group of animals is announced by one of the sons or their wives, and heralded by bugles. The melodies used in the announcements, as throughout the opera, are treated characteristically; they are memorable, made up of short, easily sung, repetitive phrases, and, in this case, built upon mildly dissonant, functioning harmonies. The melodies do not call for vocal or aural acrobatics, nor do they avoid a natural, logical flow. The tessituras are always within the most complimentary register of the child's voice with its unique capacities ingeniously reflected in the group of mice, rats, and cats which enter the Ark. By presenting their Kyrie in diminution and scoring it in that "counter-soprano" register so typical of a child's playful screams, Britten effectively represents mice, rats, and cats squeaking and mewing their way to the Ark.

Finally, in this, as in other sections, Britten demonstrates his awareness that the most easily accomplished artistic form of harmonizing is through canon. The canonic treatment of the announcement of birds takes on a sophisticated and charming quality reminiscent of an aviary, well within the grasp of children.

The Quarreling Section which follows finds the greatest use of the Flood Theme as the tension and dissonances grow with the nearing of the impending storm. Mrs. Noye refuses to come aboard. Her tipsy Gossips get involved in the confusion by interrupting the recitativic family spat with a lumpy, 6/8 drinking song. The issue is resolved when the Gossips flee and "Mother" is literally carried aboard by her sons, responding to her husband's welcome with a box on the ears.

The following Storm Section is the largest and perhaps musically the most important one in the opera. Britten chooses one of his favorite forms, the passacaglia, as the medium through which to unfold the events of the storm. The ground bass progresses through each of the twelve notes of the scale but is well grounded tonally by a recurring G as the theme itself unfolds. Each of the twenty-seven variations brings on a new aspect of the storm: wind, thunder, lightning, waves, flapping rigging, and panicking animals. Britten effectively uses recorders playing parallel 4ths and trills to illustrate the gales of winds, while bowed, open-stringed violins capture the image of billowing waves. He even incorporates earthenware mugs of various sizes slung by their handles on a string in a scale-like arrangement and played with wooden spoons to depict raindrops. Percussion and other members of the ripieno orchestra are added as the fury of the storm grows. At the height of that fury, the occupants of the Ark begin the J. B. Dykes hymn "Eternal Father, Strong to Save," a setting beautifully in relief against the turbulence of the accompaniment. The passacaglia is briefly interrupted by a traditional nineteenth century harmonization of the hymn, but resumes as the storm beats out its final thrust and then subsides.

When all is calm, Noye sends out a Raven in search of dry land. When the Raven fails to return, Noye sends a Dove. The materials used for these dances are masterpieces of thematic economy. Additionally, Britten has managed a character study of the two birds in his treatment of the material. One can feel the hesitation and trepidation of the Raven's uncertain flutterings in an asymmetrical, almost-flowing, waltz while the Dove is pictured more confidently, flying with grace and assurance. It is in the depicting of the Dove's cooing that Britten makes the most obvious and colorful use of his beloved Lydian 4th. The 4th, falling to the 3rd, is flutter-tongued on the recorder, turning out to be the most aurally picturesque sound in the entire opera.

After the Dove returns with an olive branch, God grants permission for the Ark's occupants to disembark, which they do, group by group, singing "Alleluia," escorted by the heralding bugles. God then extends His blessing and promise against a background of chiming handbells. The rainbow, sun, moon and stars appear during the recessional, "Tallis' Canon," which eventually is sung jointly by the cast and congregation in eight parts. The opera closes with God's farewell and the subdued joy of pealing bells.

The restrictions imposed on Britten by the capacities of the young performers have served not as a limitation but rather as an inspiration. He has found clever and innovative uses for his performers' natural abilities and levels of technical achievement. Certainly Britten has succeeded in creating an artistic work intended for performance by children in which he uses every element of his style, demonstrating outstanding skill in his craft.

Notes

[1] Eric Roseberry, "The Music of 'Noye's Fludde,'" *Tempo*, no. 49 (Autumn 1958), 2-3.

Originally published in *Kodály Envoy* 1, no. 4 (1975): 1, 2, 5, 8. Reprinted by permission.

CHARACTERISTICS OF WORTHY CANADIAN COMPOSITIONS FOR YOUNG PERFORMERS

Connie Foss More

Abrégé. Cette présentation tente guider des professeurs qui cherchent des nouvelles oeuvres qui sont artistiquement appropriées pour leurs étudiants, et aussi elle tente guider des compositeurs qui écrivent pour les jeunes. Les exemples Canadiens sont pour le violon, l'orchestre à cordes, le piano, et pour choeur d'enfants.

The importance of repertoire choice in the musical education of young performers is clear to Kodály-trained teachers for whom "only the best is good enough." However, how do we determine what "the best" is, especially when considering newly-composed works that have not yet had an opportunity to try the "test of time"? How also can composers and arrangers be guided to write for young students and performing groups? We know that if left to chance, our students may prefer familiar pop/rock styles or works that require little thought or practice. We also know that in the right setting they respond amazingly well to things that are the exact opposite—if the pieces are so well crafted and so appropriately challenging that they could be considered works of art.

This presentation examines several Canadian works performable by children, in a variety of media, pointing out characteristics of successful individual pieces as well as ways in which the pieces are similar. These musical examples and commentary are offered as a guide for judging the artistic and educational merits of compositions for young musicians.

SOLO VIOLIN

The first musical examples to be discussed are perhaps the simplest, because the composers were given the task of creating works for solo violin in which only 6 A-major pitches are used: from A=440 to the F# above. Of course these are the pitches used by Suzuki violinists all over the world for the famous "Twinkle Variations." The 20th Century Canadian Violin Series *A La Jeunesse* (see Bibliography/Discography) begins with pieces like these and progresses to more challenging works. I have selected an example by each of the three series composers, all of whom live in British Columbia: Jean Coulthard, Jean Ethridge, and David Duke.

Each violin part has an intrinsic shape: ABA+coda in the Coulthard; AB with a constant crescendo in the Ethridge; and AA'BB' in the Duke. Each violin part could stand alone as a finished piece. However, the composers used the piano accompaniment to enlarge the musical horizons, and the teacher's manual prepared by the composers relates their compositional technique to that of other well-known composers, in an attempt to teach contemporary "music history" as well.

In the introduction to the first piece, Coulthard's "A Quiet Moment," the composer discusses the use of parallel 5ths and an interesting C/C# cross-relation; she likens these to the music of Richard Strauss, citing his early Violin Sonata as an example. We will hear the piano/violin version; she also wrote a violin trio arrangement.

A Quiet Moment
Un Moment Tranquille

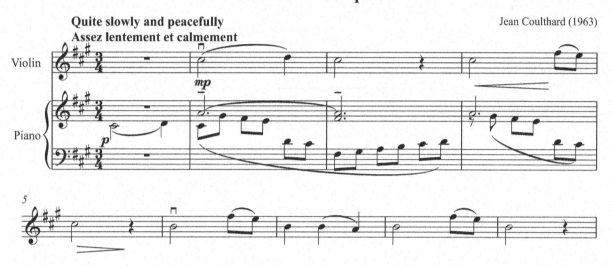

The second piece in this "created suite" is Jean Ethridge's "Subway Train." The violin plays something similar to "Twinkle Variation D," only with a crescendo programmatically designed to announce the arrival of the subway. The mildly dissonant chords of the piano express the lurching of the train through rhythmic accents modelled on the music of Prokofiev and Martinu.

THE SUBWAY TRAIN
LE METRO

The final piece in this set is David Duke's "All Alone." Notes added to triads (often 2nds and 7ths), plus a Mixolydian final cadence, evoke the style of Gabriel Fauré, according to the composer's notes.

ALL ALONE
SOLITAIRE

David Duke (1963)

Although these pieces were written for relatively young beginning violinists, the evidence of their musical worth is found in the fact that older and more experienced players find them intriguing, too.

INTERMEDIATE STRING ORCHESTRA

Suitable Canadian pieces for intermediate-level string orchestra include the three-movement work by Harry Somers, *Little Suite for String Orchestra*. An immediately-recognized difference between this work and the previous ones is the fact that each movement is based upon a folk tune that is given full exposure in the arrangements: "Lukey's Boat," "She's Like the Swallow," and "Ah! Si mon moine voulait danser!" We will hear the middle movement, which is based upon one of Canada's most beautiful Dorian mode folksongs.

Little Suite for String Orchestra

ii. She's Like the Swallow

Some of the characteristics of this arrangement of "She's Like the Swallow" that make it accessible to young players are:

1. All of the instrumental lines are somewhat independent and active, usually providing interesting countermelodies.
2. The second violin part could be played entirely in first position.
3. The first violin part has first-position divisi in all but one place in which a higher position would be required.
4. The lower parts, viola and cello, are doubled by a provided piano part. While this may seem an unwanted intrusion musically, the fact remains that orchestras of young players often include many violinists, a few cellists, and VERY few violists. The piano therefore helps to provide a musically satisfying balance of parts.
5. Rhythms, in 3/4 meter, are generally paired eighths, quarters, halves, and dotted halves. There are occasional dotted quarter-plus-eighth combinations, and tied notes.
6. In the overall ABA form, the cellists get the folk melody in the B section while first violinists experience a "decorative" part.
7. A short Violin I solo provides incentive for an advancing player.
8. The optional use of mutes provides the possibility for a special and perhaps new sound color.
9. The harmonization, though unadventurous, juxtaposes Dorian and Aeolian qualities, providing interest and challenge.

PIANO

There is an incredibly large repertoire of Canadian piano works for all levels and ages of players. The nine-book series *Music of Our Time*, first published in 1977, provides a rich and easily accessible source of material. Music in these books (pre-Book 1 through Book 8) was created by two of the *A La Jeunesse* violin series composers, Jean Coulthard and David Duke, plus another British Columbia composer, Joan Hansen of the Victoria Conservatory of Music. In this video, Hansen plays and describes two of her own compositions and two by David Duke. We have selected one composition each from Books 1, 2, 3 and 6. As in the violin series, notes written by the composers in the student books and in the accompanying teacher's manuals give structural analyses and accessible explanations of the musical idioms being explored.

David Duke's "March," from Book 1, has an F-Lydian melody with one syncopation in the right hand. The left hand almost constantly plays a pattern familiar to Kodály teachers everywhere, a "ta ti-ti" ostinato, ending with a post-World War II effect: knocking on the wooden part of the piano.

MARCH (Lydian Mode)
MARCHE (Mode Lydien)

David Duke (1977)

From Book 2 we selected Joan Hansen's "Two Tone." This staccato piece begins with the right hand in D Major and the left hand in G Major; keys are briefly reversed in the middle of the piece, where there is a sudden change in dynamics. The hands sometimes move in contrary motion and sometimes in parallel. The bi-tonal style leads to a suggested listening reference: Milhaud's "Le Boeuf sur le toît."

TWO TONE
DEUX TON

Joan Hansen (1977)

"Eskimo Song: Chesterfield Inlet" by David Duke, from Book 3, is based upon a song sung by an Inuit performer who lived near Chesterfield Inlet, on the western shore of Hudson Bay in the Canadian North. The re-pentatonic melody is passed from right hand to left hand; it is characterized here by what feels like uneven rhythm due to occasional fermatas by the "drum." It is as if the singer needs a very deep breath before each long melodic line! The Inuit drum effect created by hitting the side of the piano with the sustain pedal depressed is quite "other-worldly." (Duke's compositions actually use piano-wood percussion very seldom, despite the fact we selected two examples of this.) The use of silently-pressed and held keys is likened to the idioms created in Bartók's *Mikrokosmos* and Copland's "Piano Variations." The composer also mentions that the melody originally had microtonal ornaments that are not reproducible on our well-tempered piano.

161

ESKIMO SONG: CHESTERFIELD INLET
CHANSON ESQUIMAUDE: CRIQUE CHESTERFIELD

David Duke (1977)

Hit side of piano with open left hand
Frappez au côté du piano, la main gauche ouverte

The final piano example is Joan Hansen's "The Quarrel," from Book 6. While looking deceptively simple, the syncopated rhythms represent both a challenge and an example of a significant development in twentieth century music: displaced accents. Stravinsky and Bartók are cited as relevant historical figures. A single motive is elaborated upon by each hand separately, and then both hands together.

THE QUARREL
LA QUERELLE

Joan Hansen (1977)

While it is impossible to summarize all of these pieces in a neat way, it is probably fair to say that each one represents a combination of historical imitation and true creative innovation. In the same sense that Kodály wrote many vocal exercises in the style of other composers in order to bring those styles more easily into the classroom, this series (as well as the violin one) helps to create both an understanding and a receptive mood for various important twentieth century styles. The instrument is clearly the medium, but the message is much broader.

TREBLE CHOIR

We will discuss the five sample choral pieces in terms of difficulty and age-appropriateness. The fact that three of the pieces are by Nancy Telfer and that all of the composers are female is perhaps no accident, although it seemed so at first. Among other reasons, an association with children's choirs (as a parent, teacher, conductor or accompanist) is certainly helpful to a

162

composer who wants to write well for them, and there are doubtless fewer males in those positions.

The biggest difference between choral music and all the other genres discussed so far is, of course, that choral music has a text. The texts of the chosen examples include humor, poetic thought, the tragic ballad, and the international language of the Catholic Mass. In every case the text is at least as important as the musical setting in terms of evaluating the validity of the piece.

Our unison example, Telfer's "If You Should Meet a Crocodile," fully exploits the child's sense of fun in a pseudo-serious setting. While the crocodile wears a perpetual welcoming smile and plans his next "munch munch," the music effortlessly employs changing meter to fit the words. Fragments of musical clichés in the piano part serve to heighten the fun, as do the swooping dynamics. The second half of the song repeats the first, but in condensed form—a surprising trick.

IF YOU SHOULD MEET A CROCODILE

The same composer's arrangement of the Canadian folksong "Flunky Jim" is a good example of unaccompanied two-part singing. At first the upper part has an ostinato-like "commentary" role while the lower part takes the melody. At the end of both the verse and the refrain, the parts are sung with equal fervor and bits of vertical harmony. The refrain provides "separate but equal" tunes that sometimes share the same notes and rhythms. These unison "checkpoints" give courage to beginning part-singers and help to keep the original folk tune prominent.

FLUNKY JIM

arr. Nancy Telfer

Note: During the depression of the 1930s, when many people were out of work and money was very scarce, the Saskatchewan government offered a penny for every gopher tail turned in. (Gophers ate the already scarce grain crops.) This song was made up by a father after hearing his son talk about the clothes he was going to buy with his gopher money. It shows the type of good-humored joking that took place even when times were tough.

Ruth Watson Henderson, longtime accompanist for the Toronto Children's Chorus, has written numerous compositions for children's choir. "Slave of the Moon" is one of a series of eight pieces written to texts composed by children. Although mostly in unison, the work divides into three echoing parts when the sea (the "slave of the moon") is "sputtering, foaming, frothing." The basic 6/8 meter is juxtaposed with duplets here and also at the words "pulling at the land"—a musical "pulling" that is very effective. The composer also sets the "oo" vowel of "soon" and "moon" on high pitches, where the child's head voice is beautifully displayed.

SLAVE OF THE MOON

Words by Mary Yarmon

Music by Ruth Watson Henderson

Violet Archer's "Three Sailors from Groix/Les Trois Marins de Groix" is a French sea shanty arranged for three-part women's chorus and piano. This is a typical tragic ballad in strophic form with a refrain that forcefully states: "the wind blows; 'tis the call of the sea that torments us!" The story relates a mother's grief over her storm-lost son, whom she will meet in Paradise. Each of the four verses is set slightly differently by the composer, including a brief movement of the melody to the middle voice. The use of parallel 5ths, triads, and octaves, plus the Phrygian/Aeolian interplay, emphasizes the chilling mood. The piano introduction and interludes, sometimes accompanied by voices, seem to illustrate the waves of the sea with sighing motives. Changes in dynamics, tempi, and meter are all organic. The piece ends with a repetition of the first verse, and a powerful short coda.

THREE SAILORS FROM GROIX
LES TROIS MARINS DE GROIX

excerpt from verse 2, refrain

French Sea Shanty
arr. Violet Archer (1975)

The final choral example is the "Kyrie" from Telfer's *Missa Brevis*, written for unaccompanied SSA choir. The introduction moves easily between unison and three-note clusters. Although the lowest part has frequent pedal tones in most of the piece, it joins the other parts in equal interplay during the "Christe" B section, which features melodic and harmonic perfect 4ths. Upper and middle parts are often canonic or mirror-image in the A and A$_v$ sections. The coda utilizes clusters similar to the introduction and ends its Aeolian mode "Lord have mercy" on a questioning note: "ti."

MISSA BREVIS
Kyrie

All of these choral examples are miniature works of art. In each of them, the music and the text combine to create the mood in a natural way. They also work for young performers because the musical challenges are well matched to the type of text selected, and because the musical settings offer unexpected delights different from the kind of songs they might hear elsewhere.

CONCLUSION

I hope the musical "appetizers" that have been placed before you have stimulated your interest in Canadian compositions, and will provoke thought regarding existing and potential compositions from your own country. I am artistically moved by these musical examples, and

I know that the young people who perform them also develop a connection that goes beyond the logistical challenges of learning the music. This is the real test of worth.

BIBLIOGRAPHY

SOLO VIOLIN:
All selections taken from *A La Jeunesse* series, which exists in several books, with pieces by Jean Coulthard, David Duke, and Jean Ethridge; edited by Thomas Rolston. Waterloo, ON: Waterloo Music, 1983.   Now available at The Soundpost: https://www.thesoundpost.com/
Book 1: (maximum 6 notes - A to F#)
  "A Quiet Moment" by Jean Coulthard
  "The Subway Train" by Jean Ethridge
  "All Alone" by David Duke
[Performed by Alexis Katalin More and Connie Foss More.]

STRING ORCHESTRA:
"She's Like the Swallow" (Canadian folk song); movement II of *Little Suite for String Orchestra* by Harry Somers. Toronto, ON: Berandol, 1956. Now available at Canadian Music Centre: https://cmccanada.org/
[Performed by the Intermediate String Orchestra of the Victoria Conservatory of Music; Trudi Conrad, conductor.]

PIANO:
All selections taken from the *Music of Our Time* series, which exists in 9 volumes, with pieces by Jean Coulthard, David Duke, and Joan Hansen. Waterloo, ON: Waterloo Music, 1977 (Neil A. Kjos in USA). Now available at Mayfair: https://www.mayfairmusic.com/
 Book 1: "March" by David Duke
 Book 2: "Two Tone" by Joan Hansen
 Book 3: "Eskimo Song: Chesterfield Inlet" by David Duke
 Book 6: "The Quarrel" by Joan Hansen
[Video performance and commentary by Joan Hansen, Victoria Conservatory of Music, Victoria B.C.]

TREBLE CHOIR:
"Flunky Jim": Canadian folk song arr. by Nancy Telfer. *Reflections of Canada*, Vol. 1, *Pine Tree Gently Sigh: 45 Two-Part Arrangements of Canadian Folk Songs*, ed. John Barron. Oakville, ON: Frederick Harris Music, 1985. Now available at https://cypresschoral.com/
Library loaning copies of original edition: https://library.avemaria.edu/
[Performed by Greater Victoria Youth Choir, Foundation level; Ann-Marie Thompson, conductor.]

"If You Should Meet a Crocodile" by Nancy Telfer. For unison voices and piano; Oakville, ON: Leslie Music (Brodt in USA, Roberton in UK), 1987. Now available at https://www.lesliemusicsupply.com/
[Performed by Greater Victoria Youth Choir, Foundation level; Ann-Marie Thompson, conductor.]

"Kyrie" from *Missa Brevis* by Nancy Telfer. SSA unaccompanied. Richmond, BC: Lenel Music, 1985.
Now available at Sheet Music Plus: https://www.sheetmusicplus.com/
[Performed by Amabile Youth Singers of London, Ontario; John Barron and Brenda Zadorsky, conductors.]

"Slave of the Moon" from *Through the Eyes of Children* by Ruth Watson Henderson. Toronto Children's Chorus series G-323, for 3 equal parts with piano. Don Mills, ON: Gordon V. Thompson, 1984. Now available at Sheet Music Plus: https://www.sheetmusicplus.com/
[Performed by Mount Royal College Senior Children's Choir of Calgary, Alberta; Elaine Quilichini, conductor.]

"Three Sailors from Groix": French folk song arr. by Violet Archer. For 3-part women's voices with piano. Toronto, ON: Canadian Music Centre, 1975. Now available at https://cmccanada.org/
[Performed by the Greater Victoria Youth Choir, Senior level; Connie Foss More, Music Director.]

Lecture presented at the IKS Symposium in August 1991, Calgary, Alberta, Canada. Originally published in *Bulletin of the International Kodály Society* 17, no. 2 (1992): 22-31. Reprinted by permission.

GOOD INTONATION: EAR OR VOICE?

Edward Bolkovac

There are many Kodály-trained teachers—from the elementary through the university level—who tend initially to explain and react to out-of-tune singing as primarily a fault of the ear. In many cases these musicians have had little formal vocal training as an influential part of their study. Their Kodály training may enable them to notice and point out the intonational deficiencies of their students, but they are often unable to offer solutions that include help with how to sing more efficiently. Some ear-training specialists from other backgrounds are much less concerned about the intonational quality of their students' singing—they are focused primarily on developing their students' ability to hear and write musical sounds, not on their ability to sing musically, sing in tune and be good pedagogical role models.

On the other hand, musicians and music educators with more extensive vocal backgrounds tend initially to explain problems of out-of-tune singing as a result of poor vocal technique and the lack of ability to coordinate a series of complex muscular activities. Many are quick to point out deficiencies in the vocal mechanics of their students, but fail to engage and develop their students' aural abilities and inner hearing as important parts of the vocal process. Some studio voice teachers are seemingly unconcerned about anything but the most general intonation, focusing exclusively on teaching techniques to free up and project the voice. Choral directors with formal vocal backgrounds whose sole emphasis is the development of vocal technique may produce choirs which sing freely, but whose intonation, blend and balance leave much to be desired.

Singing out of tune may be the result of an ear that has not been systematically trained to listen carefully enough or the result of a voice that is not being properly used. Often, however, the problem is a complex combination of both. Singing in tune, however, can mean different things to different people, depending on a number of factors including one's natural preferences for sound, the compositional structure of the music, issues of historical performance practice, size of the performing forces, etc.

The Hungarian approach to singing in tune was and is today still heavily influenced by the nineteenth-century writings of Alexander Ellis and Hermann Helmholtz.[1] Their acoustical theories were adapted and applied to choral singing and in music education classrooms throughout Hungary. These practices (and their influence on vocal training and tone) were outlined in more recent times in *Kórusnevelés-kórushangzás* by Pál Kardos (1927-1978), beloved Hungarian choral conductor and music educator.[2] Kardos' treatise on developing the ability to sing with just intonation (tuning based on the frequency ratios of intervals from the overtone series) has much useful information on vertical tuning in a cappella choral music, explanations on the need to adjust the tuning of some basic structural intervals depending on their tonal contexts and many exercises for matching vowels, tuning and creating a unified choral sound. But at the heart of Kardos' philosophy (and in many respects the Hungarian approach to group singing) looms the inevitable question of what kind of vocal sound is most conducive to achieving an excellent choral tone and vertical tuning based on just intonation. Although never spelled out explicitly, the constant implication is that singing with a straight tone (or with an absolutely minimal vibrato) is imperative to achieve excellent intonation in a choral setting, because only then is it possible to listen for the beating of harmonics within the vertical structures and make the necessary, subtle adjustments.

The research of Perry Cook[3] actually corroborates the notion that singers not using vibrato can hear better and more easily adjust the intonation of their voices. However, the research of Douglas Keislar[4] finds ample evidence in research literature to contradict Helmholtz's claim that just intonation sounds more in tune and that equal temperament sounds more out of tune. In one study from 1983, Roberts and Matthews found that when asked to state a preference between chords of just intonation and chords of various other temperaments, some people preferred the 'richness' of various tempered systems, while others preferred the 'purity' of just intonation.[5] Thus, the 'beating' in an interval or chord, which to some sounds as roughness or dissonance, actually sounds richer and better to others. Keislar summarizes a few interesting points culled from his exhaustive analysis of acoustical research up to 1990:

1) In performance, a given interval can take on a fairly wide range of sizes and still be heard in tune.

2) In performance, smaller intervals tend to be compressed, while larger ones tend to be stretched relative to equal temperament.

3) Generally, people do not perform in just intonation, nor do they prefer just intervals. It is not known to what extent this is a result of exposure to equal temperament.[6]

Clearly, there is a basis in research that proves singing without vibrato enhances the singers' ability to make subtle adjustments towards just intonation, but the concept of singing without vibrato also implies the acceptance of certain tonal and vocal qualities which a great many people find unacceptable based on common vocal practices, the age of the singers, the compositional style of the music, historical performance practice issues and personal taste. Striving to achieve pure or just intonation in certain situations can be a useful exercise for maintaining the intonational integrity of a work, focusing choral singers on the sound of vertical sonorities and subtle aspects of tuning, but like anything else this approach has its limitations. Most acoustical researchers agree that singing in just intonation on a scientifically consistent basis is an impossibility. The work of Vos and Vianen has proven that the ability to discriminate various frequency ratios diminishes as the ratios become more complex.[7] Attempts at just intonation (when based on simpler frequency ratios) can have value within certain stylistic and vocal parameters, but propagating the idea of a consistently achievable just intonation—particularly across a number of historic styles and periods—has no basis in reality.

Taken to the extreme, proponents of 'pure' intonation usually focus attention primarily on achieving just intonation and the tuning of vertical sonorities. This singular focus on tuning vertical sonorities, in conjunction with an insistence on singing without vibrato (or with very minimal vibrato), may allow certain vertical structures to approach 'pure' intonation, but can cause a number of problems. These can include undue tightness, strain or damage to the voice, a strained individual tone quality, an overall group tone quality which is strident—particularly in musical situations involving extremes of tessitura and dynamics—an inadvertent emphasis on note-to-note singing and a tone quality not appropriate for certain styles of music. This approach invariably implies the acceptance of certain tonal qualities across a broad stylistic and historical spectrum. Encouraging a style of singing with no vibrato flies in the face of almost every 'school' of voice teaching and raises important issues relating to healthy vocal development at different stages of life, historical performance practice and acoustical research in the latter half of the twentieth-century.

The yin-yang philosophy from Chinese cosmology teaches that finding balance usually leads to a healthier approach. Singing with good intonation in the voice studio, on the concert stage, in the music education classroom or in the choral rehearsal is more completely achieved through a holistic approach which views the development of musical imagination, aural perception, inner hearing, a knowledge of the physiology of the voice, the physical coordination among the vocal muscles as well as a knowledge of style and theory as integral parts of the same technique. Should the vocal tone of motets by Josquin, Bach and Brahms sound the same? Should there be a difference in timbre between a motet by Palestrina and an a cappella setting by Samuel Barber? Should a large forte chord in a Bruckner motet be sung with little or no vibrato? Should the final pianissimo chord of a Lassus motet be alive with a rich vibrato? Although singing in tune in its pure essence is supposed to be a natural (and thus simple) process, simplistic solutions, dogmatic attitudes and one-sided approaches rarely lead to satisfactory results across a broader area; or they lead to very good results within a narrower technical or stylistic rubric. The age of the singers, the historical period, the compositional style of the music, the tessitura, the range, the degree of dynamic flexibility all need to be considered when deciding on a tonal and vocal approach for a specific piece of music. In other words, the tone, style and vocal approach are supposed to be derived from the music, rather than having the music made subservient to preconceived ideas of tone, an uninformed concept of style and a preferred vocal approach.

Each stylistic period of music has certain tonal, aesthetic, intonational and compositional characteristics. Within these stylistic periods and styles, one can find moments in any choral work in which the musical substance and tonal rubric emphasizes either the linear aspects of a piece or its vertical aspects. There is always a needed tension in a given work between the vertical and linear momentum and tonal integrity. It is important for the conductor, through careful analysis and introspection, to decide at any given moment of the piece WHICH aspect of the tonal structure is important. A single-minded emphasis on vertical integrity through absolute tonal purity and striving for just intonation is a very good idea, but only if the stylistic and aesthetic needs of the piece demand it. A single-minded emphasis on linear singing and the 'flowering' of the voice through proven private vocal studio techniques is a very good idea, but only if the stylistic and aesthetic needs of the music demand it. Extreme positions emphasizing exclusively the vertical or linear aspects of a piece usually result in glaring faults

172

because they often ignore the musical context. The wise conductor is one who seeks balance, utilizes a wide range of vocal techniques and determines whether the music at any given moment needs help vertically or linearly. In essence, the music should ALWAYS determine the choral sound and tone.

One of Kodály's most famous maxims is an inspiring call for musicians to be balanced: The good musician must have a well-trained ear, a well-trained mind, a well-trained heart and a well-trained hand.

A well-trained hand signifies the physical side of the musical discipline—the physical gestures of a conductor, the movements of a pianist over the keyboard, the coordination of bow with fingers, etc.—working in unity with ear, mind and heart. For Kodály-inspired and Kodály-trained vocal music educators and choral conductors, the well-trained hand must also include a striving to achieve mastery of the vocal apparatus—the physical discipline of singing working in unity with ear, mind and heart. To achieve balance in our work with voices, whether in the classroom or the choral arena, it is imperative that we adopt an approach which seeks solutions not only in the realm of the ear, mind and heart, but in the realm of the voice.

A vocal music teacher or choral conductor by definition is someone who should be knowledgeable about voice production, yet it is surprising how many music educators and choral directors feel a lack of confidence when it comes to singing and dealing with vocal problems—particularly in the Kodály movement. Lack of knowledge of vocal technique is a constant and frustrating impediment to singing with good intonation, no matter how well trained one's ear may be. (A passage may be sung in tune, but its quality and beauty of tone may be missing.) Likewise, traditional studio vocal training without the incorporation of conscious aural skills as part of the technique can be a nebulous process which does not guarantee good intonation. (The tone may be free and gorgeous for certain types of music, but possibly inflexible and filled with numerous intonational blemishes and unattended details.)

When working in the classroom or choral arena, educators need to develop the ability to analyze the causes of out-of-tune singing, giving consideration to the fact that the solution may be a problem within any one of the four areas mentioned above: heart, mind, ear or hand (or a combination of deficiencies in more than one area—ear and voice.) By elevating the importance of vocal training as an integral part of Kodály-inspired music education, we can improve greatly the effectiveness of our vocal work and heed Kodály's call for a balanced approach to music education that challenges, engages and inspires the whole person.

Notes

[1] Hermann Helmholtz, *On the Sensations of Tone* (New York: Dover Publications, 1954).

[2] Pál Kardos, *Kórusnevelés-kórushangzás* (Budapest: Zeneműkiadó, 1977).

[3] Perry Cook, *Identification of Control Parameters in an Articulatory Vocal Tract Model, with Applications to the Synthesis of Singing* (Stanford: Stanford University, 1991).

[4] Douglas Keislar, *Psychoacoustic Factors in Musical Intonation: Beats, Intervals Tuning, and Inharmonicity* (Stanford: Stanford University, 1991).

[5] Linda Roberts and Max Mathews, "Intonation Sensitivity for Traditional and Nontraditional Chords," *Journal of the Acoustical Society of America* 75, no. 3 (March 1984): 952-959.

[6] Those who espouse the attempt to sing with just intonation base most of their arguments on the fact that people are so steeped in the equal temperament of pianos that they have never learned to hear or appreciate the purity of just intonation.

[7] Joos Vos and Ben G. van Vianen, "Thresholds for Discrimination between Pure and Tempered Intervals: The Relevance of Nearly Coinciding Harmonics," *Journal of the Acoustical Society of America* 77, no. 1 (1985): 176-187.

Originally published in *Bulletin of the International Kodály Society* 23, no. 2 (1998): 21-25. Reprinted by permission.

TEACHING STUDENTS TO HEAR, SING, PLAY, IDENTIFY AND ENJOY THE MODES

Georgia A. Newlin

Introduction

Many students studying music, whether in high school, undergraduate courses, or music education programs, are introduced to the diatonic modes through learning that by using all white keys on the piano, the Ionian mode is C-C, Dorian D-D, Phrygian E-E, Lydian F-F, Mixolydian G-G, Æolian A-A, and Locrian B-B. While this might serve students in the short run for passing written music theory tests, many students do not have the ability to personally transfer this theoretical construct to further their functional aural skills as educated musicians. If instructors wish to be particularly careful about teaching the diatonic modes in a beneficial way to those new to modal theory, it is important to seek out beautiful examples of music in the art, folk, and pop genres as well as to sequence lessons exploring the theoretical concepts and aural relationships of the diatonic modes for their students' understanding.

The purpose of this article is to offer practical teaching suggestions that allow students to be able to hear, sing, play, and identify music in various diatonic modes. The tools used with this teaching/learning model include Bertrand H. Bronson's mode-star;[1] multiple musical examples (many of which are complete pieces as opposed to the small excerpts that are generally found in music theory or sight-singing textbooks) from a number of genres; and related aural skills activities. Stacey Davis, writing to music theory professors about including authentic musical experiences in their teaching, says "perspectives as musicians and pedagogues must be combined with principles of perception, cognition, and skill development. Methods of presentation and instructions to students could also better mimic typical musical situations."[2] These complete pieces of music used in conjunction with Bronson's mode-star (a seven-pointed star used as a graphic representation of the relationships between pentatonic and hexatonic scales and diatonic modes based on Cecil Sharp's modal theory[3]) have consistently helped my high school and undergraduate students to better understand modes and my graduate students to discern relationships among folk-song variants. Thus, this combination of using time-honored tools with authentic music examples from many genres suits the needs of contemporary music educators.

Sequencing the Diatonic Modes

I have used this sequence with high school students in a literacy-based children's chorus, with undergraduate music majors and minors in aural skills courses, and with graduate students in Kodály teacher-training programs. Below are the specifics for teaching individual modes, including linking them to their related pentatonic and hexatonic scales, and ways to help students learn to recognize them in their comparative modes (singing in diatonic major or minor with solfège alterations). Additionally, I introduce hypo-modes and address combinations of modes either through individual tunes set in multiple modes or through mixed modes appearing in a single composition.

Cecil Sharp set out his use of mode theory for categorizing English folk songs in 1907 in *English Folk Songs: Some Conclusions*, using the conventional names of the ancient modes to classify scales. These names were used to describe diatonic modes and to assist in the elementary differentiation of tunes that Sharp had collected in Southwest England.[4] Bronson, building upon Sharp's modal theory, created his seven-point mode-star.[5] (See fig. 1). This graphic display delineates the relationship between the seven diatonic modes and their related pentatonic and hexatonic scales. On the outer points of the seven stars, modes are labeled with the first letter of the name of the mode (in capitals); pentatonic scales are labeled with the Greek letter *pi* (π), numbered individually on the innermost section of the mode-star; and hexatonic scales, falling between modes and pentatonic scales, are labeled with the first letter of the two adjacent modes (again, in capitals). This mode-star is a visual tool that helps bring about an elemental understanding of modes and can be to be used as a springboard towards depth of analysis and understanding of diatonic modes.

[Figure 1. Bronson Mode-Star. From *The Ballad as Song* by Bertrand H. Bronson. Used by permission of University of California Press, copyright ©1970]

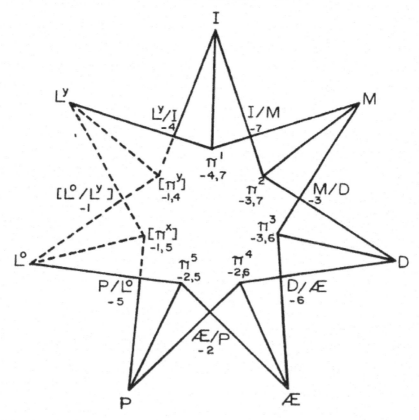

Start the process by reviewing pentatonic scales (using movable do/relative la solfège). First, students sing all of the pentatonic scales from the same starting pitch, such as B3 used as the tonal center (middle C = C4, therefore B3 is a half step below middle c; see fig. 2).

[Figure 2. Pentatonic Scales.]

d'	s'	r'	l'	m'
		d	s	r
l	m			
				d
s	r	l	m	
	d	s	r	l
m				
			d	s
r	l	m		
d	s	r	l	m
π1	π2	π3	π4	π5

Students then describe the relationships between those pentatonic scales. It is important for them to notice that they are not sung in order of *do, re, mi, sol, la* but in the relationship of perfect fifths. The students identify that the pentatonic scales are comparable in fifths because, like the circle of fifths with the diatonic scales, only one change (of absolute pitch) is made between any two adjacent scales. For example: do pentatonic (π1) becomes the absolute names of C D E G A C' and sol pentatonic (π2) becomes the absolute names of C D F G A C'. If half of the class sings do pentatonic (π1) at the same time that the other half of the class sings sol pentatonic (π2), the class sings in unison except at the interval disparity between E (π1) and F (π2)—the students sing all of the pentatonic scales adjacently in two parts to aurally discover differences and similarities.

To introduce the diatonic modes from here, the students sing many songs in each mode. Afterwards, the students create a chart (using graph paper) of diatonic modes in order to solidify their understanding of each mode as well as the relationships among them. Additionally, the use of Bronson's mode-star is helpful for visual learners to connect their eyes with their ears.

Ionian

Students sing and practice the songs in the Ionian Mode (see fig. 3, at end of article). To warm up their voices and ears, start by singing the Ionian mode in four-part canon (each note receives one beat, beginning every two beats without repeating the top note): *d r m f s l t d' t l s f m r d*. The traditional four-part canon "The Swan" (fig. 4) is used as an anchor song throughout the sequence because it can be sung in all of the modes (each new entrance starts one measure after the last).

[Figure 4. "The Swan" in Ionian.]

Sweet-ly the swan sings: "Du - dee-ah- du,   Du - dee-ah- du,   Du - dee-ah- du."

After singing many Ionian tunes in solfège by ear and from notation, students create a chart using graph paper with each block representing a half step (see fig. 5).

[Figure 5. Ionian mode]

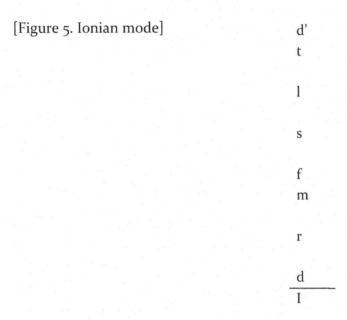

In addition, the students study Bronson's mode-star by writing the complete name Ionian at the "I" near the top of the star and by observing that when they follow the solid line from I to π^1 and subtract the fourth and seventh degrees of the mode (-4,7), as indicated, they arrive at the do pentatonic scale (π^1), a five-note subset of the seven-note mode. The students then sing the do pentatonic scale and the Ionian mode alternately to solidify the aural sound and vocal feeling of each.

A folk tune in the Ionian mode was creatively harmonized by Béla Bartók: *Three Rondos on Folk Tunes, No. 1*. Students can sing the melody as they accompany themselves with the harmonization on the piano.

At this point, it is important that students understand that the Ionian mode is not the same as diatonic major. The Ionian mode was derived from people improvising and singing tunes by combining two or more melodies made up of tetra- or hexachords. Later, the theoretical term "Ionian" was added to the resultant set of intervals that made up that mode. The Ionian mode comes from music that was generally monophonic or polyphonic so the melodies were often conceived in stepwise patterns. In contrast, diatonic major came into being over a period of time and was solidified by J.S. Bach,[6] after which composers specifically wrote within that paradigm. Composing in diatonic major is based on the tonic, dominant and subdominant harmonic functions, so the melody often outlines the chords related to those functions.

Mixolydian

Students warm up by singing the Mixolydian mode in unison and then in four-part canon (*s l t d r m f s' f m r d t l s*). Then they can sing and explore a number of Mixolydian tunes using sol as the tonal center (see fig. 3). Also they should sing "The Swan" in unison followed by singing it in four-part canon in Mixolydian (see fig. 6).

[Figure 6. "The Swan" in Mixolydian.]

Sweet-ly the swan sings: "Du-dee-ah-du, Du-dee-ah-du, Du-dee-ah-du."

The students again study Bronson's mode-star by adding the complete name of Mixolydian to the star at M and by observing that when they follow the solid line from M towards the center of the star, then subtract the third and seventh degrees of the mode (-3,7), the result is the sol pentatonic scale (π^2). Again, alternating solfège singing between the pentatonic and the mode helps solidify the notes in each.

Students update their charts (see fig. 7). To compare the first two modes, half of the class sings the Ionian mode and the other half of the class sings the Mixolydian mode at the same time from the same starting pitch. Students derive that the absolute pitches are all the same except for between the sixth and the seventh scale degrees: *la–ti* (Ionian) is a whole step while *mi–fa* (Mixolydian) is a half step. The difference between these two notes at the seventh scale degree is called the interval differential (or disparity) between the two modes (reading the chart from left to right at the seventh scale degree).

[Figure 7. Mixolydian mode.]

d'	s'
t	
	f
l	m
s	r
f	d
m	t
r	l
d	s
I	M

179

Interestingly, in bluegrass music, a common cadential pattern for Mixolydian tunes is VII–I. So, with a tune like "Old Joe Clark,"[7] the class can vocally harmonize the entire piece with VII (*fa la do*) and I (*sol ti re*) chords. They can then go on to improvise new melodies using solfège while playing the same Mixolydian harmonic progression on the piano:

refrain:

```
2/4    I   I    | I   I   | I   I  |VII VII |
       I   I    | I   I   | I  VII | I   I  |
verse:
       I  VII  | I   I   | I  VII | I   I  |
       I  VII  | I   I   | I  VII | I   I  |
```

In addition, students could sing the melody in solfège to other Appalachian fiddle tunes and improvise the Mixolydian accompaniment on piano: "Ducks on the Pond" or "June Apple."[8]

In comparison to bluegrass harmonies, during the verse of the Lennon-McCartney's song, "We Can Work It Out," instead of moving between the I and V[7] chords, as would be expected in pop music, the dominant chord is not used until the eighth measure of the section. Instead, McCartney uses the VII chord—produced by lowering the seventh degree a half step—giving a Mixolydian feel to the verses.

Another interesting Mixolydian tone set appears in a four-measure segment of the melody of the Beatles' "Norwegian Wood": *s, l, ta, d r mf s l*—this tone set (in the comparative mode) is created according to Lennon-McCartney's EM key signature. Reading comparative modes is covered later in the sequence so the students come back to this tune once they are understood.

Dorian

Dorian tunes can be quite beautiful, and some are usually familiar to students. Again, students first sing the mode in unison and then in four-part canon (*r m f s l t d r' d t l s f m r*). Students should sing a variety of tunes in Dorian (see fig. 3), including "The Swan," now sung in unison, then in four-part canon in solfège (see fig. 8).

[Figure 8. "The Swan" in Dorian.]

Sweet - ly the swan sings: "Du - dee - ah - du,   Du - dee - ah - du,   Du - dee - ah - du."

Students add the solfège of the Dorian mode to their graph paper charts. The comparison between Mixolydian and Dorian reveals that the interval differential now rests at the third degree of each of these two modes (see fig. 9).

[Figure 9. Dorian mode.]

```
d'        s'        r'
t
          f         d
l         m         t

s         r         l

f         d         s
m         t
                    f
r         l         m

d         s         r
_____
I         M         D
```

A number of composers use the Dorian mode in their instrumental compositions, for example: *Third Piano Concerto, III*; *Fifteen Hungarian Peasant Songs*, No. 8; *Mikrokosmos, Vol. I*, Nos. 14, 22, and 23, all by Béla Bartók. The English folksong "Lovely Joan" is used in *Fantasia on a Theme by Thomas Tallis* by Ralph Vaughan Williams. The medieval song "Personent Hodie" is beautifully arranged for piano by Gustav Holst.

Students now study Bronson's mode-star by adding the complete name of Dorian to the star at D and by observing that when they follow the solid line from D to π^3, then subtract the third and sixth degrees of the mode (-3,6), they find the re pentatonic scale.

Similar to Mixolydian, in bluegrass music a common cadential pattern for Dorian tunes is VII–i, so these folk songs can often be harmonized by singing VII (*do mi sol*) and i (*re fa la*). Fiddle tunes such as "28th of January," "Cluck Old Hen," "Kitchen Girl" and "Salt River" can be sung in solfège and accompanied on piano or guitar.[9] When comparing the chord qualities between the two modes students find that Mixolydian uses two major chords for the dominant (VII) and tonic (I) functions while Dorian uses a major dominant (VII) but a minor tonic (i).

Æolian

Like Ionian and the diatonic major, Æolian should not be confused with diatonic minor, as its melodies are usually stepwise while diatonic minor tunes generally outline chords associated with harmonic progressions. Sing and study some tunes in Æolian (see fig. 3) after singing the mode in canon (*l t d r m f s l' s f m r d t l*) followed by "The Swan" in Æolian (see fig. 10).

[Figure 10. "The Swan" in Æolian.]

Sweet - ly the swan sings: "Du - dee-ah- du, Du - dee-ah- du, Du - dee-ah- du."

Students again sing the adjacent modes at the same time by dividing the class in half in order to find the interval differential between the two, this time at the sixth step between Dorian and Æolian (see fig. 11). This often helps clarify the tuning of each of the two compared modes, as does alternate singing of each pentatonic scale and its corresponding mode.

	d'	s'	r'	l'
[Figure 11. Æolian mode.]	t			
		f	d	s
	l	m	t	
				f
	s	r	l	m
	f	d	s	r
	m	t		
			f	d
	r	l	m	t
	d	s	r	l
	I	M	D	Æ

While once again looking at the mode-star students add the complete name of Æolian to the star at the Æ and observe that when they follow the solid line from Æ to π^4, then subtract the second and sixth degrees of the mode (-2,6), they find the la pentatonic scale. In addition, it is time to direct students to look at a different connection made on the mode-star previously passed over.

Hexatonic Scales – A Relationship Between Modes

Between the modes there are lines connected to a dot that is further out of the star than the pentatonic scales, yet closer in to the center of the star than the diatonic modes; these are hexatonic scales. Pentatonic scales contain five notes, modes contain seven notes, and hexatonic scales contain six notes, hence the placement within the relationship of the dots on the mode-star. For example, when students follow the separate lines from Æ and D to D/Æ they find -6. If students look at the charts they are creating, they will see that if the sixth scale degree is subtracted (ti from Dorian and fa from Æolian) the absolute pitches of the two hexachords are exactly the same although the solfège is different:

	C	D	Eb	F	G	-	Bb	C'
Dorian	r	m	f	s	l	(-t)	d	r'
Æolian	l	t	d	r	m	(-f)	s	l'

Because the interval differential is missing between the Dorian and Æolian modes, there is not necessarily a way to determine which hexatonic scale should belong to the tune. Students need to understand that just because a book editor assigned a specific key signature to a hexatonic folk song, that signature does not definitively mean the hexatonic scale comes from the implied mode; rather the choice of key signature most often aligns with the easiest guitar or piano chords used to accompany the song. For example, "Joy in the Gates of Jerusalem"[10] is a hexatonic tune, so by using a key signature of F major the tune can be sung as G = *re* (re hexatonic) but by using a key signature of Bb major the tune can be sung as G = *la* (la hexatonic).

According to Bronson, hexatonic scales are not actually incomplete modes but scales unto themselves, since there is no definite way to determine which tonal center is "correct" when attempting to consign a hexatonic scale in relation to a specific mode. Interestingly, however, the origins of the folksongs can be used to determine a more authentic choice of tonal center for hexatonic tunes (a discussion beyond the scope of this article).

Students can now review the mode-star, identifying all of the hexatonic relationships previously unaddressed. (The hexatonic relationships on the mode-star are purposefully taught later in this sequence. Until students can sing, play, and comprehend these first four modes well enough to be comfortable moving among modes, they can easily become confused in moving between them). There are beautiful hexatonic tunes that fall between Dorian and Æolian, and between Æolian and Phrygian (see fig. 3).

With only a five-note scale, *Classical Canons* #21 is a pentachordal tune (missing both the sixth and seventh scale degrees) so with the written key signature of Eb major the tune can be sung as C = *la* (la pentachord) or with a key signature of Bb major the tune can be sung as C = *re* (re pentachord). A pentachordal canon, "Da Pacem Domine" by Melchior Franck,[11] is sung by entrances 1 and 3 using the do pentachord (*d r m f s*) and by entrances 2 and 4 using the sol pentachord (*s, l, t, d r*). Students discover that the intervals between of the notes of both pentachords create the same whole step/half step pattern: *d-r/s-l* (major second), *r-m/l-t* (major second), *m-f/t-d'* (minor second), *f-s/d-r* (major second). Later in the sequence, students will come to understand that when the notes of the entire canon are combined (*s, l, t, d r m f s*), they create the Hypoionian mode.

A Return to the Modes
Phrygian

Have students sing in the Phrygian mode. Again, students warm up by singing the mode in canon (*m f s l t d r m' r d t l s f m*), then "The Swan," now in Phrygian (see fig. 12), followed by numerous songs in this distinctive mode.

[Figure 12. "The Swan" in Phrygian.]

Sweet - ly the swan sings: "Du - dee - ah - du, Du - dee - ah - du, Du - dee - ah - du."

Because of the sequential redundancy in learning the modes, as well as numerical patterns produced by modes compared at the interval of the fifth, students are generally able to figure out the steps where the interval disparity occurs between the Æolian and Phrygian modes (as well as anticipating the rest of the pattern) before having to write out their charts. Students know that the interval disparity between I and M is the seventh degree, between M and D is the third degree, and between D and Æ is the sixth degree so, by having class members write a chart on the board—and without having to consult the mode-star—students figure out that the next number in the mathematical problem (the interval disparity between Æ and P) is the second degree (see fig. 13):

Ionian-Mixolydian = degree 7
Mixolydian-Dorian = degree 3
Dorian- Æolian = degree 6
Æolian-phrygian = degree 2
Phrygian-Locrian = degree 5
Locrian-Lydian = degree 1
Lydian-Ionian = degree 4

[Figure 13. Phrygian mode.]

	d'	s'	r'	l'	m'
	t				
		f	d	s	r
	l	m	t		
				f	d
	s	r	l	m	t
	f	d	s	r	l
	m	t			
			f	d	s
	r	l	m	t	
					f
	d	s	r	l	m
	I	M	D	Æ	P

A beautiful instrumental example is Debussy's *String Quartet, Op. 10*, 1st movement, with Phrygian turns in the melody. A pop music example is Britney Spears "If U Seek Amy"—the melodic outline of the hook is the descending line of *m' r d t l s f m*. Loreena McKennett's "Beneath the Phrygian Sky" comes from the pop-folk fusion genre.

When studying Bronson's mode-star, students add the name of Phrygian to the star at the P. By this time, they generally understand the relationship between each mode and its pentatonic scale so, without first having to consult the mode-star, they are able to discuss that the second and fifth degrees of the mode (-2,5) should be subtracted from P in order to arrive at the mi pentatonic scale (π^5).

Locrian

Locrian is a hypothetical mode used in a theoretical manner in order to complete the cycle of fifths between the modes. Students can sing "The Swan" in four-part canon in this mode (*t d r m f s l t' l s f m r d t*) but may need the help of a constant drone playing the tonal center when first beginning the skill (see fig. 14).

[Figure 14. "The Swan" in Locrian.]

Sweet - ly the swan sings: "Du - dee-ah- du,   Du - dee-ah- du,   Du - dee-ah- du."

Students will continue the diatonic mode chart by adding the Locrian mode (see fig. 15) and then compare the sound to the Phrygian mode.

[Figure 15. Locrian mode.]

I	M	D	Æ	P	Lo
d'	s'	r'	l'	m'	t'
t					
	f	d	s	r	l
l	m	t			
			f	d	s
s	r	l	m	t	
					f
f	d	s	r	l	m
m	t				
		f	d	s	r
r	l	m	t		
				f	d
d	s	r	l	m	t
I	M	D	Æ	P	Lo

Looking at the mode-star students will notice that most of the Locrian connections are drawn with dotted lines rather than solid lines. This is because there are few spontaneously occurring folk tunes using hexatonic scales built on *ti*. The pentatonic is marked with an x because it is not real.

When students do an internet search for the Locrian mode (in order to disprove the above paragraph) they will find that many heavy metal tunes are listed as Locrian. The reality is that the bands play in a major key signature but use the vii° chord or the seventh scale degree as a drone (thus producing the angst needed for this type of music) but many end up with a vii° to I cadence or simply fade out—most of the melodies and harmonic progressions are not actually built in the Locrian mode.

Interestingly, Crowe's *Folk Song Sight Singing Series* includes one (Polish) folksong in the Locrian mode within the entire ten-volume collection.[12] Fortunately, a few composers did write instrumental music in the Locrian mode, such as Bartók's *Mikrokosmos II*, no. 63, and Górecki's *Symphony No. 3, Op. 36* (cello, second part in F# Locrian) which the students can sing by reading the scores.

Lydian

Sing "The Swan" in canon, but now in Lydian (see fig. 16), as well as warming up with the Lydian mode in 4-part canon (*f s l t d r m f' m r d t l s f*) helping tune the students' ears for this intriguing mode. Continue teaching this mode by having students sing songs in Lydian (see fig. 3).

[Figure 16. "The Swan" in Lydian.]

Instrumental music examples include Debussy's *String Quartet, Op. 10*, 1st movement (mm 1-3) and Bartók's *Music for Strings, Percussion & Celesta*, 4th movement (mm 5-9); *Three Rondos on Folk Tunes, III*; *Mikrokosmos*, vol. I, no. 24; and *Mikrokosmos*, vol. II, nos. 37 and 55. "Sacred Song in the Lydian Mode" is used by Beethoven in *String Quartet No. 15, Op. 132*. This is an example of a modal tune being harmonized within the constructs of the mode itself but, to move out of the Lydian section, the harmonization continues on within the constraints of diatonicism.

Again, while looking at the mode-star, students will notice that most of the connections for Lydian are drawn with dotted lines rather than solid lines, mainly because *fa* is not used as a root for a pentatonic scale. Entertainingly though, when students are asked to create a hypothetical pentatonic scale based on *fa*, they discover that it creates the same melodic intervals as the do pentatonic scale:

C   D   E   G   A
d   *r*   *m*   *s*   *l*
f   *s*   *l*   *d*   *r*

Often, this exercise generates heated discussion as to whether or not the fa pentatonic scale could actually exist since no half-steps are created by this arrangement of notes.

While completing their mode charts (see fig. 17), students notice that the relationship between Locrian and Lydian is different than that of the other adjacent modes. It is because the interval between *ti* and *fa* is a diminished fifth rather than a perfect fifth. Students can be led to realize that if they move the Lydian mode to the front of the Ionian mode where the perfect fifth relationship can be maintained, the cycle of fifths actually begins with the Lydian mode.

[Figure 17. Lydian mode.]

f'	d'	s'	r'	l'	m'	t'	f
m	t						m
		f	d	s	r	l	
r	l	m	t				r
				f	d	s	
d	s	r	l	m	t		d
t						f	t
	f	d	s	r	l	m	
l	m	t					l
			f	d	s	r	
s	r	l	m	t			s
					f	d	
f	d	s	r	l	m	t	f
Ly	I	M	D	Æ	P	Lo	

Understanding Intervallic Connections Using the Mode-Star

Students can discover that when they subtract the scale degree numbers from the mode to find the corresponding pentatonic scale, the notes removed are always *fa* and *ti*. In addition, the scale degree number they subtract between each two adjacent modes to find the hexatonic scale always results in taking *ti* from the first mode and *fa* from the second; the *ti* produces a major second above *la* and the *fa* produces a minor second above *mi*, thus creating the interval differential between the two modes. Often, a thoughtful student will bring up the fact that now that they have made their way through all of the modes, they have returned to the starting place—pentatonic—with greater understanding.

Individual Tunes in Multiple Modes

An excellent aural exercise to develop strong modal singing is to have students sing "The Swan" in all of the modes in succession, beginning with Lydian and ending with Locrian. Often, accompanying this exercise with a constant drone of the tonal center (D4, for example) enables the students to sing through all of the modes without stopping. Once this is accomplished, they can sing "The Swan" in four-part canon in the same way. Singing and comparing songs with multiple modes from the same absolute pitch used as the tonal center helps many students hear and feel the differences between the modes in a way that starting each mode on a different pitch (such as using the white keys on the piano) does not.

The tune "L'homme armé" can be used to discuss the use of different modes with one melody (thus providing insight into early compositional practice) by singing the tune in three different modes from the same starting pitch. First, the tune is placed on the staff using the absolute notes G A BC D EF G' A' with a key signature of C major (making G = *sol*), thereby consigning the melody to the Mixolydian mode. Next, the key signature of F major is added (making G = *re*) putting the melody in the Dorian mode. Finally, adding another flat for Bb major (making G = *la*) results in the Æolian mode. Composers frequently used this change of mode convention in Renaissance writing—especially those who had to turn out numerous weekly masses year after year.

Mixed Modes in Single Compositions

Further study of modes can include the examination of pieces that incorporate more than one mode. "Exaudi Domine"[13] is written in the key of B minor but has characteristics of both the Dorian (phrases with G#) and Æolian (phrases with G natural) modes. "Da Pacem Domine" by Melchior Franck[14] is sung in 4 parts: entrances 1 and 3 in do pentachord and entrances 2 and 4 (starting a fourth below) in the sol pentachord. [These two scales sound the same, but use different solfa names.]

"Pleni Sunt" by J.S. Bach[15] is a clever canon for four voices with entrances at the interval of a fifth. Bach uses the key signature of C major to indicate that C = *do*, but this does not reflect the reality that each voice carries the melody in its own particular mode. The canon is written with the basses entering first on C (*do re mi fa sol*), followed by the tenors on G (*sol la ti do re*), the altos on D (*re mi fa sol la*), and finally the sopranos on A (*la ti do re mi*). Students derive that the dominant of each mode becomes the tonic of the following mode: Ionian (*d-s*)—Mixolydian (*s-r*) —Dorian (*r-l*) —Æolian (*l-m*).

Similarly, "Oh, Threats of Hell" by Paul Hindemith[16] is a modern canon for four voices in the style of Bach, also with each part sung in a different mode: sopranos begin in Ionian, altos follow in Lydian, mezzo-sopranos thereafter in Æolian, and tenors enter last in Dorian.

The first movement of Henryk Górecki's *Symphony No. 3*, Op. 36 ("Symphony of Sorrowful Songs") opens with a 24-measure theme in E Æolian. The canon begins in two parts, and eventually leads to the canon in eight parts. It begins with the second part of the double basses playing in the Æolian mode, with each succeeding entry occurring one measure into the repeat of the theme, each starting a diatonic fifth above the last. This way, each appearance of the melody in a new instrumental part is in a different mode, in this order:

E Æolian – double basses, 2nd part

B Phrygian – double basses, 1st part

F# Locrian – cellos, 2nd part

C Lydian – cellos, 1st part

G Ionian – violas, 2nd part

D Mixolydian – violas, 1st part

A Dorian – violins II, 2nd part

E Æolian – violins I, 2nd part

The eight-part canon repeats with the 1st parts of violins I and II doubling an octave higher. The voices gradually drop out one by one, from lowest to highest, with all of the strings except double basses ending on a single note of E4.

Having students sing each occurrence of the melody in solfège in the various modes from this gorgeous piece can demonstrate their musical understanding of the diatonic modes. This opening section of the first movement lasts for around fifteen minutes and is featured during the airplane crash sequence in the 1993 film *Fearless*, starring Jeff Bridges.

A familiar pop music example that moves between modes is "Eleanor Rigby," by Paul McCartney. The opening four measures of the verse are written in natural minor with a raised 6th scale degree (Dorian) interspersed with two measures of natural minor (McCartney does not use the raised seventh degree to produce diatonic harmonic minor), followed by three measures of Dorian, and concludes with one measure of natural minor that then carries through the "All the lonely people" refrain.

Hypo-Modes – A Shift of the Tonal Center Placement

Classical Canons #6[17] is the "Benedictus" of Josquin Des Prés' *Missa L'homme armé*. Part I is in Æolian, part II is in Hypoæolian, and part III, an inversion of part I, is in Hypodorian. Students are able to discern that hypo-modes occur when the tonal center is situated at the center of the tone set rather than near the bottom. First, students sing each part individually and write out the range of that part, then mark the tonal center for each (tonal center in bold):

Part I – *l td r mf s sil' t'd'* = Æolian

Part II – *r mf s l td r' m'f* = Hypoæolian

Part III – *l, t,d,di,r mf s l td* = Hypodorian.

Students then sing and derive other hypo-modes such as the Hypoionian mode in *Classical Canons #17.*

Comparative Modes

The final element of learning diatonic modes is the understanding of the comparative modes. Many current publishers will not print tunes in actual modal key signatures (using a G major key signature to signify D Mixolydian, for example) but will publish in a diatonic major/minor key signature and consistently add accidentals to the tune (such as using a D

189

major key signature with every C sharp marked as C natural for D Mixolydian). The first step in moving beyond current notational confinements of published music is for the students to derive the quality of the tonic chord of each diatonic mode. All major tonic chords can then be related to diatonic major and all minor tonic chords can be related to diatonic minor; the diminished chord (of Locrian) does not have a comparative diatonic scale. Students derive the solfège alterations (underlined in fig. 18) of each mode's comparative:

[Figure 18. Quality of tonic triad of each mode: major (M), minor (m), or diminished (º).]

Ly	I	M	D	Æ	P	Lo
f' d'	d'	s' d'	r' l'	l'	m' l'	t'
m t	t					
		f ta	d s	s	r s	l
r l	l	m l	t fi			
				f	d f	s
d s	s	r s	l m	m	t m	
t fi						f
	f	d f	s r	r	l r	m
l m	m	t m				
			f d	d	s d	r
s r	r	l r	m t	t		
					f ta	d
f d	d	s d	r l	l	m l	t
Ly	I	M	D	Æ	P	Lo
M	M	M	m	m	m	º

Students perform tunes written in the comparative mode (singing with the altered tone), then in the pure diatonic mode by adding the correct key signature at the beginning of the piece. For example, in *Music for Sight Singing*[18] number 20.17 is written with the key signature of Eb major, but every Ab encountered in the tune is marked with a natural sign. Students figure out the tone set: *t, d r m fi s l t d'* and sing the melody with this solfège (the comparative mode). Looking at their charts (if needed) the students then identify that a diatonic major scale with the raised 4th degree is the Lydian mode. They can then identify that if they subtract the Ab from the key signature, the new tone set becomes: *m, f s l td r m f*, allowing them to sing with this solfège in the natural Lydian mode. Half of the class can sing in the natural mode at the same time the other half of the class sings in the comparative mode to hear and understand that they both notate the same melody. When reading multiple tunes in the way just described, students gain insight into the fact that when reading in a comparative mode it takes the addition or subtraction of one accidental in order to put the tune into the natural mode.

Conclusion

Leading students to make cognitive connections between the theoretical constructs and the aural and kinesthetic sensations of performing music in modes often increases their desire to seek out modal music on their own. This type of innate curiosity about music is often what brought them to study music in the first place and, as educators, our hope is to provide students with a conscious awareness of this facet of their lives and lead them to develop more skills that allow them to delve deeper into their passion, making them better musicians.

Students new to modal theory can truly learn and understand the diatonic modes when numerous song materials are sung in solfège and with text. Each mode is then charted (based on Sharp's mode theory) for intervallic understanding, and the relationships between modes and hexatonic and pentatonic scales are verified by studying Bronson's mode-star. When used with multiple examples of authentic, performable music (as opposed to only small excerpts) from many genres, this sequence of teaching the diatonic modes can be highly successful in equipping students with the aural and analytic tools to hear, sing, play, identify, and enjoy music in the modes. Going through this process also aids students in Kodály teacher-training programs in their work with folk songs, particularly helping to discern relationships among and between variants. This sequence helps students of any age become more informed, musical and skill-based in their relationship with modal music, bringing about more depth and breadth of musical understanding throughout their studies.

[Figure 3. Song List]

Song	Source	Composer/Notes
Ionian Mode		
Cantate Domino—Alleluia Quodlibet	Choral Public Domain Library #01499 www.cpdl.org	Herman van Torren
Ce fut en Mai	Houlahan and Tacka, p. 133	Trouvère song
"In Dulci Jubilo" from Piae Cantiones (1582)	Houlahan and Tacka, p. 137	John Mason Neale (English text, c 1853)
"Omnis Mundus" from Piae Cantiones (1582)	Houlahan and Tacka, p. 138	Jacobus Finno, compiler of original Finnish edition
Orientis Partibus	Houlahan and Tacka, p. 132	sung today as "The Friendly Beasts"
Schön und Lieblich	CPDL #01499	3-part canon
Sellinger's Round	Houlahan and Tacka, p. 136	English dance tune
Sumer Is Icumen In	Houlahan and Tacka, p. 140	4-part canon with vocal drone
Three Rondos on Folk Tunes, No. 1		Béla Bartók/ piano
Classical Canons nos. 11, 12, 15,19	Molnar, 1983	

Mixolydian Mode

Agnus Dei	Houlahan and Tacka, p. 142	Josquin Des Prés
Ducks on the Pond	Krassen, p. 33	fiddle tune
Flowers o' the Forest		Scottish folk song
June Apple	Krassen, p. 34	fiddle tune
Serve Well the Black Sow	Bolkovac, p. 36	3-part canon
Non Nobis, Domine		attributed to Thomas Morley or William Byrd
Now Robin Lend	Bolkovac, p. 43	4-part canon
Ol' Gray Goose	Boni	American folk song
Old Joe Clark	Hackett, p. 218	fiddle tune
Pietas Omnium	Bolkovac, p. 50	3-part canon
The Red Haired Boy	Peterson	fiddle tune
Classical Canons nos. 18, 24	Molnar	

Dorian Mode

28th of January	Krassen, p. 36	fiddle tune
Beatus Vir	CPDL #26103	Orlando Di Lasso
Cluck Old Hen	Krassen, p. 35	fiddle tune
Drunken Sailor		traditional Sea Shanty
Fifteen Hungarian Peasant Songs, No. 8		Béla Bartók
Greensleeves		attributed to King Henry VIII
I Must and I Will Get Married	Sharp, p. 75	American folk song
Kitchen Girl	Krassen, p. 34	fiddle tune
Lovely Joan		English folk song, used in *Fantasia on a Theme of Thomas Tallis* by R. Vaughan Williams
Mikrokosmos, vol. I, #14, 22, 23		Béla Bartók
Noël Nouvelet	Hackett, p. 274	French carol
Nun Fanget An	Virágh, p. 8	Hans Hassler
O Belinda		American Play Party
Personent hodie		arranged by Gustav Holst
Salt River	Krassen, p. 37	fiddle tune
Scarborough Fair	Hackett, p. 258	Yorkshire ballad
Third Piano Concerto, III		Béla Bartók
Verbum Domini	Bolkovac, p. 61	5-part canon (also Classical Canons no. 14)
Classical Canons nos. 1, 7, 14	Molnar	

Æolian

All the Pretty Little Horses		Black American
Fa Mi Fa Re La Mi	Bolkovac, p. 20	4-part canon
Ghost of Tom		canon
Hine Ma Tov		Israeli round, known in English as "Jubilant Song"
Joan Come Kiss Me Now	Bolkovac, p. 30	3-part canon
Lonesome John	Krassen, p. 38	fiddle tune
Musing Mine Own Self	Bolkovac, p. 39	4-part canon
O Praise the Lord	Bolkovac, p. 49	3-part canon
Salve Mater		Jean Mouton
Sing We This Roundelay	Bolkovac, p. 53	4-part canon
Toembaï		Israeli canon
Welcome, Welcome Every Guest		early American 3-part canon
Classical Canons nos. 16, 17	Molnar	

Phrygian

A Csitári Hegyek Alatt		Hungarian canon
Beaux Yeux		French-Canadian canon
Beneath the Phrygian Sky		Loreena McKennett
"Benedictus" from Missa Sine Nomine, XVII		Josquin Des Prés
Benji No. 2 (Benji Met a Bear)	Weber, p. 23	Pat Shaw
Hey, Ho! Nobody Home	Hackett, p. 120	Thomas Ravenscroft
If U Seek Amy		Britney Spears (melodic hook)
Lady Margot & Love Henry	Niles, #27	John Jacob Niles
Pange Lingua	Houlahan, p. 135	Medieval Latin hymn
String Quartet, Op 10, 1st movement		Claude Debussy (Phrygian turns in the melody)
Tu Pauperum Refugium		Josquin Des Prés
Classical Canons nos. 2, 10	Molnar	

Locrian

Mikrokosmos, vol. II, no. 63		Béla Bartók
Polish folksong	Crowe, #36	
Symphony No. 3, Op. 36		Henryk Górecki/ cello, 2nd part in F# Locrian

Lydian

Alles Wat Adem Heeft	CPDL #01499	
Black is the Color	Hackett, p. 30	there are many versions in different modes
Mikrokosmos, vol. I, no. 24		Béla Bartók
Mikrokosmos, vol. II, nos. 37 and 55		Béla Bartók
Music for Strings, Percussion & Celesta, 4th movement (mm 5-9)		Béla Bartók
Nightingale, The	Bolkovac, p. 41	3-part canon
String Quartet, op. 10, 1st movement (mm 1-3)		Claude Debussy
String Quartet No. 15, op. 132	contains "Sacred Song in the Lydian Mode"	Ludwig van Beethoven
Three Rondos on Folk Tunes, III		Béla Bartók
Ut Re Mi Fa Me Re Ut	Bolkovac, p. 58	4-part canon with pedal point

Individual Tunes that can be sung in Multiple Modes

The Swan		sing in all modes
L'homme armé		Mixolydian, Dorian, Æolian

Mixed Modes in Single Compositions

Da Pacem Domine	CPDL #37448	Melchior Franck/ do and sol pentachords
Eleanor Rigby		Paul McCartney/ melody moves between Dorian and Natural Minor
Exaudi Domine	Bolkovac, p. 19	Dorian/Æolian, 4-part canon
Oh, Threats of Hell	Reichenbach, 1947, p. 9	Paul Hindemith/4-part canon with melody appearing in Phrygian, Ionian, Æolian and Lydian
Pleni Sunt	Reichenbach, 1943, p. 12	J.S. Bach/ 4-part canon with melody appearing in Ionian, Mixolydian, Dorian and Æolian
Symphony No. 3, Op. 36 ("Symphony of Sorrowful Songs")		Henryk Górecki/melody appears in Æolian, Phrygian, Locrian, Lydian, Ionian, Mixolydian, and Dorian

Hypo-Modes

"Benedictus" of Missa L'homme armé (Classical Canons no. 6)	Molnar	Josquin Des Prés/ part I=Æolian part II=Hypoæolian part III=Hypodorian
Classical Canon no. 17	Molnar	Hypoionian

Hexatonic Tunes

Songs that fall between Ionian and Mixolydian		
Heirlooms	Johnston, p. 189	do hexachord or sol hexachord
Resonet in Laudibus	Johnston, p. 182	do hexachord or sol hexachord
Songs that fall between Dorian and Æolian		
Katy Cruel	Johnston, p. 227	re hexatonic or la hexatonic
Joy in the Gates of Jerusalem	Bolkovac, p. 32	re hexatonic or la hexatonic, 6-part canon
Petit Rocher	Johnston, p. 234	re hexatonic or la hexatonic
Rose, Rose		English canon, re hexatonic or la hexatonic
Songs that fall between Æolian and Phrygian		
Santiano	Johnston, p. 241	la hexatonic or mi hexatonic
Pentachordal Tunes		
Classical Canons no. 21	Molnar	re pentachord or la pentachord
Da Pacem Domine	CPDL #37448	do pentachord and sol pentachord simultaneously

Song List References

Bolkovac, Edward. *Sing We Now Merrily: A Collection of Elizabethan Rounds from Ravenscroft.* New York: Boosey & Hawkes, 2007.

Boni, Margaret B. *Fireside Book of Favorite American Songs.* New York: Simon & Schuster, 1952.

Choral Public Domain Library, http://www.cpdl.org.

Crowe, Edgar, Annie Lawton and W. Gillies Whittaker. *Folk Song Sight Singing Book,* vol. 6. London: Oxford University Press, 1934.

Hackett, Patricia. *The Melody Book: 300 Selections from the World of Music for Piano, Guitar, Autoharp, Recorder, and Voice.* Upper Saddle River, NJ: Prentice Hall, 1998.

Houlahan, Micheál, and Philip Tacka. *Sound Thinking: Music for Sight-singing and Ear Training,* vol. 2. New York, NY: Boosey & Hawkes, 1991.

Johnston, Richard. *Folk Songs North American Sings.* Toronto: G. Ricordi, 1984, 1988.

Krassen, Miles. *Appalachian Fiddle.* New York: Oak Publications, 1973.

Molnar, Anton, ed. *Classical Canons: 230 Solfeggio* (2nd ed.). Budapest: Editio Musica Budapest, 1983.

Niles, John Jacob. *The Ballad Book of John Jacob Niles.* Lexington, KY: University of Kentucky Press, 2000.

Peterson, Chris. Chris Peterson's Traditional Music, www.cpmusic.com.

Reichenbach, Herman. *Classic Canons: For 2-6 Equal or Mixed Voices.* New York: Mercury Music Corporation, 1943.

Reichenbach, Herman. *Modern Canons: 38 Contemporary Canons for 2-5 Voices.* New York: Mercury Music, 1947.

Sharp, Cecil, and Maud Karpeles. *80 Appalachian Folk Songs.* Winchester, MA: Faber and Faber., 1983.

Virágh, Gábor. *Living Harmonies: Anthology of Renaissance & Early Baroque Vocal Works.* Providence, RI: Kodály Center of America, 1998.

Weber, Sol. *Rounds Galore! Captivating Rounds, Old and New.* Astoria, NY: Astoria Press, 1994.

Wikipedia entry on "L'homme armé," retrieved March 2012 from http://en.wikipedia.org/wiki/L'homme_armé.

Wikipedia entry on "Symphony No. 3 (Górecki)," retrieved February, 2013 from http://en.wikipedia.org/wiki/Symphony_No._3_(Górecki).

Notes

[1] Bertrand H. Bronson, *The Ballad as Song* (Berkeley, CA: University of California Press, 1969).

[2] Stacey Davis, "Error Detection in the Aural Skills Class: Research and Pedagogy," *Journal of Music Theory Pedagogy* 24 (2010), 62-63.

[3] Cecil J. Sharp, *English Folk-song: Some Conclusions* (London: Novello & Co., 1907).

[4] Bertrand H. Bronson, "Are the Modes Outmoded?" *Yearbook of the International Folk Music Council* 4 (1972), 23-31.

[5] Bronson, *Ballad as Song*, 85.

[6] John S. Lawrence, "The Diatonic Scale: More Than Meets the Ear," *The Journal of Aesthetics and Art Criticism* 46, no. 2 (Winter 1987), 281-291.

[7] Patricia Hackett, *The Melody Book: 300 Selections from the World of Music for Piano, Guitar, Autoharp, Recorder, and Voice* (Upper Saddle River, NJ: Prentice Hall, 1998), 218.

[8] Miles Krassen, *Appalachian Fiddle* (New York: Oak Publications, 1973), 33-34.

[9] Krassen, *Appalachian Fiddle*, 34-37.

[10] Edward Bolkovac, *Sing We Now Merrily: A Collection of Elizabethan Rounds from Ravenscroft* (New York: Boosey & Hawkes, 2007), 32.

[11] Choral Public Domain Library #37448. Retrieved from http://www.cpdl.org.

[12] Edgar Crowe, Annie Lawton and W. Gillies Whittaker, *Folk Song Sight Singing*, vol. 6 (London: Oxford University Press, 1934), #36.

[13] Bolkovac, *Sing We Now Merrily*, 19.

[14] Choral Public Domain Library #37448.

[15] Herman Reichenbach, *Classic Canons: For 2-6 Equal or Mixed Voices* (New York: Mercury Music, 1943).

[16] Reichenbach, *Classic Canons.*

[17] Antal Molnar, ed., *Classical Canons: 230 Solfeggio*, 2nd ed. (Budapest: Editio Musica Budapest, 1983).

[18] Robert W. Ottman and Nancy Rogers, *Music for Sight Singing*, 8th ed. (Upper Saddle River, NJ: Prentice Hall, 2011), 364.

Originally published in *Kodály Envoy* 39, no. 3 (Spring 2013): 6–13. Reprinted by permission.

ZOLTÁN KODÁLY AS EDUCATOR:
THE EFFECTS OF THE KODÁLY PEDAGOGY ON TEACHER AND STUDENT

Sr. Mary Alice Hein

Introduction

In the field of music education, Kodály stands as one of the great seminal figures of our time. His life, spanning over sixty years of the twentieth century, was devoted to advocating for the central role of music in education; throughout his life, he emphasized that music is unconditionally necessary to the development of a human being. Kodály's originality is evident from the rapid spread of his educational philosophy to countries on every continent of our world. Numerous books, articles, and papers have been written on his work and influence—in English, German, Japanese, Russian, Spanish, Italian, French, Polish and Czech. Conferences, local, regional, national and international have been held. Papers and books will continue to be written, conferences will continue to be held, as we explore all of the implications of this great man's philosophy for the education of children in our various countries.

The purpose of this paper, however, is not to eulogize, however fitting that may be, but rather to look at Kodály's contribution to education in a somewhat different context, based on the type of evaluation we are now conducting in our Kodály Pilot Project in the San José Unified School District, a large urban school district in California.

Very briefly, the Kodály Pilot Project is being conducted in six selected elementary schools out of a total of thirty-seven elementary schools in the district. Essentially it is a daily music program taught by music teachers who received their Master of Music in Music Education Degree with Kodály Emphasis or the Kodály Certificate from Holy Names College. The entire project is directed by Holy Names College with consistent and regular supervision given by the college faculty. Two schools have just completed their third year of the project, while four are completing their second year. Approximately 2,000 children are receiving Kodály musical training.

The following excerpts are taken from the evaluation consultant's report.[1]

The Evaluation: Phase 1

Because the Kodály philosophy stresses specific styles and modes of teaching behavior and interaction, our first emphasis has been a qualitative rather than a quantitative approach to evaluation. The focus has been on the structure of the relationship between teachers and the students in the classroom. Central to this qualitative approach to the analysis of interaction in the classroom, and its consequent results in cognitive and emotional development, is the assumption that the structure of the teacher–student interaction provides the basic context for learning and growth of the program participants. Current literature in learning and human development emphasizes that an appreciation of the educational process is important to understand its successes and its failures. Furthermore, there is a growing awareness, based on long-standing research, that intellectual content or meaning cannot be separated from the context which makes it intelligible.[2] The apparent cross-cultural success of Kodály musical training lends itself to this type of qualitative evaluation because of the concerns for cultural preservation and child development which motivated Kodály. Essentially, the evaluation is a qualitative analysis of the educational process.

The first phase of the evaluation was conducted in the spring of 1978. Prior to this time, special attention was given to insuring that all stakeholders in the district observed the pilot project. Periodic visits were scheduled for the superintendent and the associate superintendent in charge of instruction. Principals visited the classes regularly and classroom teachers remained in the classroom during the music lesson. Special demonstrations were held for the parents, who were also encouraged to visit the music classes during the day. In addition, on-site demonstrations were held for principals and teachers of all the elementary schools in the district. This orientation of the district to the pilot project was a necessary preliminary step to the evaluation, which required that all involved in the pilot project be as informed as possible about what was actually happening in the music class.

The stage was set, so to speak, for the first phase of the evaluation, which sought to elicit the reflections and impressions of administrators, classroom teachers, parents and students. All of the principals and classroom teachers in the participating schools were interviewed in person by graduate students in the Kodály Master's program at Holy Names College. At the same time, children from each classroom were randomly selected for personal interviews. All of the interviews were conducted by the graduate students, an evaluation consultant and the evaluation director. A brief one-page questionnaire was sent home to all of the parents via the students.

The vast majority of those who were polled have very favorable impressions of the Kodály music program. Classroom teachers, principals and parents who generally do not favor special programs of this type rated the program highly. They noted its success in music learning, particularly in the reading of musical notation, improvement in singing and spontaneous class performance outside the music period. They described ways in which the program has helped children to read, write and comprehend and has assisted them in listening skills, memorization, self-discipline, self-presentation, self-esteem and improved interpersonal communication. In general, they felt that the music class seemed to help those children with weak auditory memories and those who are poor readers, and seemed to give the self-confidence needed to attempt learning activities. The principals and classroom teachers felt in particular that the attitude of cooperation and peer assistance in the program, which eliminated ridicule, greatly improved the confidence and creativity of the children. This, in turn, promoted greater and freer participation in the classroom and in school activities outside the music period. Many commented on the lack of self-consciousness which the children exhibited and their willingness to stand up and perform for others. The emphasis on individual singing appears to have a direct effect on successful recitation in the class.

The benefits of the program for emotionally handicapped students were noted by both teachers and administrators. This is especially remarkable since the program was not designed for teaching handicapped students. In addition, the apparent success of the program for the participating students who represented different ethnic and socioeconomic groups implies that its basic methods closely touch and motivate the whole person to grow and develop.

The one-page questionnaire for parents which elicited their impressions had the high percentage of 73.3% return. However, since some families had more than one child in the program and since no duplicate questionnaires were received, the return rate was in fact greater. Briefly, the more specific responses of the parents' questionnaire showed that well over 90% were aware of the Kodály program and said that their child had mentioned the class, particularly that the child was enjoying the music class. Over 90% also reported that their children sing at home. This amount of singing seems to be unusual, since many of the parents had previously and spontaneously mentioned this activity to the classroom teachers as unusual and apparently linked to the Kodály music class. Although control data are lacking in order to compare how much other students sing at home, it is evident that songs from the program are echoing through the neighborhoods. Almost 90% of the parents noted that their children demonstrate the songs at home which they have learned in school and indicated that the children have tried to teach the songs to other members of the family. This seems to reflect the deep involvement the children have with music and their self-confidence in performing.

The patterns of response in this data are most interesting. Generally, there is a high degree of parental satisfaction with the program. Parents indicate that their children are singing and enjoying music. These observations correspond with the reflections of the classroom teachers and principals about the effectiveness of the program. The response of the parents regarding the influence of the program on basic learning skills is especially interesting because substantial numbers of parents noted the beneficial effects of the program in other areas. The support of the parents for the program has been commented upon by the principals in conversations with the Kodály staff as an unusual phenomenon. In the past, both parents and classroom teachers have been openly critical of special programs which they felt did not assist the children in basic learning skills.

The children participating in the Kodály Pilot Project were in kindergarten through fourth grade. One boy and one girl from each classroom were selected at random for interviews. In the bilingual classrooms, two boys and two girls were selected randomly in order to insure that mono-lingual Spanish- and Portuguese-speaking children would be interviewed. Although the data received from the children must be evaluated very carefully due to the age of these students, nevertheless the students are an important source of information, not only because they are the consumers of the program's services, but also because of their candor and the insights which their impressions convey. While acquiescence on the part of those interviewed is a research problem for any age group, those who are experienced in working with young children can testify to their candor and often stubborn independence. As might have been expected, the students' data tended to confirm the views of the classroom teachers, the principals and the parents. Over 90% said they like to sing and they also like to sing at home. This is amazingly close to the parents' responses and is more interesting since the children were interviewed prior to the parents' questionnaire. Almost 100% said they like to sing songs at school. Even if considerable allowance is made for acquiescence bias, these data speak very highly for the program and the quality of instruction. Almost all of the children responded that music made them feel happy. One discriminating second grade girl said that it depended on the mood of the song.

Several conclusions: The children enjoy the Kodály music program and it is improving their overall educational experience and enhancing their development. According to their teachers and parents and in their own words and songs, the students affirm this conclusion. Although control data and quantitative measures such as test scores were not used in this phase of the evaluation, the satisfaction of all concerned indicated that the program enriches and reinforces the quality of the educational process and appears to be strongly related to the acquisition of basic learning skills.

The positive factor in this phase of the evaluation was the opportunity for all to participate actively in the evaluation by sharing their perceptions of the Kodály Program. The overwhelmingly unanimous perceptions of administrators, classroom teachers, parents and students serve to substantiate the perceived success of the Kodály Music Program.

The Evaluation: Phase 2

The second phase of the evaluation focused more directly on an analysis of the interaction between the teacher and the student in the Kodály music classes. As mentioned earlier, our primary assumption was that the structure of the student–teacher interaction provides the basic context for the learning and growth of the program participants. The data from our first phase of the evaluation provided us with a picture of a successful program. The goal of the second phase was to make a qualitative analysis of the educational process: to try to determine just what was happening in the music class that could account for the perceived success of the program. For such successful communication to occur, we made the assumption that there must be something special in the way in which the Kodály teacher and the students relate to each other. We know that the Kodály pedagogy offers a particular pattern of interaction which may be described as having the following characteristics:

1. A consistent respect for the spontaneity and positive motivation of the student is always assumed.
2. Learning and human development occur spontaneously.
3. Honesty is highly valued. Bad singing is never called good singing. Incorrect answers are never called correct.
4. Clear demands are made by the teachers and the students. There are no mixed messages or hidden agendas. Simultaneously with the demand come the technical resources and the necessary interpersonal support to meet the demand.

5. Learning is enjoyable, collective and complementary. It is not individual, idiosyncratic or competitive.

6. Distinctions such as mind/body and nature/nurture are not made. Truth is whole, integrative, supporting, and challenging.

7. The complex integration of the person which is required for learning the communication that is music requires and motivates the basic learning skills of reading, writing, and computation.

The analysis of the pedagogy was done with both the graduate students who were doing their practice teaching in the laboratory schools connected with the College and the Kodály teachers in the San José Unified School District.

It would be well to mention here that Randolfo Pozos, the evaluation director for both the first and second phase, is an anthropologist. He observed all phases of the Kodály music education program involving both the training of the graduate students and the teaching being carried on in the San José Unified School District. His observations began in January 1978, and were completed in May 1979, with attendance being concentrated at certain times and infrequent at other times. Interviews and informal conversations with the program faculty, graduate students, Kodály teachers, administrators, classroom teachers, parents and children were extensive.

The evaluator was impressed by the precise pedagogical rituals which Kodály graduate students learned and demonstrated under watchful eyes. He noted, however, that both in the classrooms of San José Unified and at Holy Names College there was a blend of discipline and spontaneity: a sense of intellectual latitude and a very clear sense of orthodoxy. Although the classroom environment for both the children and the student teachers was supportive, there were, nevertheless, very clear and challenging expectations of performance.

What occurs in both settings seems to be clearly described in the work of anthropologist Gregory Bateson in his discussion of collective and individual modes of learning.[3] For Bateson, the structure of interaction involved in learning is either symmetrical or asymmetrical. A mode of learning places the individual in either a competitive or a symmetrical relationship. The Kodály pedagogy appears primarily to emphasize the complementarity of human relationships, behavior and ideas. This emphasis seems to be the major factor in the program's success and provides the theoretical basis for this second phase of the evaluation. For example, musical concepts and skills are introduced and perfected by combinations of rhythmic and singing activities and singing games and folk dances. The author proceeds here from the basic tenet that only the best examples of folk music, leading to art music, are the musical materials used with the children.

The pedagogy presupposes and requires the use of these types of social interactions which are based on the complementary mode of learning and cognitive development. The pedagogy also assumes that the child's natural developmental needs provide the most significant motivation for learning.

The element of respect is perhaps one of the most striking features of the pedagogy. There is a basic assumption that music and singing are a normal part of being a child and an adult. Correspondingly, there is an emphasis on structuring success and minimizing the risk of failure. The skills and concepts are presented in a logical progression, beginning with the most basic. Specific lessons are devoted exclusively to "making conscious" what the learner has already accomplished and experienced with the teacher being in control—not as an inhibitor, but as a facilitator.

The teacher as facilitator is a demanding role in the Kodály pedagogy. Each lesson is elaborately structured and ritualized. The student teachers spend large amounts of time and psychic energy in learning these rituals. A successful "make conscious" lesson must be done in certain prescribed ways. The proper use of body language including hand and facial gestures, the use of certain terms and words in precise ways and specific contexts, along with the correct arrangement of the room and furniture, are all closely watched by the master teacher. Correspondingly, there is not a slavish repetition of ritual, but a conscious sense of purpose about each lesson.

The techniques or rituals are precise ways of achieving each objective. In essence, despite its ritualistic trappings, the Kodály pedagogy is pragmatic. That which accomplishes the organized discipline and specific objectives of the lesson is accepted. The techniques which do not serve these ends are rejected.

A Description of a "Make Conscious" Lesson

The "make conscious" concept is a distinctive feature of the Kodály pedagogy. The "make conscious" lesson plan which is the subject of this particular analysis was chosen because it demonstrates the core insight of the Kodály pedagogy and because it is a good representation of a specific Kodály lesson.

The lesson plan begins with a concrete behavioral objective: "The student can identify that there is one sound on a beat." The next heading, "Musical Experience," which is subdivided into "Readiness" and "Conscious Knowledge," states the basic behavioral abilities and perceptual experiences which the children must have before they are ready to begin mastering the objective. These requirements include the ability to keep a steady beat, and to distinguish between beat and rhythm. Previous lessons have developed these required skills in a careful sequence.

The following heading, "Materials," lists all of the songs and teaching aids which are required for the lesson. Detailed preparation is a hallmark of Kodály pedagogy, along with the notion that learning occurs in a developmental stream. There are no shortcuts. The precise behavioral requirements help the teacher pinpoint the child's particular phase of musical development.

The lesson begins with the teacher greeting the children in song and thereby initiating the complementarity which will suffuse the interaction. The children return the greeting in unison. Many times this is followed by individual greetings for certain students and they respond by singing alone. In classes with bilingual children, songs and greetings in the child's first language (Spanish or Portuguese in San José) have been incorporated. This simple gesture immediately communicates acceptance to the child and a respect for his or her home. English-speaking students receive exposure to other languages and cultures and experience music as a universal language. This activity has a special meaning since the teacher picks names of individuals which illustrate four quarter beats, e.g., "Hello Mary," "Hello Bryant."

These greetings are then quickly followed by a series of songs which the children already know which contain the four beat initial rhythm patterns, thus reviewing their experience of one sound on the beat. Great care is taken to insure that everyone sings the correct pitch and interprets the mood of the song.

At this point the class is relaxed and attentive. The students will now begin to make the transition from experience to reflective awareness or consciousness. The teacher then places paper stars on the board and keeps the beat while the class sings "Starlight." The teacher's voice, hands, and total body movement are carefully coordinated. The notes are sung clearly and precisely without losing the melodic phrasing.

Individual students are selected to sing the first phrase and to keep the beat the way the teacher did. As usual, the children imitate very well and begin to act out their experience of the beat. However, this still is in the twilight between experience and consciousness.

The move toward conscious understanding is now initiated by the teacher with a very simple question, "How many beats do you hear on the first phrase?" Guessing is avoided by repeating the phrase while at the same time experiencing the beat. The four-beat pattern thus becomes obvious. The students have moved from experience to consciousness. Learning has occurred. The learning is now clearly made conscious by the next activity which is highly abstract. The beat is named "ta." The teacher again points out the stars but uses "ta-ta-ta-ta" to while keeping the beat. The specific experience of the four-beat rhythmic pattern has now become a generalized abstract concept firmly rooted in the class's experience. [This early approach to introducing rhythm was revised in the 1980's. Most Kodály teachers now introduce "ta" and "ti-ti" (quarter notes and eighth notes) in the same lesson.]

To further amplify and demonstrate the concept, the children learn a precise universal notation for communicating the four-beat pattern. Simple popsicle sticks are arranged in a series: | | | |. The students space them evenly on their desks or tables and make sure they are parallel. The students sing the text and then the "ta's" or duration syllables and keep the beat by pointing to their sticks as they sing. At this point the children are counting, writing and reading.

This brings us to the reinforcement section. The teacher holds up a flash card with the four-beat notation: | | | | and the students say "ta-ta-ta-ta." The teacher then asks the children to think of other known songs which begin with the same beat pattern, and children sing and clap the rhythm of the songs to confirm.

The students may then move on to a known singing game which includes the 4-beat rhythm pattern. The class is formally concluded by singing farewell songs, bringing the lesson to a close. The children are relaxed and ready to return to their other subjects.

Although the "make conscious" lessons do not comprise the total program, the other lessons tend to reflect the emphasis on the transition from experience to consciousness. Basically, the other lessons tend to emphasize developing the requisite skills necessary for the "making conscious" activities and reinforcing in different contexts the elements or concepts that have already been made conscious.

The Success Spiral

The highly demanding training which the graduate students receive prepares them to become successful teachers. This success improves their self-image and interaction skills. Their mastery of the strategies and techniques gives them a clearly defined experience of the relationship between discipline and creativity for the teacher as a facilitator. Consequently, the success spiral begins. Success in teaching improves self-image and interaction skills which encourage the complementary mode of learning and, in turn, promotes the mastery of music concepts and singing and performing skills. In the process, memorization, conceptualization and synthetic intellectual skills are fostered. Concomitant with these skills, the teacher develops a different, complementary epistemology. Music and education take on entirely new dimensions.

The same process occurs with the small children in the classroom. They are given tasks which relate to their social experience of play. Their simultaneous physical and psychological development is recognized by the principles of pedagogy. The discipline and precision of their neighborhood games, along with their sophisticated psychosocial meaning and motivation, is brought into the classroom. Their complementary mode of learning does not suffer the jarring discontinuity that would be brought about by their initiation into a competitive pedagogy.

The stage is set for success. The students have experienced the learning of games and songs and now the elements of that experience are directed toward the learning of music and singing. The students are able to respond to the teacher's requirements and validate the teacher in the process. At this point the circle is complete. Interpersonal communion has been established, and the classroom becomes a place of mutually supportive and related ideas and individuals. This success spiral can also occur in other areas of the lives of both the teachers and the students. For the children, such a complementary mode of interaction and learning can dissipate pathological stress. Children who were shy and withdrawn have become more outgoing and communicative; children who were aggressive have become less disruptive. The expectations of the teacher and the pedagogy itself create a beneficial "eustress" which we all experience as the challenge and enjoyment of playing and performing.[4]

The fact that large numbers of children, over 90%, sing and conduct music lessons on the playground and/or at home for their peers, siblings and parents indicates that the pedagogy has become a basic part of their epistemology. To learn how to sing is to learn how to enter into communion with others. It is demanding and enjoyable and it is fulfilling.

The Children

The implications are not lost on the children or the regular classroom teachers who have observed them during the music classes. If the classroom teachers attempt to maintain the success spiral, the results in terms of learning basic skills can be remarkable. However, if the classroom teacher still clings to a competitive epistemology, the children readily notice the difference. In fact, in one school some of the children were perplexed by the notion that the Kodály specialist was also a "teacher." The jarring differences in the social role presentation of the teachers which the children observed indicates that questions of pedagogy are far from academic. At stake here is not merely which method is better for conveying and achieving basic music literacy for elementary school children. Rather, the entire cognitive orientation of the child and his or her concomitant social behavior and notion of self-actualization can be seriously influenced by the pedagogy.

Seeing and Hearing

The success which the newly-trained Kodály teachers experience has had a significant effect. In general, the graduate students complete their training with greater expectations for their students. They are armed with an arsenal of strategies for achieving a carefully developed and articulated series of learning outcomes. More importantly, the graduate students seem to come away with a clearer sense of what exactly they want to achieve and how to achieve it. One of the Kodály specialists succinctly summarized the program's basic agenda in these words: "What we are trying to do in the program is to train the children to 'see' with their ears and to 'hear' with their eyes." Elaborating further, the Kodály specialist explained that the children should be able to visualize and write the patterns of sound which they hear, and also to be able to sing from reading musical notation.

This goal is hardly modest for any pedagogy. Perhaps, however, its simplicity and its profundity provide the basic theme of all Kodály instruction; it seems to be the fundamental criterion. This concept appears to provide the central focus and direction of all the learning activities. As a consequence, the pedagogy requires an experiential or phenomenological approach. By beginning with the most fundamental experiences of beat, rhythm, and pitch, the teacher neither lectures nor demonstrates in the conventional sense. The children are led on an elaborate journey of discovery in which they "make conscious" what they have learned experientially. Not only does this provide the children with learning's most fundamental skill, i.e., learning how to learn, it causes the teacher to be transformed from an imparter of technical skills and knowledge into a role model of self-actualized learning. In the process, however, the children learn complex musical skills at which their instrumental teachers later marvel.

This transformation is very similar to that advocated by Paulo Freire in his *Pedagogy of the Oppressed*,[5] when he recommends a conversion from the "banking" concept of education—

with its competitive, asymmetrical orientation—to an education for critical consciousness and liberation—with its symmetrical, complementary epistemology. Consequently, correctly implementing the pedagogy achieves a liberation of self-actualization for both the teacher and the student due to the basic developmental approach and the complementary relationships which are required. The overall satisfaction of Kodály specialists as music teachers seems to bear this out. The pedagogy, then, requires an abandonment of pathologically structured competitive relationships and also requires developmentally structured relationships which are the precondition for any learning in the true sense.

Notes

[1] Randolfo R. Pozos, *The Kodály Music Training Program in the San José Unified School District: Program Evaluation Report* (unpublished report) (Oakland, CA: Kodály Program, Holy Names College, 1979).
[2] Ward Hunt Goodenough, *Explorations in Cultural Anthropology* (New York: McGraw-Hill, 1964).
[3] Gregory Bateson, *Steps to an Ecology of Mind: Collected Essays in Anthropology, Psychiatry, Evolution, and Epistemology* (San Francisco: Chandler, 1972).
[4] Hans Selye, *The Stress of Life* (New York: McGraw-Hill, 1978).
[5] Paulo Freire, *Pedagogy of the Oppressed*, trans. Myra Ramos (New York: Seabury, 1970).

Originally published in a slightly different form in *Bulletin of the International Kodály Society* 5, no. 1 (1980): 40-47. Reprinted by permission.

DEVELOPING MUSIC LITERACY: KODÁLY TEACHER EDUCATION

Mary Ellen Junda

This session will describe an innovative Kodály teacher education program, Collaborative Approach to Music Instruction (CAMI). The goals of CAMI were to develop elementary general music teachers' musical and instructional skills, and as a result, to improve elementary students' musical skills. Toward this end, teachers were to develop a comprehensive sight-reading curriculum and have the skills to implement it in their respective general music classes.

CAMI was a unique two-year program that included a graduate course in conjunction with supervised teaching in the public schools. During this presentation I will describe the first-year program and the transfer of instructional techniques learned in the graduate course to the primary general music class. I also will present recommendations for teacher educators and future teacher education programs.

Project Description

CAMI was sponsored by the Frank and Lydia E. Bergen Foundation and Montclair State College, Upper Montclair, NJ. The Project Director was Chair of Music Education at Montclair State College, and I was the Associate Director and instructor. For the purposes of this paper, the term teacher refers to CAMI participants and student refers to primary-grade students. Funding for the first-year project included 80% tuition scholarships for twelve general music teachers and five site visits by the instructor to each respective district, for a total of sixty observations.

The twelve general music teachers were selected on the basis of their applications, interviews and sight-reading skills. These teachers represented suburban, urban and rural districts. Five teachers saw their classes for two thirty-minute periods per week, and seven saw their classes for one forty-minute period per week. Teacher experience varied from a first-year teacher to one with twenty-four years' experience, and one teacher was enrolled in a graduate music education program.

The core of this project was a graduate course, Sight-Reading Methodology, offered for the 1988-89 academic year. The two-semester course met one night per week, and teachers received three graduate credits per semester. The course was divided into three parts: musicianship, methodology and materials. Objectives included (1) the development of vocal, aural, sight-reading and part-singing skills; (2) the development of instructional strategies for teaching the elements of music sequentially; and (3) the identification of appropriate repertoire for grades K–3. Strategies and repertoire were combined to form the curriculum.

Materials for musicianship training were selected from *The Kodály Choral Method*[1] and varied folk song collections. Songs for early instruction were primarily from *150 American Folk Songs* and *Sail Away*.[2] Other sources included *The Kodály Method, American Folk Songs for Children, 46 Two-Part American Folk Songs*, and *Step It Down*.[3]

The methodology was based on the *Kodály Concept* and the texts were *The Kodály Method* and *The Kodály Concept*.[4] Topics included long-term planning, lesson planning, readiness skills, sight-reading strategies and curriculum development.

As part of the training process, teachers implemented the strategies and repertoire in their respective primary general music classes. Each teacher selected one primary class to participate in the observation procedures. Collectively, each grade level K–3 was represented.

I observed each teacher five times during the academic year. Initially, I gave comments on instruction and recommended specific strategies and materials for future lessons. Teachers were gradually to assume more responsibility for analyzing instruction.

Videotapes of primary-grade classes, recorded four times during the academic year, were used to document and evaluate instruction. Teachers reviewed their own videotaped lessons and the videotaped lessons of one peer selected randomly. I reviewed the first two videotaped lessons with each teacher and selected excerpts to share with the graduate class. Teachers reviewed their last two tapes independently.

During this session, data from classroom observations and excerpts of videotaped lessons will be used to highlight the use of specific teaching techniques in the classroom.

Procedures

The first observations, held the last week of September, were primarily goal-setting sessions, and teachers planned their lessons without my guidance. The observations revealed that eleven teachers adhered to an activities-oriented approach in the classroom, and students sang, listened to music, and played instruments. Songs were primarily from older music series books or teacher-composed. Teachers based their lesson evaluations primarily on student participation.

Observations indicated that, with one exception, teachers did not focus on skill development, nor did they sequence instruction taking into consideration long-term planning. These teachers performed songs incorrectly, did not correct inaccuracies in the students' performance, and seldom included opportunities for individual student performance. In addition, teachers lacked procedures to assess instruction and the students' skills. The first videotaped lessons revealed similar results.

I will present a five-step plan that summarizes how the teachers learned the teaching techniques needed to develop music literacy.

Step 1: Musical environment

Before students learn about music notation, they must first have a variety of musical experiences. Toward this end, I directed teachers to (1) perform music from memory accurately and stylistically; (2) implement age-appropriate songs in regard to vocal range, musical patterns, and text; (3) teach songs a cappella and limit the use of accompaniment; (4) include movement and singing games in each lesson; and (5) encourage students to take responsibility for singing.

Results of the observations and videotaped lessons indicate that each teacher memorized songs, taught songs a cappella and included movement and singing games in each lesson. Improvements were noted in repertoire because teachers used songs learned in the graduate class. However, teachers tended to supplement instruction with composed songs that were either trite or too difficult. During the graduate class, I reviewed the criteria for selecting songs and required teachers to keep song lists and to substantiate their choice of repertoire to their colleagues and me. This assignment promoted numerous discussions in the graduate class.

Another concern that was immediately obvious was that teachers sang constantly with the students. This habit caused three problems: (1) teachers overused their voices, which caused vocal fatigue; (2) they did not correct inaccuracies in the students' singing; and (3) they did not encourage students' vocal independence. In the graduate class, I continued to concentrate on score study and aural perception so that teachers would know the songs well and be able to discern errors in rhythm and pitch. In the classroom, it took some teachers the entire year to correct this habit, and one teacher never did. (VIDEOTAPE #1)

Step 2: Readiness skills

Once students know a repertoire of songs, the next step is skill development. The prerequisite skills to music reading, called "readiness" skills, are organized into four categories: intonation, aural perception, rhythm and inner hearing. Behaviors which demonstrate these skills include the ability to reproduce sounds vocally; distinguish between differences in pitch, tempo, dynamics and form; keep the beat or rhythm; and internalize musical patterns.

During the graduate class, teachers observed demonstration lessons, learned an instructional sequence for readiness skills, and developed strategies. I directed teachers to teach students (1) to use their singing voices and match pitch; (2) to demonstrate the beat in varied ways and to clap the rhythm of the words; (3) to discriminate between higher and lower sounds, faster and slower tempi, louder and softer sounds, and same or different patterns; and (4) to inner hear using chants and songs.

The first concept most of the teachers taught was the beat, but they did not spend enough time practicing and evaluating students' skill development. As a result, when they introduced rhythm, students confused the two concepts. To remedy this situation, teachers learned four long-term instructional steps: (1) modeling: teacher models the skill, students imitate; (2) guided-practice period: teacher performs skill with students; (3) independent-practice period: students perform skill without teacher; (4) evaluation: individual students perform skill independently. To evaluate rhythm and beat, teachers clapped the rhythm while students tapped the beat and vice-versa. These steps improved teacher effectiveness in the classroom. (VIDEOTAPE #2)

Teachers implemented strategies for students to distinguish between differences in pitch, tempo, dynamics and form. These strategies could have been successful except that the students did not know the songs well from which the concepts were derived. For example, teachers would teach a song and immediately ask questions about higher and lower notes.

Students could not answer the questions because they were still concentrating on learning the words.

I reminded teachers that, before they use a song to teach concepts, students must know the song thoroughly. Teachers recognized that they should not teach songs and concepts simultaneously, nor should they just plan from lesson to lesson. As a result, teachers, with my guidance, began to develop long-term plans.

Most of the teachers implemented inner-hearing strategies, but they tended to select random notes or groups of notes for the students to sing internally. I reminded teachers that the purpose of inner hearing is to develop the internal ear and musical memory, and to tune specific patterns or intervals. Furthermore, it was important for teachers to work in motives or phrases, not random notes. (VIDEOTAPE #3)

It took much longer for teachers to address the development of vocal intonation. Although intonation was a frequent topic of discussion in the graduate class, the results were not evident in the classroom. The primary reason was that, during the lesson, teachers paid attention to adhering to the lesson plan rather than listening to the students' performance. Teachers also were hesitant to correct the students' singing because they feared that if they were critical, students would not want to sing anymore. In addition, one teacher admitted candidly that she did not think she could diagnose differences in pitch.

Clearly, sight-reading programs will not succeed if teachers do not develop vocal intonation. As part of the formative evaluation in February, I required teachers to rate each student's vocal skill on a four-point scale. By assessing each student, teachers began to attend to their vocal performance and to tailor instruction to meet the needs of individual students. Teachers realized that students needed both opportunities to perform individually and feedback from the teacher in order to improve their skills.
(VIDEOTAPE #4)

Step. 3: Planning

Long-term planning involves teaching a concept over a period of time. Teachers organized long-term plans that included concepts, goals, objectives, repertoire, procedures and evaluation. The procedure includes three steps: (1) preparation: students recognize a new rhythm or tone aurally and visually; (2) presentation: students learn the name and symbol for the tone or rhythm; and (3) practice: students practice the tone or rhythm by sight-reading, notating and improvising. Evaluation occurs after each instructional step.

The distinction between long-term planning and lesson planning was not easy for teachers to comprehend. More than half of the teachers had difficulty using the long-term plans to write lesson plans. The tendency was to prepare, present and practice a new concept in one lesson rather than over a period of time. It was important for teachers to realize that they should prepare a concept during several classes over many weeks and that they must evaluate each instructional step before proceeding. At the conclusion of the program, nine teachers could organize and implement long-term plans; three others had difficulty with the implementation. (VIDEOTAPE #5)

Step 4: Tools

The tools used to develop sight-reading skills include movable-do sol-fa, hand signs and rhythm names. During each graduate class, teachers practiced using the tools so that they would gain expertise in performance, understand the function, and learn to use the tools effectively. Teachers learned that rhythm syllables represent duration; therefore, students should clap the rhythm and say the rhythm syllables simultaneously. Sol-fa syllables represent tonal function, and students use sol-fa to memorize melodies and intervals. Hand signs are a physical representation of sol-fa syllables and aid the memory of pitch patterns; therefore, students perform sol-fa and hand signs together.

Although teachers used the tools during every graduate class, many had difficulty using the tools effectively in the classroom. They would confuse when and how to use the tools.

(VIDEOTAPE #6) During this activity, students sang the song, clapped the rhythm, then added rhythm syllables. Discussion in the graduate class was about the sequence of the activity and use of the rhythm syllables during the initial stages of reading.

(VIDEOTAPE #7) In this activity, the teacher had the students sing a song using hand signs. This is a difficult task because students have to think the sol-fa while singing the words. Clearly, this teacher did not understand the relationship between sol-fa and hand signs; therefore, he did not use the hand signs appropriately with the students.

(VIDEOTAPE #8) In this activity, the students read a familiar song from the staff with inner hearing and guessed the song. The teacher was confused as to whether the students should sing with the words or sol-fa next. She had the students sing with words first, because the students knew the song and wanted to see if they were correct. If the students could not guess the song, the teacher should have had them read with sol-fa first. This demonstration also shows that the students needed more work on vocal intonation before they learned so-mi.

I continued to focus on the appropriate use of the tools, but at the conclusion of the course not all of the teachers could use the tools effectively in the classroom. A few teachers perceived the students' use of the tools as a goal in itself rather than as an aid to develop sight-reading skills.

Step 5: Sight-reading

Music reading varies in difficulty from reading a known song with sol-fa to reading unknown melodies. The sequence of the activity frequently determines whether the students will read successfully. Teachers learned to sequence sight-reading activities, moving from the aural to the visual. The recommended steps are listed in Figure 1.

Figure 1: Sight-Reading Sequence

1. Aural Preparation

2. Visual Preparation

3. Sight-Reading

4. Evaluation

5. Closing

1. Students sing previous song in same key as sight-reading example or sing scale and specific intervals from hand signs or tone ladder.
2. Students review staff placement in the appropriate key. Students analyze tonality, form and patterns of sight-reading melody.
3. Students clap rhythm (optional), read with inner hearing, sight-read.
4. Students read individually or in small groups.
5. Students sing with words.

Initially, teachers did not follow this sequence in the classroom, and students were not sight-reading successfully. We reviewed the sequence in the graduate class, and teachers had the opportunity to practice conducting sight-reading activities. Teachers showed improvements in the classroom on the last videotape in April. (VIDEOTAPE #9)

These sight-reading demonstrations are of the two teachers whose students achieved the highest level during the first year of CAMI. At the conclusion of the program, the first-grade teacher's class was able to sight-read tritonic songs and the third-grade teacher's class could read simple pentatonic melodies. Given the variety of teaching situations, not all teachers were able to conduct sight-reading activities in their primary music classes during this academic year.

Project Evaluation

Teachers participated in midterm and final program evaluations, which consisted of questionnaires with open-ended questions and a checklist. Data from the observations and graduate course also were analyzed. The videotaped lessons provided a means for the teachers, instructor, project director and an independent consultant to evaluate the change in teachers' musical and instructional skills and the students' musical skills. The effectiveness of the in-service program in meeting the intended goals was determined by examining the results of the data analysis.

Data from the graduate course and classroom provided evidence of the change in teachers' musical skills. Initially, only two teachers could sight-read using movable-do sol-fa. At the conclusion of the program, each teacher could sight-read with sol-fa and rhythm syllables, and hold his or her own voice part in two-part music. Observational data revealed that teachers' vocal skills improved and they performed a cappella songs accurately. An improvement in aural skills was indicated by the teachers' ability to correct intonation and errors in their students' performance.

For the purpose of this program, instructional skills focused on sight-reading pedagogy. Teachers demonstrated knowledge of readiness skills, sight-reading pedagogy, long-term and lesson planning and curriculum development on course assignments and examinations. Teachers also selected repertoire based on the learners' needs, instructional setting and musical concepts. They combined the strategies and materials to form a Teacher's Manual for Sight-Reading Pedagogy, which is a guide for developing sight-reading programs in the primary grades. Each teacher organized a sight-reading curriculum for his or her respective music program based on this manual.

Clearly, knowledge of pedagogy is only the first step; the second step is the application of the techniques in the general music class. This process takes time, practice and constant reinforcement. For example, responses on the first-semester examination indicated that teachers had an understanding of children's vocal development; yet only one teacher focused on pitch accuracy in the general music class. The other teachers did not consistently address the development of vocal intonation until after they evaluated the students' vocal skills in February. Other techniques that teachers gradually acquired included the use of the tools, readiness and sight-reading strategies, and methods of evaluation.

At the conclusion of the program, an improvement in teachers' instructional skills was evident in the primary music class. The most substantial increase was in the number and variety of strategies to develop readiness and sight-reading skills. Improvements also were noted in the selection of repertoire, sequence of activities, and organization of the sight-reading activity. Furthermore, nine teachers were able to plan, implement and evaluate the instructional process independently. The other three teachers had difficulty planning and evaluating objectives.

The improvement of teachers' skills was directly related to the improvement of students' skills. Students demonstrated substantial improvements in readiness and sight-reading skills as a consequence of the strategies and materials implemented in the general music class. In addition, each class knew a memorized repertoire which they performed independently. Positive changes also were noted in students' participation in class.

Teachers indicated that the supervisory observations were one of the most important components of the project, and that the instructor's comments helped them to develop their instructional skills and adapt the curriculum to their program. By working with the instructor throughout the year, teachers gradually assumed more responsibility for evaluating instruction and the students' musical skills. Viewing videotaped lessons also developed teachers' observational and instructional skills, but there was a consensus among teachers that videotapes be used only to enhance, not replace, the supervisory observations.

Teachers suggested modifications to the program that included adding an introductory summer course, offering more graduate credits, dividing the class into two levels, and having school districts assume responsibility for videotaping classes. They also indicated that participation in the project and review of videotapes was time-consuming, but this did not deter them from requesting a second-level course.

These results confirm the results of previous studies that long-term, sequential programs which include the implementation of strategies in the schools and supervision by the instructor are effective in making substantial changes in teacher behavior in the classroom. Furthermore, what these results make obvious is that CAMI improved the quality of instruction in the schools and the students' musical skills.

Conclusions

It is a unique and exciting experience to work with a select group of teachers over a period of two semesters. Given this amount of time and the teachers' commitment to the program, substantial changes in their skills were observed during the course of the year. In addition, specific areas of difficulty also were noted.

It was important that CAMI was structured to focus on the development of both musical and instructional skills. Improvements were observed in teachers' vocal, aural, and sight-reading skills. By developing their own musical skills, teachers also showed improvement in their instructional skills and were able to assess their students' skill development more accurately.

As the program progressed, I recognized that a combination of skills is necessary to be effective in the music classroom. For example, the most advanced musician was not the most effective teacher, because s/he thought the students would achieve skills very quickly. Teachers with less advanced musical skills sometimes had a clearer understanding of the practice needed for skill development, yet they had to be careful not to become overly repetitive. Also, teachers who wrote excellent long-term plans did not necessarily implement the plans effectively. On the other hand, teachers who excelled in the classroom often did not write detailed plans. It was important for me to recognize each teacher's strengths and weaknesses in order to help them improve their skills.

Developing new teaching techniques is a long-term process. For most of the teachers, teaching songs a cappella, diagnosing musical errors, using the tools, and implementing sight-reading activities were new techniques. As teachers acquired one skill, they would begin to concentrate on other ones. At the conclusion of CAMI, six teachers could implement a sight-reading program effectively: three teachers had the knowledge, but needed more practice in the classroom; and three needed further study. One teacher admitted candidly that she needed more time to make the suggested changes in her instructional techniques. A first-year teacher felt that she needed more effective classroom management before she could concentrate on music-teaching techniques.

The change in teachers' and students' skills also was predicated upon the specific teaching situation. Six teachers taught at two schools, one teacher taught at three schools, and three teachers traveled from classroom to classroom. Nine teachers taught between 600 to 800 students each week. Teachers who met with their classes twice a week had more opportunities to introduce concepts, work with individual students, and evaluate skill development. Teachers who met with their classes once a week found it more difficult to implement a skill-oriented program. Also, the change in students' skills was less noticeable. Yet the results of the evaluation indicate that students in every setting showed improvements in their music skills.

Two of the strongest components of CAMI were the supervisory observations and videotaped lessons. The benefit of scheduling five observations was that teachers received feedback on each phase of their development. During the supervisory conferences, teachers learned to make informed decisions about goals, objectives, strategies and materials, and to assess instruction based on the results of student evaluation. Teachers found the sharing of videotapes beneficial because they rarely have the opportunity to observe their colleagues in the classroom. One teacher said that this was the first time she had observed another general music teacher since her student-teaching experience twenty-four years before.

The results of this study indicate that Kodály teacher education programs and courses should include supervisory observations or videotaped lessons to ensure that the techniques learned in the graduate class transfer to the general music class. Supervisory observations gain importance for music teacher education programs because elementary music teachers seldom are observed by a supervisor who has expertise in elementary music education. Also, teachers prefer observations because they get immediate feedback on the lesson. If observations are not practical because of time, travel or financial constraints, teachers should videotape numerous activities or lessons. Videotapes provide the means to review the lesson more objectively, replay segments, and share excerpts with the class.

For the videotape review to be efficient, teachers should videotape specific techniques such as teaching a song or game, developing readiness skills, or preparing a concept. Once they have mastered these skills, they can videotape more advanced techniques and complete lessons. The instructor should inform the teacher how to analyze instruction when reviewing the videotape. Initially, teachers may just check behavior or listen for musical errors. More advanced techniques involve analyzing the instructional sequence, use of the tools, and sight-reading activities. Furthermore, teachers should always critique their own lessons because they will learn to be more reflective of the teaching-learning process.

One of the benefits of an academic-year program such as CAMI is that the relationship between the instructor and teachers is modified as the year progresses. Initially, I presented theories and teaching techniques in the graduate class and teachers learned the information. Once the teachers implemented the techniques in their general music classes, they would ask me specific questions about materials and strategies. As the year progressed, teachers began to address their questions to their colleagues. This promoted group discussions and the shared interaction among teachers that was an essential part of this project. As a result, I became more of a facilitator as teachers used their colleagues as a resource.

This project was a learning experience for all involved. Clearly, teachers must have a strong foundation in instructional and musical skills to implement the Kodály concept successfully. Yet teachers also must have the freedom to make decisions, explore different techniques, and develop their own style. As teachers gained confidence in their skills, they became more creative in their use of materials and techniques.

Conducting this project also gave me a broader understanding of public school music education. As teachers learned to be more structured, I learned to be more understanding of each teacher's needs and the requirements of his or her program. Conducting CAMI was a wonderful educational experience for me, and I appreciate the opportunity to share what I have learned with other teacher educators.

Notes

[1] Zoltán Kodály, *The Kodály Choral Method* (New York: Boosey & Hawkes, 1962).

[2] Peter Erdei and Katalin Komlós, eds., *150 American Folk Songs to Sing, Read and Play* (New York: Boosey & Hawkes, 1974); Eleanor G. Locke, ed., *Sail Away* (New York: Boosey & Hawkes, 1988).

[3] Lois Choksy, *The Kodály Method*, 2nd ed. (Englewood Cliffs, NJ: Prentice-Hall, 1988); Ruth Crawford Seeger, *American Folk Songs for Children* (Garden City, NY: Doubleday, 1948); Denise Bacon, *46 Two-part American Folk Songs* (Wellesley, MA: Kodály Center of America, 1973); Bessie Jones and Bess Lomax Hawes, *Step It Down* (New York: Harper & Row, 1972).

[4] Lois Choksy, *The Kodály Context* (Englewood Cliffs, NJ: Prentice-Hall, 1981); Choksy, *Kodály Method*.

This paper was based on the author's doctoral dissertation at Teachers College, Columbia University, 1990. Originally published in *Bulletin of the International Kodály Society* 20, no. 1 (1995): 26-34. Reprinted by permission.

MUSIC, EDUCATION, AND THE BRAIN

Sean Breen

In December of 2013, newspapers, magazines, television stations, and countless Internet sites reported the results of a Harvard University research study into music and intelligence.[1] Media reactions were evident from the dramatic headlines: for example, "Music doesn't make you smarter, Harvard study finds"[2] and "Do, Re, Mi, Fa-get the Piano Lessons, Music May Not Make You Smarter."[3]

Many outside of the music education community responded with "I told you so." To this group, the Harvard study confirmed something that they suspected but had yet to prove: that claims concerning the cognitive benefits of music education were at best inflated, or at worst unfounded. Within the music education community there was, predictably, a much different response. Here the dominant sentiment was that the authors of the study were not in a position to reach any conclusions that dealt with the cognitive value of music education. How could university-based researchers possibly claim to evaluate the cognitive benefits of classroom music education? If researchers at Harvard (or anywhere else) wanted to investigate the cognitive benefits of music education, they could do no better than to ask music educators, who witness and can confirm the positive effects in their classrooms. How could academia expect to capture the richness and wealth of music's contribution to children's cognitive gains without spending time in the classroom with the real experts?

Professional music education organizations responded with varying intensity and expediency. One typical reaction came from the National Association for Music Education (NAfME): "Mehr's findings do not actually say anything new about the value of music education, but rather reaffirm the difficulty of showing causality in describing academic benefits. Contrary to what the negative headlines report, the jury is still out on the extrinsic value of music study."[4]

Online discussion groups also provided the opportunity to weigh the merits of the findings. One such forum included comments from the first author of the Harvard study. In Mehr's own words, "We did not debunk anything!"[5] In general, Internet sites emphasized the same point: that the media reporting of the study did not accurately reflect the actual conclusion. As is no surprise, media outlets that originally employed sensationalized headlines did not choose to issue corrections. In fact, media attention died down rather quickly. A Google search on April 14, 2014 (Mehr+Harvard) produced no new articles relating to the original research.

Kodály teachers reacted even more pointedly. Informal responses from attendees of the 2014 Organization of American Kodály Educators (OAKE) National Conference focused on the value of teacher experiences. Additionally, strengthened by the tenets of Kodály's vision of music education, OAKE members cited their personal experiences to counter the Harvard findings as reported in the media. The wealth of experience acquired by these teachers through generations of careful, expert application of Kodály principles is of far more real-world value than the observations of university researchers. As before, the prevailing opinion was that if people want to know about the cognitive benefits of music education, they should ask those who work with it and experience it every day: in this case, those who teach in the Kodály way.

Immediately following publication of the Harvard study, a slightly different, but no less prevalent, response appeared. This response built on the idea that the arts are valuable for children regardless of any proposed non-art benefits.[6] Perhaps Winner and Hetland said it best: "We don't need the arts in our schools to raise mathematical and verbal skills—we already target these in math and language arts. We need the arts because in addition to introducing students to aesthetic appreciation, they teach other modes of thinking we value."[7]

Somewhat surprisingly, the lead author on the Harvard study joined the chorus with a telling statement from the conclusion of the study: "Regardless of any potential transfer effects, we echo the view of Winner and Hetland that the primary benefit of music education for parents and children is self-evident: to improve the musical skills and repertoire of parents and children along with their appreciation and enjoyment of musical activities."[8]

To many music educators these responses make a valid point. The value of music education should not depend on transfer effects; it should be valued for its impact on a child's lifelong appreciation of music. In the short run this may not be a bad way to relieve some of the pressure. Unfortunately, there may be an unintended consequence of this focus on "art for art's sake": a reluctance of music educators to confront the more pressing question of whether or not music education actually makes children smarter. Given that many within the Kodály community face the almost daily challenge of justifying the allocation of educational time and material resources to the cause of music, it becomes imperative not only to champion the intrinsic benefits of music, but also to be prepared to respond to those who look to minimize its curricular presence due to a perceived lack of extrinsic benefits. While there may be parents, administrators and school board members who need no reassurance as to the place of music in the school curriculum, there are also many who will find themselves swayed by media reports such as those concerning the Harvard study.

The Big Question

What are Kodály teachers to do? Ideally, we would be able to point out the strengths and weaknesses of topical research, as well as provide perspective through our own classroom experiences and expertise. Unfortunately, there are very few teachers (and administrators) knowledgeable about the many current research techniques. Without such knowledge, it would be difficult, if not futile, to attempt to refute or challenge many research conclusions. Fortunately, there are steps that we can take to establish a stronger position.

First, music educators must approach the challenge as true professionals: that is, we must become knowledgeable about the science and methods behind the research. Second, music educators must acknowledge that their personal expertise and experience are equally valid sources of research data, comparable to laboratory results. Third, we must develop a theory based on both the research and personal observation. Fourth, we must also be willing and ready to adjust our theory based on new research and personal experience.

Become Knowledgeable

Much of the research reported by mainstream media outlets falls either into the category of neuroscience or of cognitive neuroscience. Unfortunately, educators often confuse neuroscience with cognitive neuroscience in spite of significant differences.[9] In order for educators to determine the value and relevance of neuroscience and cognitive neuroscience research, they must know how the two fields are similar and how they differ.

Neuroscience

Neuroscience is, by definition, the study of the nervous system. This includes not only the brain, but also the spinal cord and all components of the nervous system. Modern neuroscience investigates many facets of how the nervous system functions, including its architecture, mechanisms, development, malfunctions and alterations. However, the great majority of educational neuroscience research focuses on brain function. To comprehend such research, educators must develop a basic understanding of brain architecture, starting with neurons. Neurons are cells that communicate to other cells through connections called synapses. The human brain has one hundred billion neurons and one hundred trillion synapses that organize into networks. Researchers investigate these neural networks in an effort to gain insight into questions concerning which parts of the nervous system are active when a specific behavior is present.

Neuroscientists use a variety of imaging technologies in order to ascertain the location and time of brain activity associated with a behavior. The names for these imaging technologies are well known outside of neuroscience. fMRI, PET, EEG, and DTI are the most commonly employed technologies.

What is important to remember about neuroscience imaging technologies is that each has strengths and limitations. fMRI (functional Magnetic Resonance Imaging) measures blood oxygen flow within the brain. The thought is that oxygen flows to those areas of the brain that are active while a person is engaged in a specific mental behavior. By measuring and analyzing the blood oxygen data, researchers look to construct models about regions of brain activation associated with specific psychological processes.[10] An advantage of fMRI is that it is basically risk-free. However, fMRI can only show limited areas of brain activation, and only in a relatively broad time frame.[11] Additionally, interpreting fMRI data can be problematic because of the difficulty in determining which psychological functions are represented in the brain activity.[12] fMRI also is limited by the need to have the subject remain still in a loud, often intimidating machine. All fMRI data must be considered in light of these limitations.

PET (Positron Emission Tomography) utilizes a radioactive tracer to show the workings of the brain (fMRI only reveals the structure). PET suffers from similar area resolution limitations as fMRI (http://hopes.stanford.edu/neuroimaging/).

The expense of preparing the tracer as well as the PET unit limits the extent of PET imaging. Similar to fMRI, PET imaging requires the subject to lie still in a machine, limiting its use in real-world scenarios.

DTI (Diffusion Tensor Imaging) does not provide a dynamic accounting of brain activity. The strength of DTI lies in its ability to identify pathways of activity in the brain through the imaging of water movement. DTI imaging is limited by the fact that it is a "...gross oversimplification of actual anatomy."[13] However, used in conjunction with fMRI, DTI has a promising future in the realm of neuroimaging. Media reports often reference these and other imaging technologies (EEG, CAT, MEG) when reporting music education research findings. With a working knowledge of neuroimaging techniques, teachers can be in a position to consider the research in light of the strengths and limitations of the techniques employed. As impressive as current neuroimaging technology may be, it is vital to always consider that each imaging technology has inherent limitations and that mainstream media outlets commonly ignore these limitations in their reports. Beyond these limitations there lies a different type of problem. Common in neuroscience research, "reverse inference" is the inferring of a behavior because it is associated with a particular pattern of brain activation. The problem of "reverse inference" will be discussed in greater detail in a later article in this series. According to Poldrack, "The goal of reverse inference is to infer the likelihood of a particular mental process M from a pattern of brain activity A, which can be framed as a conditional probability."[14] Many of the theories and conclusions of neuroscience research arise from the use of reverse inference to "read minds." Reverse inference is also common in mainstream media reports of neuroscience studies.[15] The problem comes when these theories are presented as facts.

Bridging the Gap

Neuroscience research also faces an additional yet no less significant challenge in the form of "level of analysis," which refers to location, size or scale of a research target. The leap from neurons and synapses to classrooms and students is, as Bruer famously stated, "a bridge too far."[16] From this point of view, drawing music education conclusions from neuroscience studies is as appropriate as treating a common cold by describing cellular properties of viruses. While the information is valuable, and in some way may contribute to the final desired outcome, there needs to be a way to relate the many levels of analysis and bring the information and desired outcome together.[17] In our case, there needs to be a science that can connect neurons and synapses to students and classrooms.

Cognitive Neuroscience

Cognitive neuroscience focuses on how the brain produces cognitive functions, including learning. Therefore, cognitive neuroscience is based on theories that link psychology and neuroscience in order to answer how cognitive functions arise. Cognitive neuroscience has the potential to bridge the gap between the worlds of education and neuroscience[18] by facilitating the sharing of questions and data between the two fields. In the case of music education, the experiences and concerns of music teachers would play a part in developing the research directions of neuroscientists, and not exclusively the other way around. Cognitive neuroscientists would translate the questions and experiences of the educators or neuroscientists into theories that then inform the research directions and practices of both fields. This multi-disciplinary, "two-way street" approach allows for both education and neuroscience to appreciate the perspectives and contributions of each other. [19]

The field of cognitive neuroscience needs to develop theories that connect the classroom and the neuroscience lab. These connections may then allow educators to consider how such theories either do, or do not, reflect the reality of their music classroom. The bridge then allows travel in the opposite direction. The observations of music educators become data for new cognitive theories that then contribute to research directions of neuroscientists. Unfortunately, this promising interdisciplinary two-way model has not yet found general acceptance. To date, neuroscience has been reluctant to take advantage of the wealth of possible contributions from the world of education.

Teacher Perspectives

There has been relatively little research into teachers' views on the value of neuroscience and cognitive neuroscience in the classroom. What research has taken place sends a cautionary message. While a majority of surveyed educators acknowledge the value of neuroscience research in the classroom, a closer look at their responses shows that the value comes when the research confirms the teacher's classroom pedagogy.[20] Additionally, while many teachers believe that they currently incorporate neuroscience findings in their classrooms, the incorporated practices are often misapplications of study findings.[21]

Further caution is suggested when considering the sources of educators' neuroscience information. Media outlets such as Dr. Phil and Oprah are frequently cited as the primary source of teachers' neuroscience information.[22] Therefore, it may come as no surprise that many educators confuse cognitive neuroscience and neuroscience. As a result, music educators, including Kodály music educators, may find themselves inadequately prepared to respond to research claims that depict music education negatively.

What can Kodály music educators do to effectively counter media misrepresentations of neuroscience and cognitive neuroscience research? How can we provide perspective to the debate of the value of music education?

Step one: We must do our homework. As mentioned above, knowledge is key. By taking time to become familiar with the basic terminology, techniques, strengths and limitations of neuroscience imaging techniques, music educators will be able not only to point out problems and misrepresentations, but also to recognize valid findings and theories that could potentially have a place in the classroom. To become knowledgeable, we must:

• Develop a fundamental understanding of the imaging technologies used and be aware of the strengths and limitations of each.

• Appreciate the distance (levels of analysis) between neuroscience and the classroom, and be aware of the value of cognitive neuroscience and the underlying theories it can provide.

• Understand that neuroscience is but one scientific source that can contribute to education, but should never be confused with educational science.[23]

The next step is to recognize that you are an expert. Remember, there is no research laboratory that can replicate the experience, and experiences, that music educators possess. Just as health care providers balance technical knowledge with their own practical experience, so should music educators. This does not mean discounting what neuroscience studies offer. On the contrary, music educators would do well to critically evaluate the research and be willing to adjust their own pedagogy when appropriate. While we, as experts in the day-to-day appreciation and application of Kodály music education, have access to the most extensive data set on the cognitive benefits of music education, the general public, including administrators, politicians and school board members, may be more likely to have their opinions shaped by mainstream media reports that merely need to reference neuroscience in order to produce an effect.

Like other educators, music educators, including Kodály music educators, face the challenge of evaluating research from the fields of neuroscience and cognitive neuroscience. This article is intended to provide tools and strategies to help decipher seemingly intractable neuroscience and cognitive neuroscience data. The next article ["Making Sense of Neuroscience Research," published in the *Kodály Envoy* 41, no. 1 (2014)] will demonstrate how to evaluate neuroscience and cognitive neuroscience research to determine its validity and applicability. With these steps, Kodály teachers can move confidently toward constructive response to the challenges of neuroscience research and its representation in the media.

Notes

[1] Samuel A. Mehr, Adena Schachner, Rachel C. Katz and Elizabeth S. Spelke, "Two Randomized Trials Provide No Consistent Evidence for Nonmusical Cognitive Benefits of Brief Preschool Music Enrichment," *PLoS ONE* 8, no. 12 (2013), e82007. doi:10.1371/journal.pone.0082007.

[2] *Boston Globe*, December 11, 2013.

[3] *Time*, December 11, 2013.

[4] "Harvard Study Challenges 'Mozart Effect'," *The Advocacy Bulletin* (December 12, 2013), http://advocacy.nafme.org.

[5] Comment posted on December 12, 2013 re "Two new studies by Harvard researchers show no effect of music training on the cognitive abilities of young children," http://www.reddit.com.

[6] Lois Hetland and Ellen Winner, "The Arts and Academic Achievement: What the Evidence Shows," *Arts Education Policy Review* 102, no. 5 (2001): 3–6, doi:10.1080/10632910109600008.

[7] Hetland and Winner, "Arts and Academic Achievement," 4.

[8] Mehr et al., "Two Randomized Trials," 12.

[9] Sarah D. Sparks, "Study: Teachers Like Neuroscience, But Confusion Abounds," *Education Week: Inside School Research* (April 14, 2011). Retrieved from http://blogs.edweek.org.

[10] Marc G. Berman, John Jonides and Derek Evan Nee, "Studying mind and brain with fMRI," *Social Cognitive and Affective Neuroscience* 1, no. 2 (October 2006): 158–161, doi:10.1093/scan/nsl019

[11] Robert Turner and Terry Jones, "Techniques for Imaging Neuroscience," *British Medical Bulletin* 65, no. 1 (March 2003): 3–20, doi:10.1093/bmb/65.1.3.

[12] Nikos K. Logothetis, "What We Can Do and What We Cannot Do with fMRI," *Nature* 453, no. 7197 (June 2008): 869–878, doi:10.1038/nature06976.

[13] Susumu Mori and J. Donald Tournier, *Introduction to Diffusion Tensor Imaging: And Higher Order Models* (Oxford: Academic Press, 2013).

[14] Russell A. Poldrack, "Inferring Mental States from Neuroimaging Data: From Reverse Inference to Large-scale Decoding," *Neuron* 72, no. 5 (December 2011): 692, doi:10.1016/j.neuron.2011.11.001.

[15] Poldrack, "Inferring Mental States."

[16] John T. Bruer, "Education and the Brain: A Bridge Too Far," *Educational Researcher* 26, no. 8 (November 1997): 4, doi:10.3102/0013189X026008004

[17] Sergio Della Sala and Mike Anderson, *Neuroscience in Education: The Good, the Bad, and the Ugly* (Oxford: Oxford University Press, 2012).

[18] John Geake and Paul William Cooper, "Cognitive Neuroscience: Implications for Education?" *Westminster Studies in Education* 26, no. 1 (June 2003): 7–20, doi:10.1080/0140672030260102.

[19] John Geake, "Cognitive Neuroscience and Education: Two-way Traffic or One Way Street?" *Westminster Studies in Education* 27, no. 1 (April 2004): 87, doi:10.1080/0140672040270107.

[20] Cayce J. Hook and Martha J. Farah, "Neuroscience for Educators: What Are They Seeking, and What Are They Finding?" *Neuroethics* 6, no. 2 (August 2013): 331–341, doi:10.1007/s12152-012-9159-3; Susan J. Pickering and Paul Howard-Jones, "Educators? Views on the Role of Neuroscience in Education: Findings from a Study of UK and International Perspectives," *Mind, Brain, and Education* 1, no. 3 (October 2007): 109; Lauren Serpati and Ashley R. Loughan, "Teacher Perceptions of NeuroEducation: A Mixed Methods Survey of Teachers in the United States," *Mind, Brain,and Education* 6, no. 3 (August 2012): 174– 176, doi:10.1111/j.1751-228X.2012.01153.x.

[21] Debby Zambo and Ronald Zambo, "Teachers' Beliefs about Neuroscience and Education," *Teaching Educational Psychology* 7, no. 2 (Fall 2011): 25–41.

[22] Zambo and Zambo, "Teachers' Beliefs."

[23] Sala and Anderson, *Neuroscience in Education*.

Originally published in *Bulletin in the International Kodály Society* 40, no. 1 (2015): 3–8. Reprinted by permission.

THE APPLICATION OF INVENTED SYMBOLS RELATING TO SIGHT-SINGING

Megan Ankuda and Margaux Lux, with David Fulton

In our Kodály-inspired model of instruction and learning, we often observe that students sing more accurately when tracing the melodic line. Beyond tracing with one hand while singing, the use of Curwen hand signs enhances and refines a kinesthetic response to intervallic relationships. John Curwen developed hand signs in 1870 as he continued to refine the movable-do sol-fa method adapted from Sarah Glover.[1] Hungarian pedagogue Erzsébet Szőnyi described the impact of Curwen's innovation in England, in particular the addition of movable-do sol-fa syllables written under traditional notation, which "facilitated enormously a hitherto complex maze of tonalities."[2] In this article, we will describe how one student's invented symbols helped a class of second-graders in New Haven, Connecticut, learn to sight-sing more fluently using hand signs and positively impacted the learning environment.

Although hand signs are considered synonymous with the Kodály approach, their use was never mentioned specifically by Kodály himself in publication. The first mention of hand signs in Hungarian methodology was by Jenő Ádám, in a pedagogical book written at Kodály's request.[3] Nevertheless, hand signs are a commonly accepted pedagogical tool for accurate singing. They were first introduced to Hungarian pedagogues in 1937, when German educator and folklorist Fritz Jöde presented his teaching methods—including movable-do solfège—in Budapest, greatly influencing the developing Hungarian methodology.[4] Zoltán Kodály's multiple observations of the English choral tradition, and specific references to John Curwen's method, emphasize their validity in our pedagogical mindset.[5] The pedagogical writings of Lois Choksy underline that the hand signs "have been incorporated, with only minor changes, to reinforce intervallic feeling. They present a visualization in space of the high-low relationship among the notes being sung."[6]

Our challenge as teachers is to provide a context where hand signs function to assist, rather than overburden, our students. We dislike the stereotype that any teaching involving solfège is labeled as "the Kodály Method," and we also want to make sure we are teaching music, not solfège. Although differentiated instruction is built into a good Kodály teacher's practice, new students entering rigorous music programs require special attention. In the opinion of the author, who has taught in two public school systems with high-frequency instruction, pedagogical techniques for new students must be continuously developed and refined in high-frequency teaching situations.

Like many communities in America, our urban school's population in New Haven is transient. On a monthly basis we receive new students, expecting them to integrate into a program where music notation has been constructed sequentially from Kindergarten, and students attend music class three to four times weekly. This is a curious problem for high-frequency music programs, because they are so few and far between in public education: How do we help new students to acclimate to solfège, hand signs, and traditional music notation without frustrating them?

We met David Fulton in the fall of 2016, when he began second grade at Worthington Hooker School in New Haven. David's family had recently returned to their neighborhood school after spending a year away, and David rejoined a cohort that attended music three times (100 minutes total) per week. At the beginning of second grade, his classmates' literacy practice included a pentatonic tone set in three positions.

Fig. 1. Pentatonic tone sets for David Fulton's 2nd-grade class.

F=*do*   G=*do*   C=*do*

David is a dedicated cello student who values both music and literacy. Upon his return to our school, he struggled to combine solfège and hand signs when reading traditional music notation. Looking back, David remembered feeling frustrated by music reading, and decided to invent a solution.[7]

One Friday afternoon, David approached us with an idea. His class had sung a two-part exercise based on the melody of "Wallflowers," and David asked if he could write the hand signs on his music. We responded that it might be cumbersome to actually draw pictures of hands beneath each note, and inquired what he actually meant. David showed us: Under *so*, he drew a square. Under *mi*, a dash. Under *do*, a circle. Our interest was piqued. For each of the five notes of the pentatonic scale, David had in mind a symbol to correspond with the shape of his hand:

Solfa syllable	Curwen Hand sign	David Fulton's Symbol
do	🖐	o
re	🖐	\
mi	🖐	—
so	🖐	□
la	🖐	∩

According to David, the symbol ∩ enables the singer to immediately retrieve the hand sign for *la*. He uses these symbols, which we dubbed the Fulton Symbols, sparsely: often at the beginning of a phrase, or after an interval larger than a second. David's invented symbols replaced the sol-fa syllables traditionally placed below music notation. Note this example

228

(Figures 2 and 3) from Kodály's *333 Reading Exercises*.[8] The Fulton Symbols replace the sol-fa letter name with a symbol corresponding to the hand sign.

Fig. 2. Zoltán Kodály: *333 Reading Exercises*, no. 216

Fig. 3. The same exercise using Fulton symbols.

As the result of a carefully sequenced sound-before-sight approach to music, students hear *la* within the established tonality when their hand forms the corresponding sign. The Fulton Symbols allow students to transition directly from symbol back to sound using the shape of their hand without first having to intellectualize the sol-fa syllable.

We were initially skeptical that an additional layer of symbolism would help students internalize the music. Over the course of the school year, we experimented with use of the Fulton Symbols and became convinced that enabling students to access hand signs directly from the page allows the singer to "fully concentrate on correct intonation and the aural image of the pitch,"[9] and to more immediately and directly derive music from the staff. The Fulton Symbols improved the sight-singing of the entire second grade cohort, especially those who were new to our school or were struggling with fluency.

Aside from their musical benefit, David's symbols created an unprecedented opportunity for social interaction, evocative of the interactive play space of learning in the Vygotskian frame of reference.[10] David's ownership of his learning through his own invented musical notation became contagious: Students in his class began to apply the Fulton Symbols to traditional notation and became—in a sense—musical connoisseurs[11] in the process. Before sight-singing a new exercise, students engaged in peer-to-peer conversation with David and each other about the need for Fulton Symbols in particular spots, gaining a sense of camaraderie and ownership of the sight-singing process as they struggled together through cognitive disequilibrium.[12]

Invented children's notation is uncommon in the Kodály teacher's scope and sequence, but our experience with the Fulton Symbols reinforced the need for students to lead and construct their musical understanding. Jeanne Bamberger's conclusion to her book, *The Mind Behind the Musical Ear: How Children Develop Musical Intelligence*,[13] serves as a reminder that we must remain open to new ideas, especially those from our smallest teachers.

My hope is that teachers can maintain their integrity and at the same time be willing to take risks, to query their own beliefs, to become more intimate with what they know how to do well; and that by looking at the window that shapes their view of a child's world instead of always looking through it, they will come to know better what their students know.[14]

Notes

[1] Celia Waterhouse, "An Appraisal of the Norwich Sol-fa Method and Materials for Choir Training and Music Teaching, Devised by Sarah Anna Glover in 19th Century Norwich" (paper presented at the 19th International Kodály Symposium, Katowice, Poland, August 17, 2009). http://kodaly.org.uk/blog/an-appraisal-of-the-norwich-sol-fa-method-by-celia-waterhouse

[2] Erszébet Szőnyi, *Kodály's Principles in Practice: An Approach to Music Education through the Kodály Method* (London: Boosey & Hawkes, 1973), 20.

[3] Lois Choksy, *The Kodály Context: Creating an Environment for Musical Learning* (Englewood Cliffs, NJ: Prentice-Hall, 1981), 10.

[4] Mary Alice Hein, SNJM, *The Legacy of Zoltán Kodály: An Oral History Perspective* (Budapest: International Kodály Society, 1992), 19-20.

[5] Zoltán Kodály, foreword for a publicity brochure following publication of the first English version of the Kodály Choral Method in July 1962, in Bernarr Rainbow and Gordon Cox, *Music in Educational Thought and Practice: A Survey from 800 BC* (Woodbridge, UK: Bowdell Press, 2006), 386.

[6] Lois Choksy, *The Kodály Method: Comprehensive Music Education from Infant to Adult* (Englewood Cliffs, NJ: Prentice-Hall, 1974), 2.

[7] David Fulton, interview by Megan Ankuda and Margaux Lux, New Haven, CT, May 2016.

[8] Zoltán Kodály, *333 Olvasógyakorlat* (Budapest: Editio Musica Budapest, 1941), no. 216.

[9] László Dobszay, *Teacher's Book to Volume I of the World of Tones* (Budapest: Editio Musica Budapest, 1966), 23.

[10] Lev S. Vygotsky, *Mind in Society: The Development of Higher Mental Processes* (Cambridge, MA: Harvard University Press, 1978).

[11] Debbie Carroll, "Children's Invented Notations: Extending Knowledge of Their Intuitive Musical Understandings Using a Vygotskian Social Constructivist View," *Psychology of Music* (Article first published online: July 14, 2017 DOI: https://doi. org/10.1177/0305735617716532): 15.

[12] For a discussion relating to the term cognitive disequilibrium, see Jeanne Bamberger, *The Mind Behind the Musical Ear* (Cambridge, MA: Harvard University Press, 1995), 102.

[13] Bamberger, *Mind Behind*, 283.

Originally published in *Kodály Envoy* 44, no. 2 (2018): 5–6. Reprinted by permission.

THE KODÁLY SPIRIT

Katalin Forrai

Zoltán Kodály was a soft-spoken, reserved man. Sometimes he would take many seconds to answer, yet his reply was always straightforward, clear and short.

Imagine Kodály standing on the top of a hill. From here, he had the ability to see great distances and remote places in the future, as well as the value of time. His patience was rooted in the love and respect of nature, learning from it that time would yield fruit, invisibly, yet definitely. He was not afraid to let his compositions and writings ripen over a long period of time.

Kodály's criticism was a source of strength and motivation to improve. He never instructed, but generated professional arguments from which the hearer deduced unambiguously the unspoken answer.

Kodály was a multi-faceted genius, composer, ethnomusicologist and linguist: a man of public life, of international recognition, who fought for public education.

What is the secret of Kodály's spirit that motivates his followers, his students and their students to teach subsequent generations with a sincere obsession and pleasure? Could this spirit be the rich happiness that teachers and students realize through cultivating and listening to music?

Hungary is a small country in Central Europe, a drop in the sea of the nations of the world. In 1996, it will celebrate its one thousand one hundredth anniversary of existence. For centuries it was the scene of various power struggles. The armies of the East and the West clashed on its territory, leaving behind demolished villages. Hiding in the hills and on the river banks, the people had to start anew over and over again. Overcoming difficulties gave strength to survive. In this struggle, preserving the language and specific traditions was a matter of life and death. This historical past was perhaps one of the reasons why the respect for tradition and a sense of belonging together developed.

Written evidence of the Hungarian's pleasure in singing survives from the eleventh century onward. Singing has always given strength to the people, and teachers wanted to transmit the pleasure of the beauty and force of singing to others, as is true even today, at the end of the twentieth century.

At the beginning of this century, Béla Bartók and Zoltán Kodály recognized—as composers, folk song collectors and professors of the Academy of Music—that musically educated people were unfamiliar with the Hungarian musical tradition, while most people were completely ignorant of the masterpieces and culture of the musically educated world. Bartók and Kodály turned toward musical education from the twenties and thirties onward, when they were already acknowledged and appreciated as composers and scholars. Their objective was to realize in the people's consciousness an appreciation for the specific qualities of Hungarian music and to make them musically better educated. Zoltán Kodály composed children's songs and Béla Bartók compiled the series *For Children* and *Mikrokosmos* for young ones learning to play the piano.

When Kodály's interest turned toward public education, about five to six percent of children learned to play an instrument. For the sake of raising the level of general education, he advocated for letting every child partake in musical education at school. He determined the contents of education leading to musical culture. He was looking for an effective and simple method of musical reading and writing which could reach all those who would not study an instrument but would be dependent on their ear and singing voice alone.

The human voice expresses the beauty of melodic lines by singing. The symbolic potential of words originates from and affects imagination. The magic of singing together is a socializing factor, forging together communities and making people friends. Starting from the common chanting of mother and child, through various phases of singing, to performing choruses by Bach, singing may bring uplifting moments in life.

Kodály firmly believed that music had a force in shaping personalities and even a transfer effect. Paradoxically, music induces discipline: It happens in time, has a precise pitch in a required tempo. Its inner mathematical laws have been known for centuries. At the same time, its lifelong emotional effect cannot be expressed in words.

Throughout the world, those who have created philosophies of music education have recognized the importance of starting music education early. However important the susceptibility and imitation faculty of small children may be, it is a dangerous concept to think that what they like is good for them and in accordance with their age. Children like and imitate anything and everything, for their ability to choose has not yet developed. They will prefer the music which surrounds them, which they get to hear. One single deep emotional experience may suffice to kindle their interest in, and turn their imagination to, good music. Kodály recalled from his childhood a memory when, sitting under the piano, he was listening to his parents performing music. As he came to know later, they were playing Mozart's F Major violin sonata. He was convinced that he would not have become the kind of musician he turned out to be if his parents had played a fashionable "hit song" then and there.

Properly chosen music material may be a means of supplementing and counterbalancing the many-sided musical influences received from the mass media. It is to be feared that the youth of our days have more experiences of music from mechanical sources than of live music. They would rather listen to than make music—though there is a demand not only for singing and entertainment while they are young, but later in adulthood as well. As a beginning, Kodály suggested using the folk tradition for the cultural force carried by the language and folk songs. At the same time, he thought that it was important to transmit the knowledge of composed music—the masterpieces of world music literature— and the characteristic music of other nations as well. In his opinion, good and valuable music was everything that, when listened to or performed, had a positive effect, an additional nourishment for the soul, which contributed to the strengthening and enrichment of the personality.

One of the major, most essential driving forces of the "Kodály spirit" in education is the idea that the teaching process should be based on aural sensations and singing. According to his advice, the audible tone, the melody, the rhythm and the harmony should come first and only later should the musical elements and phenomena be named. It is just dry theory to explain to the children the intervals of the major scale in words instead of having them sing melodies in that key, hear the key in a piece of music, and then attach to it the concept of the key. A well-developed ear provides the foundation for musical memory, promotes a better understanding of musical works, and contributes to enjoying them.

Kodály suggested a method of musical reading and writing that was used in the tenth century. The system of relative sol-fa stood in the service of vocal culture for centuries and was still known in England and the United States in the last century. In this system the relation of the notes defines the intervals, the movement of keys on the staff, and the simple forms of writing figures and demonstrating pitch visually are used to prepare relative solmization.

As a linguist, Kodály held the rhythm and accentuation of speech in high esteem. He suggested not to begin musical notation with the notes of the scale, step by step. Every language and country should construct a sequence for musical reading and writing starting from its own specific intonation and rhythm, from simple children's songs to difficult choral parts. For example, the typical turns in the majority of European children's songs are *slsm* and *sfmrd*—within the range of a major hexachord. On the other hand, the pivot interval of Japanese children's songs is due precisely to linguistic properties. Here we find *rdl*, with the end of the songs often returning to the starting note *(re)*. In "Kodály's spirit" then, the Japanese start reading and writing with the interval *re-do* and not *sol-mi*. Similarly, 6/8 time and the upbeat must appear in the kindergarten in countries where this is a natural element of the language. Since they do not occur in Hungarian, children encounter them only later, at school, when they learn to sing other people's songs or listen to excerpts from composed music.

Foreigners are often astonished by the consciousness, creativity and teaching preparation of Hungarian teachers. This pedagogical attitude is a prerequisite—and the basis of a good education. Having an overall view of the whole process, extending over several years, excludes the possibility of a teacher ever using the same song material for three or four years. Developing long-term objectives and planning the level of attainments in advance help to create the individual teaching units and ensure their success. This conscious approach must be paired with a constant readiness to carry out changes whenever the original concept must be adapted to the requirements of a given situation, matching the musical experience and mood. Recognizing the actual state of affairs during teaching, and finding new ideas and manners of realization quickly, demands continuous task-solving ability and creativity from the teacher.

Kodály often quoted Jenõ Ádám, the eminent Hungarian music teacher, who compiled the first school book series in 1948 under Kodály's guidance. Ádám said that the means, procedures and methods of teaching must be worked out by the teachers themselves. To be able to do so, they must be well-educated in music, educational theory, and practical teaching. They must take their own personality into consideration and adapt themselves to the age and composition of a given group of children. They must be familiar with the concept and find the most suitable music material and most effective forms of teaching. Only a well-trained, educated teacher with a deep knowledge of his or her subject can make a proper decision concerning the various methods and choose the most appropriate one. This background is needed to make teaching joyful and enjoyable, both for the teacher and for the children.

Kodály's personality attracted enthusiastic Hungarian music teachers. With excellent sense, he selected from among them experts for the various age groups and levels. During the past fifty years they proved the viability of Kodály's ideas by teaching in the schools, writing school books and manuals, and educating generations of teachers. They emphasized the importance of human relationships in the alienated, mechanized atmosphere of the twentieth century, as well as the beauty and joy of education and learning.

It was on the occasion of the Budapest ISME Conference in 1964 that the world met with and was astonished by the achievements of Hungarian music education, which by that time had been carried on for 20 years. After the well-intentioned stumbling of the first adaptations abroad (for example, the translation of Hungarian children's songs into other languages, or beginning with pentatonic music in places where this was not present in the local culture), the situation has changed. Instead of two-day Kodály courses, after which all participants were convinced they had become Kodály experts, there are now Kodály training courses offered for academic years and continuing summers to satisfy increased musical demands, and to prove that the "Kodály spirit" is something more than only hand signs and *ti-ti ta*.

Kodály's personality united the folk music collector, the composer and the cultural politician into one. His intention was (1) to raise youth to the high arts rooted in and nourished by folk arts and (2) to show people harmony and beauty among the shocking events of the present. Good music has a positive charge, inspiring confidence and encouragement.

Kodály was able to discover a diamond among the ashes and set it into a golden frame. The original folk song, the simple peacock melody sung by an old peasant, is the diamond. (The peacock is the symbol of freedom for those who are in prison and also a symbol of the quest for truth.) I would like to demonstrate Kodály's musical setting, which is the golden frame of the diamond found among the ashes. Listen to the folk song and then to the last bars of the *Peacock Variations*, arranged for orchestra, as they unfold from the simple melody.

Originally published in *Bulletin of the International Kodály Society* 18, no. 2 (1993): 3–6. Reprinted by permission.

DEVELOPING MUSICAL CREATIVITY: MUSIC AS A LANGUAGE

Helga Dietrich

We seem to have lost the natural need for daily human communication and the magic of turning towards each other. At least the acknowledgment of its usefulness and right seems to be banished or ignored nowadays, especially in the development of the *personality in early childhood education*.

Perhaps it is not too late to stress the importance of building and shaping our *personal* human relationships and the *joy* they imply in our everyday life. We must do so because the development and formation of the personality of the children entrusted to our care is a great responsibility for the teacher.

Lack of communication is a worrying phenomenon, the examination of which is pressing. This is the question: who needs, and how important is, communication based on the human voice, face-to-face contact and moving together with regulated postures?

Infants' interest in their surroundings begins already in the womb as an innate inclination. The *early interaction* with the baby, melodious and rhythmic speech, idiosyncratic intonation and the mother's heartbeat exert a compound impact on emotional bonding and security. Infants respond more and more often with movement to early stimulation influencing their emotive and cognitive development. Motivation—its playful modes—need not only be verbal: it can and ought to be musical as well. A special language may develop between mother and child.

To be able to live, we have to discover ourselves and learn how to live in our environment. We do so every day, both spontaneously and with careful planning. To establish contact with someone, we need a language to communicate by.

Let us find out how music/ singing can become an authentic tool and medium of expression from early childhood: how it can be a language that, in the course of acquisition, becomes essential in laying the foundation of the child's personality.

Music as a kind of language is organized in tones, carrying tension caused by various changes; a channel between partners, a form of metacommunicative signaling. Its complement is movement, which also assumes a unique role as signal: the play of the eyes, the expression of the glance. Non-instrumental music, as is the case here, includes words and verbal images, but messages are also conveyed by the *intensity of sound, timbre, the length of sound, the pitch of the note*.

If music/singing is a sort of language, it mediates messages that express first of all emotions —joy or sorrow, quiet or clamorous moods; hence it mainly affects the feelings. As a language, however, it varies from culture to culture and from age to age. Even the simplest songs differ— in tone set, compass, articulation, rhythm, basic pulsation—on various continents.

In Hungarian music education, one of the basic principles is that music should be an everyday experience and a living, direct form of expression. It should also help the child develop conscious musical memory and attention, through the joy of playful movements and singing together.

The starting point is the adult playing with the child. The above-mentioned facts are especially important when the infant's environment is organized. In the phase of learning to speak, instances of music/singing—just like speech—serve as *models* for the child. The acquisition of the *musical mother tongue* also begins with imitation, so a model worth imitating is indispensable.

The cooing of the infant is a kind of extemporized production, improvisation at a basic level. Its main characteristics are imitation and repetition. From the *melodious and rhythmic speech patterns* that the infant hears, he/she is especially attracted to pitch and melodious intonation, and later to articulation, differing from country to country.

There is an active road to the discovery of the realm of sound. At the beginning, the child plays with sounds instinctively, *strongly motivated by the rhythmic character of the language*. The heard and remembered rhythmic patterns of sound and the patterns of experience are decisive. As in games, this is also organized by certain rules after some time, after much imitation and repetition.

There is increasing systematization in the infant's vocal production, implying the basic elements of music, such as rhythm, melody, dynamics, etc. This can also be observed in two or three note patterns followed by a pause, and attempts at their varied repetition. This activation of the vocal chords already points to other basic elements of speech and music: carrying tension, presupposing a recipient. While practicing, the child also learns that the sound is "audible mimicry." It may express an *inner need*, a feeling of comfort or anxiety, with its intensity, repetition, duration, pitch, timbre. The gradual learning of the main elements of singing—both the inclination and the physical possibility—can be observed even in early infancy, as well as in the *cooing monologues*. This is an enjoyable process for the child: learning to hear and to act. At the beginning, the child does not say but sings the human sounds in imitation, trying to fix the range of sound just heard. At first he/she repeats each sound at a given pitch, followed by their combination. Often enough, a dialogue evolves between mother and child. The ear is helped by the eye: the child watches the mouth of the speaker, trying to fix the sound source. He/she often remains immobile while doing so.

Imitation gets richer and richer every week and the child is filled with a sense of security through this game. The child's perception, the ability to grasp something and keep it in mind, is improved by imitation. It pleases the child to be able to produce sound sequences; the joy of activity is immediately apparent. It is actually a "functional game" in which the child learns, practices sung sequences, testing the capacity of his/her ear and voice production and performance—all this instinctively. Thus the child becomes open to receiving and storing further experiences.

About the age of one year, irregularly swinging rhythmic two-bar movements can be observed, such as swaying the body, wagging the head left and right, lifting the arms, and later, the alternation of left and right feet. This natural kinetic movement will later help develop real musical rhythm—the sense and skill of coordinated rhythm—but at this level it is *not* musical rhythm.

The child acquires the basic elements of speaking and singing playfully, through imitative "functional games," copying the models in its environment. And in the process, the speech organs also are refined.

The arousal of the need to act is only the beginning in the child's development. The emotional bonds tying the child to his/her surroundings and to the persons around him/her are of great importance. An adult capable of entering into delightful contact, face to face, with the child has an easy job: the eye contact, together with the sound stimuli, is an enjoyable daily occupation. It reinforces the child's emotional security, especially when the playful singing, the tiny situations repeated day by day, are also coupled with shared movement, and when the child can clearly perceive the non-verbal communicative signs of the adult facing the child. An emotionally motivated child is open to cooperation, for example, when you tickle, caress, exercise, tap or rock him/her.

The adult—as the human representative of the child's environment—provides the child with experiences to be perceived by his/her senses (heard, seen, touched). This is done spontaneously, but it is advisable for the adult to consciously select experiences for the child as well. Their further contact will depend on the multitude of personal patterns that make the child open to action; the mediating force is the instinct to imitate.

By creating a playful situation in a relaxed atmosphere, in natural, unaffected situations of speech and song, total communication may evolve between adult and child, with lively facial expressions, constant eye contact, carefully created gentle tone colors, clear articulation, authentic gestures, relaxed posture and regulation of distance.

All this means the giving of one's entire personality. That is important because when a contact is established with a child, one's deepest personal traits must be brought to the surface, offered as a gift. Singing that we give to them with emotional openness relaxes them and makes them free.

Another important factor in creating a playful situation is what to find—that is, offer—for *imitation*. In spontaneous situations, whether the adult is the mother, father, nurse, kindergarten teacher or other, one's deeds flow unrestrained. Naturally melodious/rhythmic utterances and simple repeated sentences are most frequent, when, for example, you tend to the infant's needs, lull him/her to sleep, lure the toddler to take another step, etc.

In addition, rhythmic nursery rhymes and simple children's folk songs, facilitating the formation of a playful situation suited to the child's age, play an important role. It is noteworthy that a competent teacher with a responsive ear will only choose songs and rhymes that are perfectly suited to the children's level of linguistic development, and to the physical state of their vocal chords.

Zoltán Kodály, the great music educator of the twentieth century who was also a professor of philology, often stressed in his writings that *rhythmic rhymes and songs of a narrow compass have equal importance* in the early phase of a child's learning to speak.

Children can instinctively absorb the *intonation* and *natural melody of the mother tongue*, its *unwritten rules of accentuation*, while they play in concerted motion with the adult in riding, swinging and rhythmic plays, or in playing the palm or tickling games that lead to an exhilarating climax. The chosen tempo of speaking is slower than normal speech—for the sake of articulation, to be read from lip movement as well, and to match the kinetic movement (clapping, fist-hitting, etc.), serving to stress the pulsation accompanying the text.

It is well known that in the "lap-child" and "knee-child" periods, the child's main activity is playing. The child's mind is disposed towards playing; he/she carries on every activity playfully, through which he/she gathers valuable experiences.

Singing also comes to life during playing. Singing causes joy in the play. A child of two often sings songs of his/her own invention, "found out by him/herself." This playful production is closely connected to the play activity. It is most often continuous humming, with motifs repeated again and again. At the age of two to three, words still play a subordinated role; the text may be constantly repeated groups of sounds, clusters of recognizable phonemes or series of words without definite connotation. It possibly expresses the general emotive state of the child. It is a fact, however, that this process rests on the reconstruction of once heard and remembered elements.

From three onwards, children sing meaningful texts with increasing frequency, studded with playfully coined phrases. Onomatopoeic words are more and more often used. The contents of these singing manifestations are always determined by the activity of playing, such as baking or rocking a doll to sleep. A child may "perform" a whole story adorned with songs, whose basis or background is usually some experience in the child's life elaborated at his/her level, for example, the birth of a brother or sister.

In terms of music, the products of creative melodious playing are often no more than the recitative enumeration of tones, within which the child repeats a few shards of the musical experiences—e.g. typical intervals—he/she has obtained from the environment. For quite some time, no motivic articulation can be observed. Sometimes a sentence takes off and meanders along, and the next time, the story and the tune round off bluntly. Rarely are tonal rules observed. Some rhythmic commitment can, however, be observed in children who have heard many live examples. Such children soon respond well to the rhythmic rules of the mother tongue; prosody is soon correctly included in their playful word and sentence creations, as when they dance a doll, knock with a wooden-spoon doll, imitate a growling bear, etc.

Some children add a self-made melody to a part of a poem or nursery rhyme they have heard often. Their vocal performance may span almost two octaves, gliding up and down along this range, creating sounds and sound sequences.

In the course of adaptation to the sounds of the environment, gradually distinct intervals and motifs can be discerned in the child's performance, which he/she tries to copy repeatedly. This process is facilitated in the adult environment by the basic forms of the melodic intonation and accents of speech, which vary from language to language.

One cannot stress enough the influence of early children's songs restricted to very simple intervals. It is also important to emphasize that these motifs suit the physiological conditions of the child's speech organs. Success in imitation is also most complete through these simple tunes.

In Europe the inviting-calling thirds (so-mi) have salient importance in the auditory experience of children. The minor third is a pleasing interval to them, and appears in their recitations as a relatively constant, recurring element. The words sung to it are often just "padding words," such as the initial "and then" or "once upon a time." Children keep returning to these notes even when the rest of their sing-song consists of gliding transitions of tones.

With the advance of time, both the number of tones and the number of consciously intoned intervals increase. Naturally enough, there are individual differences in the process of the articulation of notes and in melodic invention. Being *constantly repeated*, some motifs stand out from the initially incoherent singing and become reinforced. These will be used by the child when he/she imitates a tune but simplifies a too difficult section by substituting familiar and easier melodic turns (e.g., *s-f-m-r-d* or *l-s-m*). This is especially common in the middle of a song. There is a close correlation between the reproduction of known songs and the child's own song-creating activity.

For adults, there is much to be learned by observing the songs and singing of little children—by observing, for example, how they experience these activities, or how they form their singing games, even from the early age of three years. If we are observant as teachers, the child can give us the signal or feedback that will provide an indication of a group's level of maturity in more than one personality area.

"Fictional games" are a qualitatively higher form of playing—by comparison to the previously mentioned "functional games"—a transfer of the observed world into the child's world. Everything that children can observe in their environment is acted out or "played out" in a "pretend" situation, and this ability or tendency to creatively incorporate personal experience applies equally to singing games.

Such games have great significance in the course of a child's personality development. What the child can formulate becomes contextually more colorful and kinetically richer; simultaneously, musical development begins through the child's expression of melody and song lyrics. In optimal situations, a stable emotional environment may foster this development.

The singing of folk songs and rhymes helps young children to discover the basic rules and common usages of sentence structure and grammar, eventually allowing such rules and structures to become second nature in their speech patterns. The "motif construction" of simple sentences linked together builds up compositions from two-bar (4 beat) motifs. Let's see some English rhymes as examples:

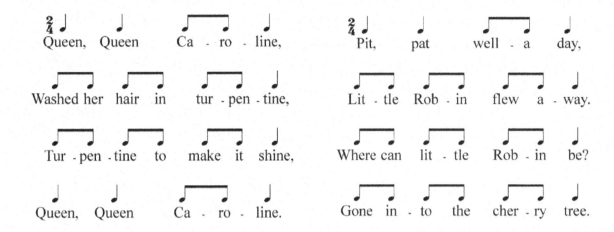

The *musical sentence*—even in the most simple child's song or nursery rhyme—comes to life as the smallest *musically meaningful unit, in the form of the motif.* The rhythmic pair or two-bar composition can be filled by different rhythmic elements. With the help of the rhythm of the words and the interpretation of the musical rules, the child begins to understand that the accent comes on the first sound or syllable of the motif, and within that is the first beat:

or:

Chop, chop, choppity chop/Chop off the bottom and chop off the top,
What there is left we will put in the pot/Chop, chop, choppity chop.

Each singing game and rhyme coming from the folk tradition is a complex unit, integrally interconnected, combining lyrics, rhythm, melody, movement and action into one complete experience. Together, these elements, in most cases, support and enhance the phrasing of the musical motifs. It cannot be stressed enough that, in the course of the singing games, the accompanying movements, the physical activity itself—so important for children's involvement here—become, for the child, directly associated with the melodic, line-by-line structural phrasing: for example, "Teddy bear, Teddy bear / Turn around. . ."

The peculiarities of "fictional games," mentioned above, also begin to appear in the singing games of three- and four-year old children playing in small groups. This development comes from the strong influence and modeling of primary caregivers, and later from the children's own peer groups. The child's developing musical memory becomes evident in recreational play and in a variety of *recreated singing games*, as both lyrics and melody reflect a continually evolving precision and richness of expression. Therefore, the transition from one level of game activities to the next—and its contextual enrichment—is the direct result of the modeling behavior of adults and the guiding direction from more mature peers.

Throughout the duration of these activities, the "living imagination" is continuously present and develops as creative singing leads to "playful buildup." This "buildup" uses mainly melodic elements drawn from well-known and frequently repeated children's songs. These melodic elements are filtered, stored and saved as a *passive musical vocabulary*. From this "vocabulary" the child instinctively recalls those melodic elements he/she thoroughly knows and sings correctly. Favorite, often-heard fragments of melodies are committed to memory and, during spontaneous games, children often recall these fragments and "dress" them with invented words and very simple sentences—an activity which is *emotionally motivated*. The observer can often discover "borrowed melody turns" that children learn, select from, and use in their musical environments. These are generally adapted—transformed to their own capabilities. This explains why, in the spontaneous singing of four- or five-year olds, the basic traditional structure of musical forms appears.

Depending on the individual child—approximately at the beginning of the fourth year—*sound-synthesis* becomes the *unconscious way of creating* free melody improvisations. This ability leads to the *synthesis of the chain of sounds* which incorporates the imitated intonation of speech. Should these two conditions exist, they may be followed by the third stage of this process, *motif synthesis*—but only if the child has developed a *musical mother tongue* and strong language roots. Through his musically imaginative singing experimentation, the child's basic traditional *structure of musical forms* solidifies, going beyond the previously favored "organ grinder" melody-turns and the so-called "type" tunes. The child now begins using his *original* ideas with greater *flexibility* than before, ideas that are forthcoming with increasing *fluency*.

By the age of six years, within this process of individual development, the desire to create more elaborately stuctured tunes gradually evolves. Of crucial importance for the achievement of this stage is the strong presence of modeling behavior and an *encouraging environment*.

Given the important role that musical education can play in the fostering of growth and the shaping of character in small children, the responsibilities of adults providing musical teaching must be addressed. Children, *from laptime through kneetime and beyond* into the larger social world, are primarily influenced through their emotions. This notion is summed up by Katalin Forrai, a prominent Hungarian pedagogue and an internationally recognized expert on early childhood music education:

Emotion is a phenomenon caused by sensory perception. Everything that we hear and see connects with our inner reaction. This inner reaction is influenced by the attitude of adults, and this, in turn, contributes to the shaping of the child's "value system." Susceptible, interested in everything, refusing nothing equally, children accept the opinion and value system of the beloved adult.

Therefore, at their young age of development, we cannot argue about what has artistic value based upon the child's taste, a taste that completely surrenders itself to the forces and effects of the environment.[1]

The child's personality or character can be developed in different areas, and the best method for encouraging this development is to awaken the *desire for action*. Again, we emphasize the importance of the encouragement and support of the modeling adult. Children who have the opportunities both to take part in creative activities and to practice and play within these activities will be comfortable in three major capacities:

- communication
  - verbal and non-verbal
  - singing
- kinesthetic
  - movement; the body's spatial awareness
  - coordination of different parts of the body
  - then movement linked to sound, and, with practice, acquiring the ability for self-expression
- cognitive
  - thinking with understanding on different levels, development of memory, and the enrichment of imagination

While we can examine these capacities analytically to further our understanding of childhood learning and development, in the reality of our everyday lives such capacities are intrinsically interrelated, forming a closed unit.

The degree of development of the above capacities is strongly dependent on the openness and empathic ability of the adult, an ability which is a vitally important component for establishing a *mutual language*. This language also helps in the establishment of a community (daycares, preschools) where verbal means of communication (speech and singing, including tone, color, dynamics) are complemented by nonverbal means: mime, posture, hand movement, the great varieties of body movement. . . through interactions.

Katalin Forrai reminds us in the above-mentioned article:

Overall aesthetic appreciation is not confined to works of art or to the beauty of nature, but can include our response to social environments and human interactions. Art is a unique reflection of the world of colors, sounds, emotional effects of words, and the individual interpretation of symbols.[2]

Well-articulated, melodious speech, rhythmical sentences, and especially individual intonation, help in the development of the child's aesthetic sense, the enrichment of his vocabulary, and the continuing formation of his linguistic comprehension.

The use of *imaginative activities* serves as a good example for children who are eager to imitate. Their feedback proves to us how much pleasure is gained from the freedom of handling their own very individual ideas and imaginative activities. This pleasure is expressed in musical self-expression as well. Its components are originality, flexibility, fluency and later, the ability to elaborate in the creation of musical ideas.

The power of imagination belongs to the *divergent thinker.* . .

Words, songs, and the various means of metacommunication are all forms of expression—forms that, in their mutual effect, continually impact upon each other, evolving and maturing into an individual ethnocultural method or tool for communication. This "mature" communication, when combined with the use of a carefully chosen, specific method, will progressively allow the child at first to develop the ability for being receptive towards communication, then actively to imitate or imitatively respond to this communication, and finally to become independently creative in his own individual play-activity. In the introduction and application of this method, great attention must be paid to its *planning* and execution, so that each activity sequentially builds on the previous and firmly established step, providing a series of firm plateaus in the child's development. Yet it is important for the child's attitude and involvement that each activity remain thoroughly enjoyable and playful within a relaxed, nurturing environment.

Notes

[1] Katalin Forrai, "A művészetre nevelés lehetőségei az óvodai zenei nevelésben [The opportunities for art education in kindergarten music education] (Óvodapedagógiai nyári egyetem 18). Unpublished summer course materials, Kodály Institute, Kecskemét, Hungary (1991), 34.
[2] Forrai, 34.

A version of this article appeared in the Conference Book of the Kodály Music Education Institute of Australia (KMEIA) 2012 Biennial Kodály National Conference, Prince Alfred College, Adelaide, South Australia.

IT CAN BE A JOY, NOT A TORTURE:
MUSIC DICTATION WITH FRAMES

Ildikó Herboly Kocsár

The skill of musical writing is interdependent with and inseparable from other musical skills: rhythm, hearing, inner hearing, reading, memory, etc. Thus the best proof and control of hearing ability is music dictation in classes. Every music teacher knows that dictation is a nightmare for students in many cases. To avoid a bad experience, the method of music dictation with frames will help. This way of writing gives a very strong feeling of safety and security, because the students can see WHEN and WHERE the music starts and ends. There is no more tension, panic and fear in music classes, because the students are not facing a blank white paper.

In this article the following examples are taken from 32 different types of exercises used by the author in her teaching. They are suitable from primary level up to the tertiary one. (The numbers in brackets refer to their place within the range of the 32 graded examples.)

1. The paper given to the students shows a simple short rhythm phrase with one bar missing.

2. This is a known tune. The students fill in the missing notes.

3. The student example shows an unknown melody. The teacher sings the whole tune with la-la. Students must write the sol-fa syllables and rhythm as well.

4. The melody has pitches only. After listening to it sung or played by the teacher, students need to add time signature, rhythm values and bar lines.

5. "Row of notes" dictation. Signs show the missing notes; students fill them in first in staff notation, then with letter names.

6. "Technical writing." Put the two rhythm lines together into one score.

7. "Technical writing." Fit the two melodies into one score.

Mozart KV 465

8. The class is divided into two groups: they sing the sustained D and A while listening to a 4-note tune played by the teacher. The task is to write the melody sung by the teacher.

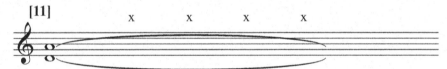

9. The teacher plays or sings a series of notes starting on D. The students must write figures indicating the interval from note to note.

10. This exercise is similar to the previous one, but now the instrumental students must write the fingering number of the melody.

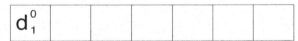

Thus far we have been dealing with single line dictation. Two–part dictation can be introduced systematically in much the same manner:

245

1. While singing the lower notes from the score, listen to and write the upper part.

[16]

2. While singing a known song from the score with text, make marks under the words indicating the rhythm played by the teacher on drum.

[17]

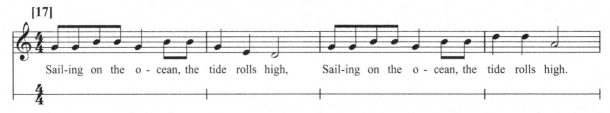

Sail-ing on the o - cean, the tide rolls high,   Sail-ing on the o - cean, the tide rolls high.

Sail-ing on the o - cean, the tide rolls high,   You can get a pret-ty girl,   by and by.

3. While singing the lower line in solfa, the students write the intervals played by the teacher above the sung notes.

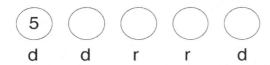

5

d   d   r   r   d

4. Fill in the missing intervals.

[25]

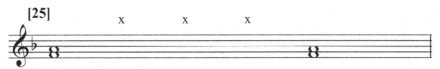

5. Add the missing accidentals.

J. Haydn

[28]

246

6. Fill in the missing upper and lower notes.

W. A. Mozart

7. While listening to the CD, fill in the melody.

G. Fauré: REQUIEM
Pie Jesu

8. While listening to the CD, fill in the missing notes.

HAYDN: Quartet Op. 76, Nr. 4 (Sunrise)

Students led in this way to musical dictation will find it a joy rather than a torture. They will have the sense that writing music is no more difficult than writing language and that the language of music belongs to them.

Summary of workshop presented at the 16th International Kodály Symposium in July 2003, Ourimbah (The University of Newcastle), Australia. Originally published in *Bulletin of the International Kodály Society* 29, no. 1 (2004): 35-39. Reprinted by permission.

HIGH-LEVEL MUSICIANSHIP IN FOCUS

Erzsébet Hegyi

In Kodály's conception of music education we encounter two fundamental purposes. One is the aim of cultivating a music-understanding general public, which appreciates and is receptive to valuable music, and the other is the training of a generation of musicians with a wide horizon, endowed with concrete and thorough professional knowledge. Although we are faced with different tasks in these two areas of cultural life, still the two cannot be separated from each other. After all, the ultimate aim of artistic manifestation is to help more and more people to attain a sincere enjoyment and understanding of beauty and artistic values.

One of the primary fundamental conditions for a high standard of a given human community's musical culture is that the teachers actively participating in musical instructions should be not only good pedagogues, but also good, or even better, musicians. But who might we regard as good musicians?

In his article "Who is a Good Musician?" (1953), Kodály said the following: "[T]he characteristics of a good musician can be summarized as follows: 1. A well-trained ear; 2. A well-trained intelligence; 3. A well-trained heart; 4. A well-trained hand. All four must develop together, in constant equilibrium. As soon as one lags behind or rushes ahead, there is something wrong."[1]

The question might occur to us when reading these lines: How are we to ascertain whether these components of the content of our musical nature are indeed in proper balance? What is the standard to which we can and must relate ourselves in this regard? The answer: If we are able to meet all the musical and intellectual requirements which Kodály poses for us in his vocal series (the so-called "Choral Method"), composed with a pedagogical purpose for future musicians, then we may claim we are versant in all four components of the conception of a good musician. Because whoever performs the pieces of the volume of *Epigrams* so as to sing the melody while playing the piano accompaniment himself, moreover in an artistic rendition, or intones the most difficult pieces of the *Tricinia* volume infallibly, and transposes them by heart wherever he wishes, because he has a clear grasp of the work's chord progression, its musical logic, and is able to pursue it mentally, has indeed developed within himself at a high level the unity of accomplished hearing, comprehension, the heart and the hand.

Naturally this aim can be attained only with consistent, tenacious and conscious work. But we will be rewarded for all our pains by the awareness and fact that, in possession of absorbed and sound professional grounding, we may boldly and purposefully advance in our career on the way we deem to be the best.

The frame of this opening lecture does not make it possible for us to point out all the essential music-, logic-, artistic- and knowledge-conveying moments of the way that Kodály has revealed to us. A few random examples are perhaps sufficient, however, to illustrate even from the standpoint of our own development how much we can draw from this rich treasury of musical culture.

In the following we hear a melody with a *s-m-r-d* tone set from the *333 Reading Exercises*:

333 Reading Exercises/253

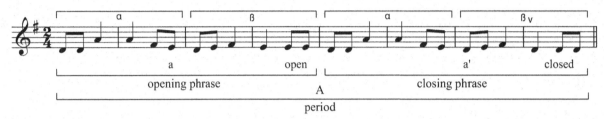

The pentatonic tetrachord melody with a *do* ending has the form of a typical period. The first half-melody consisting of two motives is open, the second half-melody containing similar material, but closed, replies to the first.

Another curiosity of the exercise is that the two successive rhythmic patterns of the paired bars making up the individual motives are heard in retrograde inversion:

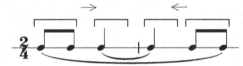

The period containing a a' presented in the foregoing is extraordinarily typical of the formal realm of Viennese Classicism. For example, both periods of the melody of Beethoven's "Lied des Marmottenbuben" have this kind of structure. We hear the first period of the song:

Beethoven: "Lied des Marmottenbuben"

250

We find this very same structure in the Trio section of Mozart's "Rondo in F Major" (K.15hh), but with formal elements of twice the length:

Mozart: "Rondo in F Major," K.15hh

Shall we return to the previously sung melody of the *333 Reading Exercises*? We can sing it also in canon if we hear the interval relationships of the given tonality unerringly:

333 Reading Exercises/253

If we possess sure inner hearing, the dissonance of the clash of seconds is not able to disturb our pure intonation of the melody as a tonal course of music.

We are able to solve the presentation of the following excerpt from Britten by relying on this very same sure inner hearing:

Britten: *Peter Grimes* (or.: I)

251

In this instance the melody that is sung sounds within the pentatonic tone set connected with C as *do*, while the accompaniment alternates an also C-rooted seventh chord [incomplete] and an A major 6/4 chord. Thus essentially two kinds of "maggiore-minore" vertical sounds occur in the musical material: one with an E—E flat coincidence based on a C keytone and another with a C—C sharp coincidence based on an A keytone. Nevertheless, intonation of the given pentatonic melody, when we possess the corresponding tonal sense, presents no difficulty.

Our next example from Kodály is the folksong theme of the 57th piece in Volume I of the *Bicinia Hungarica*. Its tonality is the *m-r-d-l,* pentatonic tetrachord ending on *la*. Its attraction is represented first of all by the changes of meter. For an intensive illustration of this, accommodating our singing to the accent relationships, we accompany it with metrical unit beats of differing timbre:

Bicinia Hungarica 1/57

An excerpt from Stravinsky's *The Wedding* shows a great affinity with this melody. We find in it also a pentatonic tone set of four tones (*d'-l-s-m*) and alternating meters with different metrical units. Let us solve the singing similarly to that of the previous folk song:

Stravinsky: *The Wedding* (or.: 6#)

Returning to the previously sung melody of *Bicinia Hungarica* Vol. I, let's listen to the two-voice arrangement by Kodály:

Bicinia Hungarica 1/57

Since the D la-pentatonic melody sounds simultaneously with its A la-pentatonic canon at a fifth, the complete musical material is bitonal. Pure intonation will present no difficulty here either, if we hear the given theme within its own tonal frame securely, and make ourselves conscious of the dissonances stemming from the tonalities of the two different keytones sounding simultaneously.

Essentially a similar basic principle is to be seen in the 62nd piece of Bartók's *Mikrokosmos* cycle. Within the 12-bar starting period of the musical material we hear the very same minor trichord in a two-voice texture. Yet its intonation is more difficult than in the previous arrangement, for several reasons. First of all, the theme appears not in a pentatonic tone set, but a minor trichord, including a minor second as well. Secondly, the distance between the two tonalities is not a perfect fifth but a minor sixth; thus its frame tones make up a diminished octave. And finally, its manner of construction is not canon-like, but results in a vertical sound of mixture. In vocal and piano performance this 12-bar musical unit sounds as follows:

Bartók: *Mikrokosmos*, No. 62

The reason the sounding together of the B and G minor trichord themes is so peculiar is that their main tones produce a chord having two different thirds: In this case the pure intonation of the individual voices can be realized exclusively by concentrating on the given minor trichord. Otherwise the minor sixth distance of the keytones will diminish to a perfect fifth on account of the clash of the B and B flat tones. The key question again, therefore, is the presence, or lack, of a sure tonal sense.

We find a sort of synthesis of the two latter compositions (*Bicinia Hungarica* No. 57 and *Mikrokosmos* No. 62) in the second movement of Bartók's *Piano Concerto No. 2*. The thematic material of this excerpt is to be heard in three Phrygian hexachords with different keytones sounding a perfect fifth apart from each other. Hence between the extreme voices of the three-voice texture the major ninth, heard generally as a dissonance, is constantly present. This fact, however, still does not disturb the sure intonation of the individual voices of Phrygian tonality, because the melodic tones—in a root-overtone relationship—do not weaken, but reinforce each other.

We hear first the theme, then the three-voice progression of a perfect fifth mixture:

Bartók: *Second Piano Concerto, II.*

In the 113th piece of the *Bicinia Hungarica,* Kodály made an arrangement of a mediaeval Hungarian Gregorian chant. The three-line theme moves in a diatonic tone set colored by *ta,* thus containing within itself the typical 8-note Gregorian tone set:

The last stanza of the two-voice arrangement has also preserved the 8-tone frame:

At the same time the cadential succession of the melody recalls the Renaissance style modal key changes. The first line ends in the Ionian, the second in the relative Mixolydian, and the last in the Aeolian mode colored by *ta*. The *ta* tone appearing in the cadential element alters the Aeolian mode at the last moment into one of Phrygian character; thus the theme ends not in the *la* Aeolian, but in the *la* Phrygian mode. We repeatedly encounter this manifestation in Renaissance motets—first of all those of Lassus. For example, among the *24 Two-Part Motets* of Lassus, an excerpt from No. 20 sounds as follows:

Lassus: *Two-Part Motet*, No. 20

The lower voice of the excerpt, with its descending second step, and the suspended counterpoint sounding with it arrive at a form-dividing cadence. But as a consequence of the *ta* coloring tone, the musical material here too, instead of remaining in the Aeolian mode, acquires a Phrygian character. Thus, similarly to the 113th piece of the *Bicinia Hungarica,* it ends not in the *la* Aeolian, but in the *la* Phrygian mode.

We encounter the characteristic fifth-answer type in Renaissance music in the 37th piece of the *66 Two-Part Exercises*. The first paired themes in the A-Aeolian composition sound in the E-Phrygian and A-Aeolian modes, whereas their transformed variants appear in the C-Ionian and the G-Mixolydian modes. Therefore, the paired themes consistently preserve the D—T and T—D relationship, but instead of modulations with changing key signatures, with the alternation of modes of diverging character belonging to the sphere of the same key signature.

The paired themes mentioned above:

66 Two-Part Exercises/37

This specific fifth answer is one of the most characteristic style traits of Renaissance music, which is known by the name: modal answer. Among others, for example, Palestrina's motet starting with "Fecit potentiam," similarly to the above mentioned exercise, begins with the fifth answer of the Aeolian and Phrygian tetrachords:

Palestrina: "Fecit potentiam"

We find modal answers and other Renaissance characteristics in the 4th piece of the volume of *Tricinia*. In connection with this work, perhaps let us now dispense with analysis and just observe the playfully light, madrigalesque sound realm of the composition:

Tricinia/4

In a new phase of historical development, in Baroque music, imitation technique arrives at the fugue-like mode of construction containing severe and restricted marks of style. We come across this Baroque polyphony in numerous exercises by Kodály in the most diverse variations. In a few instances, in some of his works having this character, he used original Baroque themes as basic musical material. For example, in the 12th piece of his *Fifteen Two-Part Exercises,* the Vivaldi theme selected by Kodály sounds like this:

15 Two-Part Exercises/12

Its foremost characteristic is a striving for inner balance. In the 1st unit we hear a sequentially articulated dynamic start and a momentary arrival. The 2nd unit sounds a natural minor Baroque sequence descending all the way in the tonality from the exposed top note. The 3rd unit brings the final close with a return of certain elements of the start of the theme.

In this exercise Kodály sets the Baroque theme not only into musical material of polyphonic construction, but also into a Baroque formal framework. The introduction of the theme—reminiscent of two-part inventions—is accompanied by double counterpoint, rhythmically amplifying and harmonically supporting the theme. This new musical material, partly with the stylistic restrictions of double counterpoint, and partly with lesser or greater variations, is present each time the theme is heard.

The tonal construction of the work follows a typically Baroque formula, known otherwise as a plagal order of keys: It modulates first from A minor to E minor, that is, from the tonic to the dominant minor, then through the tonic and its relative major it arrives at the subdominant key, to rise from there back to the original tonic level:

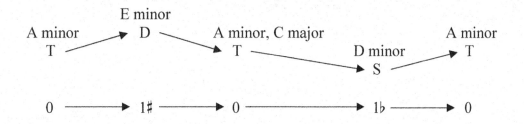

Now let us listen through the whole composition:

In the course of the performance of the work we could also observe the harmonic elements of the musical material. A fourth-chain authentic sequence runs through the whole work, both in the natural minor typical of the Baroque, and in the major key. The logical element of this harmonic passage is given to us by the musical material of the theme's second unit with the melody proceeding downward by the step of a fifth, and upward by a fourth. The chord series appears in several kinds of variants and sound types, depending on which voice carries the theme, and on whether it is heard in a minor or major key. We find the most beautiful variants of the chord progression perhaps in the opening and closing sequences of the composition:

The Neapolitan sixth and the turn of deceptive cadence make the closing section of the latter series a truly convincing and finally closed Baroque cadence.

Stepping out of the musical sphere of the Baroque, which is worthy of admiration even in its inner logic, let us take a glance at the pieces of Kodály's pedagogical series that recall Romanticism, or that are conceived in an artistic atmosphere of Romanticism. The relatively easily surveyable musical material of these works, and their mostly brief scope, make it possible for us to comprehend clearly, and to follow the otherwise often seemingly complicated, or indeed intricate tonal and harmonic order of Romanticism in them.

From the standpoint of harmonic occurrence, the pieces of the *Tricinia* are the most characteristic, because the harmonic succession establishing the musical material, impelling it onward and forming it, unequivocally rings forth from the three-voice texture.

In No. 18 of the *Tricinia* we come across incomparably exquisite, typically Romantic sounds and chord successions. Even in its form the work is clearly articulated, its order of keys simple. In contrast, No. 15 embodies more complicated harmonic and more extreme tonal elements of Romanticism. No. 25 unites with marvelous concentration the lightly undulating theme of Romantic intonation with a form of folk music conception and chord turns striving for Romantic simplicity.

If we take into consideration the possibility of only a single hearing, perhaps the first mentioned *Tricinia* piece, No. 18. can best engage the musical sympathy of the audience. Since Kodály wrote the composition—similarly to most of the pieces of the *Tricinia*—using C-clefs, we perform it with the letter names:

From a harmonic standpoint the work just heard belongs among the most easily memorizable ones. But only someone who has thoroughly mastered the most essential stylistic traits of the Renaissance, functional, and Romantic harmonic worlds, theoretically and practically—hence in the sphere of hearing too—can attempt it with success.

As our last example we hear the 3rd piece of the volume of *Epigrams*. In the piano accompaniment of the work, the musical elements of Impressionism and of the twentieth century unite, giving a home, as it were, to Kodály's warmly accommodating and yet boldly soaring melody:

Everything that has been heard here relates to the essence of Kodály's conception addressed to us, the teachers. Even through his pedagogical works Kodály expects of us, beyond the development of our musical ability, that we be conversant with various musical styles, that we grasp their melodic, rhythmic, harmonic and formal characteristics, the laws governing them, and clearly see the historical development. The teacher's pedagogical sense, his passionate desire to teach, his professional knowledge, musical erudition and broad horizon are the assurance that he will guide his pupils, within the given possibilities, with concentrated work and sure hand towards an acquaintance with the most essential musical elements and their mastery, while offering an enduring experience.

Finally I feel, however, that if we have met here in the name of Kodály, we cannot take leave of each other without some kind of common singing. My choice is the theme of the *Psalmus Hungaricus*, which in its simple and noble beauty is sure to lie close to the heart of every musician. Let us first hear it with the original Hungarian text, then as a repetition linked organically to this introduction let us all sing it, in the international language of solmization:

Kodály: *Psalmus Hungaricus*

Notes

[1] Zoltán Kodály, "Who is a Good Musician," in *The Selected Writings of Zoltán Kodály*, ed. Ferenc Bónis (London: Boosey & Hawkes, 1974), 197.

Keynote address presented at the 11th Organization of American Kodály Educators Conference in March 1985, Philadelphia, Pennsylvania. Originally published in *Bulletin of the International Kodály Society* 10, no. 2 (1985): 36–48. Reprinted by permission.

MAKING MUSIC TOGETHER

Judit Hartyányi

Since nought so stockish, hard, and full of rage,
But music for the time doth change his nature.
The man that hath no music in himself,
Nor is not mov'd with concord of sweet sounds,
Is fit for treason, stratagems, and spoils;
The motions of his spirit are dull as nigh,
And his affections dark as Erebus.
Let no such man be trusted. Mark the music.[1]

Allow me to complete Shakespeare's words—and make music!

Dear colleagues and guests from all over the world, gathered here for the sixteenth symposium of the International Kodály Society, I bring greetings from Zoltán Kodály's faraway country to you who are spending the next few days in the spirit of "Making Music Together"; who busy yourselves day by day pursuing your profession devotedly to cherish some indelible values, to foster the conviction of your environment, of your pupils. Culture in general, and music in particular, is one of the most important tools of personality development. Plato said the following in *The Republic*:

Is music not the best possible educating agent? There is nothing that gets as close to the soul as rhythm and melody, they captivate and ornament the soul, make it noble-minded, if a person has been brought up the right way—if not, they have the opposite effect. . . Indeed: In the depths of music there is education, hidden.[2]

The major thinkers of the following centuries, who have been committed to the building of a qualitative human existence, all expressed similar opinions. The title of this conference is close to one of Zoltán Kodály's most famous sayings: Music belongs to everyone. If that is true, then the participants and possessors of music are not only those who listen to it—the audience—but also those who make music together. They possess it even more profoundly, since the most direct way to possess, to know, to love music is to make music, and make music collectively. To quote Kodály's advice: "Let us arrive at musical geniuses through the instrument available to all: the human voice, singing. It is that which can guide the masses, and not only a select few, to music."[3] So: make music together in order to be able to perceive the works of the great composers so that we can be enriched by them.

But what is the quintessence of music that influences a person so strongly? What are its distinctive features through which it exerts its power and effect? Why do we need it? At the beginning, music meant harmony, or, to speak with Shakespeare's words: "concord of sweet sounds." Kodály, the thinker, composer and ethnomusicologist, and the determining personality of Hungarian musical education, aimed to improve society, and his concept extended all over the world. Kodály was convinced that music was one of the best tools to make people live in harmony with themselves and their environment. An answer to these questions can possibly be found in the words of William Collins, whose text Kodály used in his choral work "An Ode for Music":

> O Music! Sphere-descended Maid,
> Friend of Pleasure, Wisdom's Aid! . . .
> Arise, as in that elder Time,
> Warm, Energic, Chaste, Sublime! . . .
>
> "Tis said, and I believe the Tale,
> Thy humblest Reed could more prevail,
> Had more of Strength, diviner Rage,
> Than all which charms this laggard Age. . .[4]

This piece, composed in 1963, was meant by Kodály as a greeting and encouragement for the tenth Cork International Choral Festival in Ireland. It was the year in which Kodály revealed his childhood joys caused by music in an interview with Denijs Dille. He recalled with nostalgia the rich experience of melodies he had obtained from the most diverse strata of society: operetta melodies, folksongs, the music of the Gypsies of Galánta and the chamber music of his parents. It was also the year before the ISME world conference in Budapest, where participants from around the world were amazed by the incredible achievements of Hungarian music education. Now, forty years later, we may rightly think that no encouragement was needed at that time; the power of music was alive and effective. Today, when an international company of musicians has come together again, we are living in calamitous times all over the world. We are indeed badly in need of the power of music; the message of the cited poem is acutely timely. We need delight, wisdom, warmth and energy as the sources of peace; we need music emanating chaste and sublime emotions. We need something that "charms this laggard age." This something is good music. But what is good music? How can we recognize it? Kodály said in 1953:

> In the overwhelming chaos of music produced today only a past master can find his bearings. It is a hundred times more difficult to acquire sureness of taste today than it was a hundred years ago. Often the genuine can scarcely be distinguished from the counterfeit. But a good musician knows what good music is. He is guided by his familiarity with

literature, his theoretical and practical knowledge and his/her educated taste—all acquired over the course of many years.[5]

But, does an educated taste mean the same today as it meant fifty years ago when Kodály commented on it? Is today's taste a good guide?

I think we are far worse off now than we were fifty years ago. We are experiencing a crisis of values: The criteria of quality have changed. Culture has become a commodity, and a good commodity is defined not by quality but by sales numbers. Competition is the rule; money has the decisive role. We have been witnesses to dumbfounding technological advances, but this process is trying to oust man from his earlier position and subject him to impersonality, to the market, technological development, money, to the logic of material things. To avoid this, to keep the world an authentic and living place, our task as music teachers is to bring people closer to one another with the help of music, to turn the face of the individual towards his fellows again: to make music together. Let us teach and learn good quality music. That is how music can heal the illnesses of the modern age. "Good music certainly has a general character-forming influence, as it radiates responsibility and moral solemnity. Bad music lacks all these; its destructive effects can go as far as to undermine the faith and standards in moral law."[6] At another place, you can read: "He who begins life with music will have this reflecting on his future like golden sunshine. The gift received with this will provide such strength that it will help to overcome many difficulties."[7]

The century of reason has dehumanized the world. As a result of the most sublime thought, man has turned against man, or has chosen individual existence, believing it to be genuine freedom. Apart from reason—believed to be omnipotent—emotions must also be reckoned with. When teaching, and when singing together, "the aesthetic-emotional (effect) can come before—before you analyze and understand all that is to be analyzed in music. The emotional experience must be as spontaneous as the singing."[8] The best school for "emotional education" is a choir.

Kodály deemed choral singing of paramount importance. As he wrote, "Is there anything more demonstrative of social solidarity than a choir? Many people unite to do something that cannot be done by a single person alone, however talented he or she may be."[9]

Looking back into the history of pedagogy, you may find among the principles of Johann Heinrich Pestalozzi (1746-1827) that a whole nation must be led to singing, to making music. This is the more astonishing as Pestalozzi is said to have been musically untrained, even downright ungifted. The collective feeling, the joy over the fine result of a common effort, develops disciplined and noble people, so this role of choral singing is invaluable. Apart from moral gain, the musical profit is not negligible, either: Discipline results in rhythmic and intonational precision, attention results in tonal adjustment in harmony, thus multiplying the emotional charge of the expression and intensifying the impact of the performance on the audience. Making music in many parts improves the sureness of intonation. Kodály noted in the preface to his singing exercises *Let Us Sing Correctly:*

What can support the first steps of the beginner in the infinite realm of sounds? I tell you: It is not the different timbre of a tempered instrument but a second vocal part. In other words: No one can sing clearly if he or she only sings in one part. Singing clearly in one part can only be learnt surely by singing in two parts. The two parts correct and counterpoise each other.[10]

So again: Make music together. Let us effect and influence the audience through a musically precise style and intonation and through suggestive performance.

Let us see now a few fine examples of singing together.

The following ensembles emerged against backgrounds of various motives, musical knowledge and goals of functioning. Yet we are impressed by what they share in common: being nourished by deep roots in the soil of tradition. Be it folk music or church songs, especially psalms, they have been preserved to this day by the people's inclination to sing.

It was not only the improvement of their individual abilities but also membership in a community, development through collective experience, that enabled the choir members to make music at a high level. Though the level of performance may vary, the main point is not performance but the unification of the mental and spiritual energies at a high degree. These singers and their predecessors have always sung: In the family, in school, in church, the desire, joy and sorrow of a community was expressed in their singing. Just as the tiniest twig and last little leaf of a tree gets sap from the roots via the trunk, the legacy of a singer is conveyed by the community of the chorus. Thus, in collective music making, the educative influence of music through great composers' works, the understanding of good (valuable) music in the process of music education, and the social and musical consequences of music making are all fed by the roots.

Kodály's philosophy is imperishable because he worked out valuable principles not only for Hungarians. It is on the basis of its own respective culture that any nation—involving ever larger masses and generations in singing—may arrive at the knowledge of universal culture in which all the nations may be united.

The following musical examples reflect these principles.

1. Cultures of peoples living at a geographical distance meet at summer seminars based on Kodály's pedagogical principles. So it was on several occasions in Manila. The Philippine music teachers sang Mozart and Kodály, and sang and played their own folk song arrangements. The musicians were united by the productions requiring different tone and phrasing.

2. Protestant songs—this has been the title of two concerts held at the Music Academy. Two church choirs of high standards sang psalms and congregational songs in unison, as well as a few arrangements. Since the scores of the songs were distributed among the audience, some strophes could be sung by the choir and the audience jointly.

3. On the next recording the mixed choir of the Liszt Academy is singing. Its members are studying at different departments; they are future instrument players, choir conductors,

composers: the future professional musicians. Choir is a required subject for all of them. At the end of each semester they give a concert.

4. Generations—pupils and parents—sang together at the concert held on the twentieth anniversary of the Kodály Zoltán Primary School in Nyíregyháza. The school was founded in 1975 by an exceptionally gifted pedagogue who professes Kodály's statement:

> Evolution is a gradual process without leaps, and there is no progress without accepting the natural laws of nature. As a house must be built from the foundation upwards, the base of music culture must also be rooted in the instinctive expressions of the people. This is the only way to gradually create musicians. An understanding, inspired and inspiring group must be formed around them from all layers of society and in this way the seeds of hope can be sown so that future generations will be susceptible to even higher quality music.[11]

5. The Banchieri Vocal Ensemble are former pupils of the above school, and to my delight, their leader was also my student at the Music Academy. The six young men, who otherwise did not choose a professional musical career, stayed together to make music and founded the ensemble to sing Renaissance and twentieth-century a cappella works. They also gladly sing light music arrangements. From the moment of establishment, they have consciously advocated Zoltán Kodály's spiritual legacy and music pedagogical principles. Their aim is to popularize the form of collective singing they have chosen and the new perspectives of sound implied by the folksong-based arrangements they sing.

Finally: What can we pass down to posterity?

Roots and wings. The tradition of creating, building and fostering culture which has always and everywhere developed in communities. Our songs and tales determining and expressing the character of our nation, which bind us like roots. But making music together, nurtured by the inexhaustible emotional richness of singers united for a common goal, will soar boundless through space and time.

Notes

[1] William Shakespeare, *The Merchant of Venice*, Act. V, Scene 1

[2] Plato, *The Republic*, Book III, 402-403. In Hungarian in *Régi muzsika kertje*, ed. Bence Szabolcsi (Budapest: Zeneműkiadó, 1957), 22.

[3] Zoltán Kodály, "Gyermekkarok" [Children's Choruses], in *Visszatekintés*, ed. Ferenc Bónis (Budapest: Zeneműkiadó, 1974), 1:42.

[4] Zoltán Kodály, "An Ode for Music," in *Choral Works for Mixed Voices*, ed. Péter Erdei (Budapest: Editio Musica Budapest, 2018), 122. The text is taken partly from a poem, "The Passions: An Ode for Music" by William Collins (1721–1759), and partly from a poem ["Orpheus with His Lute Made

Trees"] that has been attributed both to William Shakespeare (1564–1616) and to John Fletcher (1579–1625).

[5] Zoltán Kodály, "Who Is a Good Musician?" (1953–1954) in *The Selected Writings of Zoltán Kodály*, ed. Ferenc Bónis (Budapest: Corvina, 1974), 199.

[6] Zoltán Kodály, "Tanügyi bácsik! Engedjétek énekelni a gyermekeket!" [Education Gentlemen! Let the Children Sing!] (1956), *in Visszatekintés*, ed. Ferenc Bónis (Budapest: Zeneműkiadó, 1974), 1:306.

[7] Zoltán Kodály, "A kecskeméti ének-zenei általános iskola új épületének felavatásán" [At the Inauguration of the New Building of the Kecskemét Singing Elementary School] (1964), in *Visszetekintés* ed. Ferenc Bónis (Budapest: Zeneműkiadó, 1989), 3:120.

[8] Zoltán Kodály, "Music Education, Educating Human Beings" (unpublished interview recordings, in English, 1966).

[9] Zoltán Kodály, "Children's Choirs" (1929), in *Selected Writings*, 121.

[10] Zoltán Kodály, *Let Us Sing Correctly!* (London: Boosey & Hawkes, 1967), 2. Note: This quotation is a translation from the Hungarian edition.

[11] Zoltán Kodály, "Kecskemét példája" [The Example of Kecskemét] (1930), in *Visszatekintés*, 3:23.

Keynote address presented at the 16ᵗʰ International Kodály Symposium in July 2003, Ourimbah (The University of Newcastle), Australia. Originally published in *Bulletin of the International Kodály Society* 28, no. 2 (2003): 21-24. Reprinted by permission.

Contributors

Megan Ankuda, KSC '16, teaches elementary general music and chorus at Worthington Hooker School in New Haven, Connecticut, where she is also a member of the Yale Camerata. Megan began summer study at Holy Names while teaching in the Kodály program in the Cambridge (MA) Public Schools, where she was inspired by HNU alumna Katie Bach. After completing the Kodály Summer Certificate at Holy Names, she attended the International Kodály Seminar in Kecskemét, Hungary, as a Fund for Teachers Fellow in 2017. She enjoys collecting new songs from the many international families at her school and integrating them into her teaching sequence.

Betty Bertaux, MM '75, founder and director of the Children's Chorus of Maryland, was an authority on vocal and musical development in children. A former faculty member of the Peabody Conservatory in Baltimore and of Holy Names College, she was professionally active for over 40 years, working with music students of all ages. Betty often served as a guest conductor and workshop clinician with children's choruses and choral conferences. She received an MM in Composition from Rice University in 1992, and is well-known as a composer of music for treble choirs. Her works are available via the Betty Bertaux Music Series with Boosey and Hawkes of New York and Alliance Music Publications, Houston.

Edward Bolkovac is the professor of choral music at The Hartt School of the University of Hartford and the artistic director of the New Haven Chorale. Prior appointments include senior lecturer in Music at the University of Queensland in Brisbane, Australia; artistic director of the Brisbane Early Music Festival; artistic director of the California Bach Society; and director of the Kodály Music Education Program at Holy Names University. He conducted the 2001 and 2004 OAKE National Concert Choirs and has been featured at many international music conferences. Ed studied conducting in Hungary and completed his doctorate at Stanford University.

Sean Breen, MM '06, has been a music educator for over 40 years, the past 35 at the Cathedral School for Boys in San Francisco. After joining OAKE and NCAKE in 2004, he received the MM in Music Education with Kodály Emphasis at Holy Names in 2006. In 2011 Sean completed a Masters in Cognitive Neuroscience from the Harvard School of Education, where he was recognized with the Intellectual Contribution Faculty Tribute Award and named the Chester Pierce Fellow. His articles have appeared in the *Kodály Envoy* as well as the *Bulletin of the International Kodály Society*. Sean presents internationally on neuroscience and music education, among other topics.

Lois Choksy, professor emerita and former head of music at the University of Calgary, is author of six seminal books in music education, the most familiar of which to music teachers everywhere is *The Kodály Method*. She served on the organizing committees of the Organization of American Kodály Educators and the International Kodály Society, and was president for two terms of the Kodály Society of Canada. After fifty years of teaching at every level from kindergarten to graduate school, Dr. Choksy retired to the small fishing village of Gibsons Landing in British Columbia, where she lives in quiet seclusion.

James Cuskelly, KSC '91, is head of music at St Aidan's Anglican Girl's School, Brisbane; president of the International Kodály Society; director of the Summer School Music Program, Brisbane; and director of the Cuskelly College of Music. He is founder and musical director of the Queensland Kodály Choir and conductor of the auditioned girls' choir, Ensemble Volar. James has taught at the pre-school, primary, secondary and tertiary levels, and is involved in teacher training programs in Hungary, Scotland, Britain, Malaysia, South Africa, New Zealand and Australia. He is internationally recognized for his ability to inspire and bring about effective learning in students across all ages or abilities.

Helga Dietrich received a diploma as a violoncello and singing teacher from the Liszt Ferenc Music Academy of Budapest in 1972. Following graduation, she taught in a music elementary school (Marcibányi Children's Center) in Budapest and began her work with Katalin Forrai, teaching in postgraduate courses for kindergarten teachers. She also served as a lecturer at the Teachers Training Faculty of ELTE University, Budapest from 1986. She currently teaches groups for mothers and toddlers at the International Children's Center in Budapest. Helga has taught in Kodály courses in Scotland, England, Canada. Australia and the U.S. A member of the Early Childhood Commission of ISME, she has presented papers at conferences in Poland, England, Australia, Japan, the United States and Hungary. Helga has taught regularly in HNU's Kodály Summer Institute, beginning in 1999.

Miriam Factora, MM '84, received her BM in Music Education at the University of Santo Tomas, Philippines; MM in Music Education at Holy Names University; PhD in Music at the University of Queensland, Brisbane, Australia and was an International Kodály Society scholar at the Liszt Academy of Music, Budapest. She has taught a wide range of levels—early childhood, elementary, middle school, high school and university. Miriam has presented lectures, keynote addresses and in-service training to students and teachers in the Philippines, U.S.A, Japan, Hong Kong, Australia, Mexico, England and Scotland. She was a keynote speaker at the International Kodály Symposium in 2007 and in 2015. Miriam joined the faculty of the Kodály Summer Institute in 2014.

Katalin Forrai's first priority was the music education of Hungarian preschool children. With Kodály's encouragement, she traveled to countries throughout the world, teaching in Japan, Canada, Australia, the United States and Britain, among others. Wherever she went, she always ensured that beautiful music from each culture suitable for preschool children was used. Kati established the Early Childhood Commission of the International Society for Music Education, and later became President of ISME. Kati's inspirational legacy lives on to this day, helped by the biennial presentation of the International Katalin Forrai Award established by the IKS in 2011 and presented to excellent preschool music teachers throughout the world. She taught at Holy Names during several summers, including the 25th anniversary institute in 1994.

Judit Hartyányi taught choral conducting at the Liszt Academy of Music in Budapest from 1985 to 2010. She has taught frequently in the HNU Kodály Center's academic year and summer programs, as well as in summer courses in Italy, Slovenia, Ireland, the United Kingdom, Malaysia, the Philippines and the United States. She was a founding member of the Hungarian Kodály Society (1978) and co-president from 2012–2018. Judit also served as vice president of the International Kodály Society (2005-2013), and is a member of the presidency of the Association of Hungarian Choirs and Orchestras. She received the Artisjus prize (1997) for contemporary music and the Apáczai Csere János prize (2016) for outstanding educational work.

Erzsébet Hegyi was instrumental in formulating the Hungarian tradition of teaching solfège and music theory according to the Kodály concept. She taught several generations of musicians at both the Liszt Ferenc Academy of Music and the Leó Weiner Conservatory in Budapest, as well as at Holy Names University's Kodály Summer Institute. Through her scholarly activities, dedicated teaching and extensive publications that have been used widely in Kodály-based musicianship training courses around the world—*Stylistic Knowledge according to the Kodály Concept* (3 vols.), *Solfège according to the Kodály Concept* and *Bach Examples*—she made a major contribution to the world-wide dissemination of Kodály's pedagogical legacy.

Sr. Mary Alice Hein met Zoltán Kodály and Erzsébet Szőnyi at Stanford University in the summer of 1966. Following studies in Hungary, she founded the Kodály Program at Holy Names College in 1969 and directed the program till 1991. In 1973, Sr. Mary Alice developed an academic year program offering an MM in Music Education Degree with Kodály Emphasis, making Holy Names the first institution of higher learning in North America to offer an advanced degree in Kodály music education. She was the co-chair with Erzsébet Szőnyi for the first International Kodály Symposium (IKS), held at Holy Names in 1973, and was a founding board member of both the IKS and OAKE. With the assistance of a Fulbright research grant, she wrote *The Legacy of Zoltán Kodály: An Oral History Perspective*, an IKS publication (1992).

Jerry L. Jaccard, MM '76, discovered the Kodály concept of *musical* education just prior to his first year of teaching in 1969 and has taught in the Kodály way for 50 years, in rural Arizona schools and in inner-city and suburban Connecticut and Utah schools. Jerry gratefully defines his 1976 graduation from the Holy Names Master's degree program as the watershed event in his career. He was the director of the Kodály Musical Training Institute at the University of Hartford (1980–1983) after which he obtained his doctorate from the University of Massachusetts-Amherst. He now enjoys professor emeritus status after 21 years on the faculty of the Brigham Young University School of Music, where he founded the BYU InterMuse Academy for Kodály Certification. Jerry has been the Lead Editor of the *Bulletin of the International Kodály Society* for several years and is the current President-Elect of the IKS.

Judith Johnson, MM '84, was for twenty-six years Head of Visual and Performing Arts at Clayfield College, Brisbane, Australia, where she founded a Kodály-based program teacher education program. During her tenure at the College, she was invited to teach for one academic year at Holy Names University. She was later appointed to the University of Queensland as a lecturer in music education and aural studies. Judith is the author of a number of music education textbooks used extensively in Australian schools. She has been president of the National Councils of the Kodály Music Education Institute of Australia, state president of the Queensland Branch of the Institute and served for eight years as a vice president of the International Kodály Society.

Mary Ellen Junda, MM '82, professor of music at the University of Connecticut, is recognized as an innovative music educator. Her recent research and teaching has focused on issues related to social consciousness and justice through performances with Earthtones Vocal Ensemble; four NEH Landmarks of American History and Culture programs, including *Gullah Voices*; articles on pedagogy in *The Choral Journal, College Music Symposium* and *General Music Today;* and as co-author of the lead chapter in *Songs of Social Protest: International Perspectives*. She recently presented at "Choral Symposium: Relevance," co-sponsored by ACDA, and has presented internationally at conferences in Australia, Portugal, Ireland and Canada.

Thomas Kite, MM '77, is a lifelong and devoted user of Zoltán Kodály's philosophy. A native of California, he now lives in Minnesota. He holds degrees in music performance (organ), music education and music theory from California State University, Northridge, Holy Names University and University of Houston. Kite's professional contributions include thirteen years in lower division music education (pre-school & K-12) as well as twenty-five years of University teaching, including University of Houston, University of Texas, University of Calgary, and University of Wyoming. In retirement, Kite devotes his time to writing (and attempts at publishing). A hobby in retirement is cake decorating, which allows him to sing while working. Singing, always close to Kite's heart, is summarized in the words of Ronald Blythe, set to music by Steven Sametz: "I have had pleasure enough. I have had singing!" Kite agrees and Kodály would have approved.

Ildikó Herboly Kocsár was a professor and conductor at the Teacher Training Institute of the Liszt Academy from 1968 to 1976, heading the theory department and supervising all music primary and secondary schools in Budapest. From 1976 to 1987 she taught at the Zoltán Kodály Pedagogical Institute of Music in Kecskemét. Ildikó has presented at seminars and symposia in Australia, Canada, England, Estonia, Finland, Greece, Ireland, Japan, Korea, Norway, Philippines, Poland, Sweden, Taiwan and the United States. She is the author of *Teaching of Polyphony, Harmony and Form in Elementary School* and *Music Should Belong to Everyone"—120 Quotations from Kodály's Writings and Speeches*, and served on the IKS Board as a Director from 1999 to 2007. She taught at Holy Names during several summers, including the 25th anniversary institute in 1994.

Eleanor G. (Toni) Locke was a member of the 3-year Ford Foundation training program at the Kodály Musical Training Institute in Wellesley, MA in 1969. The first year, Peter Erdei taught solfège and conducting and taught a fourth grade music class in Winchester, MA, for which the members researched appropriate songs and games. The second year was spent in Hungary observing teaching at all levels in Kesckemét and Budapest. In year three, Toni worked with Katalin Komlos, musicologist and editor of *150 American Folk Songs*, researching folk music at the Library of Congress and other institutions. In 1976, she joined the faculty at Holy Names where, over 10 years, she led faculty and students in creating the American Folk Song Collection for Teaching. This collection of over 2,000 songs gained the official recognition of the Archive of American Folk Song at the Library of Congress in 1984. She is the author of *Sail Away: 155 American Folk Songs*, which was published in 1987.

Andrea Matthews, MM '86, BM '72, from Crane School of Music at University of Potsdam, NY. She taught K-5 general music in Keene, NH, for 28 years before retiring in 2008. She spent a sabbatical year studying at the Liszt Academy, '87–88, where she also observed music classes in the public primary schools in various locations around Budapest. While teaching in Keene, she directed a women's community chorus for nine years in Brattleboro, VT. At a later date, she directed a mixed community chorus for five holiday concerts for a local music organization, Friends of Music at Guilford (VT). While her husband was in Malawi, Africa on a Fulbright, she spent seven months there, in 2002, collecting songs and teaching a music literacy class to locals. In Malawi in 2006, she transcribed the songs of an elderly story teller for publication in *Old Nyaviyuyi in Performance*, by Tito Banda. She has been singing and performing locally in Singcrony, a female a cappella quartet, for the past ten years.

Connie Foss More, MM '75, Certificate, Liszt Academy, lived in the eastern USA, Hungary and Nanaimo, British Columbia before becoming founding artistic director of Victoria's VIVA Choirs, for singers aged 6-18. She was a Kodály-inspired teacher from 1969 until her 2009 retirement, with students in childcare centers, public schools, universities, and at the Victoria Conservatory of Music. A Kodály Society of Canada Honorary Member, she was also a member of the Early Childhood Commission of the International Society for Music Education. Now described as a "lifelong citizen" who is primarily working against perilous climate change, she has brought the power of meaningful music into many lives.

Gail Needleman, MM '98, has taught at Holy Names for twenty years and is the creator of HNU's integrated undergraduate curriculum, based on the Hungarian model of music education. She is the co-developer (with Anne Laskey) of Holy Names' acclaimed American Folk Song Collection website, which is used by thousands of teachers and musicians throughout the world. Gail has presented papers and workshops on folk song and musicianship at regional, national and international conferences, and was a keynote speaker at the 2017 International Kodály Symposium in Alberta, Canada. In 2018 she received the OAKE Lifetime Achievement Award.

Georgia A. Newlin, MM '88, music education consultant, is past president of the Organization of American Kodály Educators and teaches in Kodály programs in Indiana, Hawai'i, and Virginia. Music Is Elementary has published her book, *One Accord: Developing Part-Singing Skills in School-Age Musicians*, as well as her lesson plans for teaching music literacy through choral singing in *The Crooked River Choral Project*. Georgia is also published with the *Ruth Dwyer Choral Series* from Colla Voce. Georgia is frequently called upon as a conductor for choral festivals, as a clinician for choral workshops and reading sessions, and as a consultant for curriculum planning.

Lily Storm, MM '14, is a singer specializing in traditional music, with particular emphasis in Eastern European styles. She is a member of Kitka Women's Vocal Ensemble and also performs as a solo artist, collaborating with Bay Area musicians such as accordionist Dan Cantrell, the Circadian String Quartet, and Armenian singer and duduk-player Khatchadour Khatchadourian. Last year she released a second solo album, a collection of European lullabies called *Louloudhia*. Lily teaches math and music at a K-8 public school and evening community workshops for adults.

Frank A. York, MM '80, grew up in a multicultural environment in Pennsylvania, which fostered a lifelong love of ethnic music and dance. Frank studied with Lois Choksy (with whom he has coauthored) and with Ivy Rawlins at Holy Names, and with Erzsébet Hegyi in Budapest. He taught in primary and secondary schools in both the United States and Australia, at the Bendigo College of Advanced Education, Victoria, Australia, and later at James Cook University, Queensland, Australia, where he also received his PhD in Ethnomusicology for research into the music and culture of the Torres Strait Islands, particularly Iama (Yam Island). He was director of RATEP, a distance education program for remote Aboriginal and Torres Strait Islander students which allowed them to earn a degree while studying in their home communities.